Reproductive Medicine and the Life Sciences in the Contemporary Economy

Reproductive Medicine and the Life Sciences in the Contemporary Economy

A Sociomaterial Perspective

ALEXANDER STYHRE and REBECKA ARMAN

Routledge
Taylor & Francis Group

LONDON AND NEW YORK

First published in paperback 2024

First published 2013 by Gower Publishing

Published 2016
by Routledge
4 Park Square, Milton Park, Abingdon, Oxon OX14 4RN

and by Routledge
605 Third Avenue, New York, NY 10158

Routledge is an imprint of the Taylor & Francis Group, an informa business

Publisher's Note
The publisher has gone to great lengths to ensure the quality of this reprint but points out that some imperfections in the original copies may be apparent.

Gower Applied Business Research
Our programme provides leaders, practitioners, scholars and researchers with thought provoking, cutting edge books that combine conceptual insights, interdisciplinary rigour and practical relevance in key areas of business and management.

British Library Cataloguing in Publication Data
Styhre, Alexander.
  Reproductive medicine and the life sciences in the
  contemporary economy : a sociomaterial perspective.
  1. Fertility clinics. 2. Human reproductive technology--
  Economic aspects. 3. Business and medicine.
  I. Title II. Arman, Rebecka, 1976-
  338.4'761669206-dc23

The Library of Congress has cataloged the printed edition as follows:
Styhre, Alexander.
  Reproductive medicine and the life sciences in the contemporary economy :
a sociomaterial perspective / by Alexander Styhre and Rebecka Arman.
      pages cm
  Includes bibliographical references and index.
  ISBN 978-1-4094-5350-5 (hardback) -- ISBN 978-1-4094-5351-2
(ebook) -- ISBN 978-1-4724-0831-0 (epub) 1. Human reproductive technology.
2. Human reproductive technology industry. I. Arman, Rebecka, 1976- II.
Title.
  RG133.5.S79 2013   2012046483
  618.1'7806--dc23

ISBN: 978-1-4094-5350-5 (hbk)
ISBN: 978-1-03-292556-1 (pbk)
ISBN: 978-1-315-60550-0 (ebk)

DOI: 10.4324/9781315605500

Contents

List of Tables

Preface

Infertility and human reproduction are undoubtedly a major concern not only for women and men suffering from involuntary childlessness but also for social planners and policy-makers. Like perhaps no other human activity or condition, human reproduction has influenced the culture and organization of human societies. Customs, law, taboos, traditions and economic accumulation are all structured on the basis of how human societies are capable of reproducing themselves.

Over centuries, human reproduction has been subject to systematic study and specialized expertise and especially the women developing a first-hand experience and know-how regarding the delivery of babies in agrarian and rural societies were quite knowledgeable regarding the mysteries of human birth and life. However, medicine did not become an experimental scientific discipline until the first half of the nineteenth century and the development of many sub-disciplines in medicine in the twentieth century has led to a more systematic and scientific understanding of human reproduction. The irony is that the pursuit to understand reproduction was triggered by the threat of overpopulation, still a major concern as natural resources are depleted and global warming may lead to unanticipated changes for human societies, while the very same know-how is today used to fertilize embryos in the laboratory. Science is indeed, as Bruno Latour once suggested, Janus-faced—always being two-sided.

This book sets out to explore and theorize the development and organization of assisted fertilization clinics, the clinical branch of reproductive medicine. It is written from an organization theory perspective and while one of us (Rebecka) has formal training and experience from medicine and healthcare work, we do not intend to primarily examine the medical aspects of assisted fertilization practice. On the other hand, it would be meaningless to study the clinics and the everyday work without saying at least something about reproductive medicine, and consequently we try our best to explain the various practices involved in the work.

When searching for literature and studies of assisted fertilization clinics and its practices, we have learned that there is little within the social science literature to draw on. While much is written in general about assisted fertilization and especially from certain favoured theoretical perspectives (e.g. feminist theory), there is still a shortage of ethnographic studies of the field. Also in the field of organization studies there is almost nothing written about this domain of the life sciences.[1] This is perhaps somewhat surprising given that the field of reproductive medicine and assisted fertilization clinics contain many of the issues that organization theorists concern themselves with: innovation, entrepreneurship, the role of law, regulations and institutions, professionalism, and so forth.

Since this book is one of the first works produced addressing assisted fertilization therapies and clinics in organization studies, the theoretical framework developed and used is multidisciplinary and includes contributions from many different social science and humanities disciplines. The aim of the book is still, as is being argued in the final chapter, to make an organization theory contribution to the study of the commercialization and institutionalization of the life sciences. Without making too bold a statement regarding our possible contribution, we think this is one early effort to understand the expertise, know-how and entrepreneurial foresight needed to advance assisted fertilization to the position it has entrenched today as a safe, credible and very much appreciated contribution to society, especially for women and men suffering from infertility.

The long-standing call for making business school research more "socially relevant" (here we could reference a long series of worried editorials and "discussion papers" published over the last few years, but we will skip that routine this time—readers craving examples can check the first section of the last chapter) is perhaps best handled by studying things that matter to people. Reproduction of course does. We thus believe that assisted fertilization clinics are worthy of more scholarly attention outside its traditional disciplines (e.g. gender theory and science and technology studies) and hope that we are capable of setting an example or at least provide some inspiration for further research with this research volume.

---

1   Brewis and Warren (2001) discuss pregnancy from an organization theory perspective but more from a conceptual angle than an empirical study.

*****

We would like to thank all the representatives of the field of reproductive medicine and assisted fertilization for participating in the study. Alexander would like to thank all his colleagues in the organization and management section at the School of Business, Economics and Law, University of Gothenburg, for commenting on various texts-in-the-making over the last few years. In addition, seminar participants at University of Innsbruck and at the Norwegian Business School in Bergen where research work appearing in this volume was presented should be recognized for their helpful comments and questions. Rebecka would like to thank Professor Gideon Kunda and the Visiting Professor Program Post-doc group at the School of Business, Economics and Law for comments and a fruitful exchange of ideas.

This book was financially supported by a research grant from the Bank of Sweden's Tercentenary Fund. We would like to thank Kerstin Stigmark at the Bank of Sweden's Tercentenary Fund for helping us make use of the money wisely.

PART I
Theoretical Perspectives

Introduction:
The Predicament of Childlessness and the Baby Business

Experiences from Assisted Fertilization

> *Firsthand thinkers mediate upon things; the others on problems.*
> *We must live face to face with being, and not with the mind.*
>
> *E.M. Cioran (1998: 43)*

Reproductive medicine and assisted fertilization are dealing with human reproduction, the elementary processes of life, and a central concern in any culture or human society (Ginsburg and Rapp, 1991). Indeed, we need to live our lives in the immediate connection to things. In Platonist thinking and in the Christian tradition, the material, everyday life world is downplayed and instead the "higher" and "eternal" issues beyond this crude and unfulfilled world are acquiring prestige and status.[1] However, there is nothing that makes human beings more acutely aware of their own material and biological existence than the loss of health (Frank, 1995). Instantly, the world around us crumbles as our human bodies cease to function as anticipated and we easily surrender to faith and folk belief as we hope to be able to restore ourselves. When the body hurts and aches, the higher values and intellectual discourse quickly loses its relevance for us. Rather than starting a research monograph on assisted fertilization with the theoretical domain, we will thus first encounter a few persons, couples of women and men, with first-hand experience of lending themselves to the practices of assisted fertilization.

---

1   In Plato's ideal state, presented in *The Republic*, the world of economy and commerce supports the world of politics and legislation which in turn supports the world of philosophers, the literati and intellectuals. Society is constituted as a hierarchical arrangement based on strict division of labor and responsibilities. *Skholē*, the freedom from work, is for Plato the highest degree of prestige, enabling reflection and what Martin Heidegger speaks of as *philosophieren*.

Rather than outlining a sophisticated conceptual framework or pointing at statistics indicating the relevance and scope of assisted fertilization, we will now enter this inquiry through a few life stories. These life stories, being told by two couples, one couple with positive experience from assisted fertilization inasmuch as they eventually became parents and today have a son, and one couple with a more negative experience filled with exhausting years of hope and despair ending with the insight that they would not be able to become parents, are by no means representative of anything else but their own experiences. Nevertheless, these stories being told may help us enter a more complex narrative including a variety of heterogeneous resources and conditions that taken together constitute what is called assisted fertilization. If nothing else, these vignettes from the world of assisted fertilization may help us think of these advanced technoscientific procedures and field not as an abstract system of interrelated and in many ways obscure and esoteric activities but as series of encounters and activities that in their own ways constitute assisted fertilization as what it is, as an encounter with technoscientific expertise that in many ways is impressive in what it is capable of accomplishing or at times even intimidating but that nevertheless is dealing with human reproductive materials under highly specific conditions. Hopefully assisted fertilization, its accomplishments and limitations, may become intelligible in this volume.

The first couple suffered from the female's illness, endometriosis, a medical condition reducing fertility. When deciding to seek assisted fertilization help, they were not naïve regarding their chances of becoming parents: "They [clinic staff] did not make any promises given [the woman's] diagnosis. They have never been able to say very much besides general statements … So I thought they conveyed adequate information and there were no false expectations but they were rather straightforward" (Male IVF patient, Couple 1). The initial hope that the assisted fertilization therapy would be able to help them become parents soon led to disappointment and despair. The couple endured a four-year period where they returned to the clinic for repeated treatment cycles after failing to get pregnant. After undergoing a few failed treatment cycles the woman learned to anticipate and feel the reactions and shivering of her body:

> In the beginning, I was full of hopes and really believed in this, analyzing every single little feeling, that "this might be something this time," but then you were devastated when it didn't work. After a few times, I tried to convince myself that this time I mustn't become sad if it fails but nevertheless you were totally broken just the same. Every single time! Those days when you realized that

> *this won't work this time either, you were broken down … but then through the denial or repression that I used [I could continue]. (Female IVF patient, Couple 1)*

She continues:

> *Either you start to bleed or if time passes you can take a [pregnancy] test at home. But I have been able to sense it every single time. I get this ache … I get certain symptoms, like an ache in my thighs and being heavy in the legs and all sorts of things, so I have been a hundred percent sure that this is it! A few days before the actual event [the miscarriage]. (Female IVF patient, Couple 1)*

Every single miscarriage was a painful, emotional event wherein the couple suffered a wordless sense of disappointment regardless of their understanding of the woman's medical condition. To cope with the situation in an orderly and somewhat emotionally detached manner was therefore of great importance. When they asked the clinicians why there was such limited progress, they were not able to get any clarifying answers:

> *After a few treatment cycles, we were starting to … become concerned regarding the lack of progress, then I asked a few questions to the doctors … then they were telling us that "there are better chances with the fresh trials rather than with the frozen [embryos] and that the success rate was higher in such cases" … When we have done like, six, seven, eight embryos, they were starting to tell us that they were concerned regarding the lack of progress. (Female IVF patient, Couple 1)*

Rather than telling their families and friends, the couple had decided not to tell anyone, potentially making the ordeal an even more demanding experience as they had to maintain a secret everyday life. The reason for this secrecy was to avoid further disappointment among, for example, their parents: "We didn't want to carry their [parents'] expectations as well … Of course we knew … and they have given us a few hints as well … that my parents were wondering why there were no grandchildren coming," the woman argued.

As the years passed, the couple almost lost count of how many cycles they had undergone. After the second campaign of treatment, around the tenth cycle, they both lost their faith in fulfilling their dreams of parenthood but continued until the fifteenth cycle, just to be sure that they "had done everything they possibly could": "It felt definite after the second round of treatments. The third round was just a mere formality, more than a real, serious attempt" (Male IVF patient, Couple 1). He continued: "We have done what we could and we cannot go any further. Now we have to live with that. There's nothing we could have done differently. And that feels good" (Male IVF patient, Couple 1). Even though the man claimed that he feels good about having the energy and determination to be able to do all that was asked from them, there is still a strong sense of disappointment and disillusion: "I suppose we were prepared, more or less, but it felt like … well, we had tried for many years … consuming so much energy both from us and from work … ruining the body, and things felt … well, unfulfilled" (Female IVF patient, Couple 1).

Needless to say, for the couple these were not happy years, years filled with joy and laughter. Instead, the period was exhausting as everyday life had to be maintained at the same time as therapy continued:

> I don't think I had any regular everyday life during these years. Things have been exhausting and both of us have been tired because of all the hopes and the sadness you have to live with when things came out this way. The medication hasn't been particularly mild … You get emotionally labile … It is tough. (Female IVF patient, Couple 1)

There are few possibilities for identifying any positive experiences from these years in the clinic. At least, being able to keep their relationship despite the pressure was regarded as a joint accomplishment:

> The best part is that we're still in a relationship, that it did last … It is quite demanding to endure this kind of situation. First, the grief in itself in not being able to become parents when you want to and then the sense of guilt on my part, being the source of all this. It is not a happy situation. (Female IVF patient, Couple 1)

When being asked about their view of the work in the clinic, the couple lacked a sense of an integrated view of their case, moving back and forth between the woman's endometriosis specialist and the clinic: "There is no integrated perspective. But we have been very well treated by all midwives. If it's been one professional category that has been nice throughout, it is them—every single one of them!" (Female IVF patient, Couple 1).

Despite their inability to become parents, they believe the Swedish healthcare policy is quite "generous" in letting them undergo no less than 15 treatment cycles:

Female IVF patient, Couple 1: Today, I'd say it is quite generous, actually.

Male IVF patient, Couple 1: Yes, I think so too … We have been given like fourteen or fifteen treatment cycles and that is amazing when you think about it. You need to say that it is generous.

Adoption is not necessarily the solution for the couple as they regard that as an "entirely different thing" than having a child of one's own. "That would be another issue to handle and think through if we would be willing to do that," the woman responded. "It is like night and day. There are like eleven new issues popping up in comparison to having children of one's own … So it's very different," the man added. Adoption is at best a form of substitute to giving birth to one's own biological children. In summary, the couple was pleased they had the stamina and energy to follow their path chosen to its very end but besides that the assisted fertilization therapy was, despite limited expectation, an exhausting and ultimately disheartening experience. Also the time spent in the clinic was complicated to predict: "When we started, we did not know how long time it would take … We did not believe it would last for four years," the man reflected.

The second couple could tell a less heartbreaking story inasmuch as they managed to become parents, but their story also includes failures and despair. As with the first couple, the female is suffering from a medical condition but in contrast to the first couple, the second couple started to consider adoption but they were turned down because of the man's age: "We were quite confused [after being turned down by the adoption bureau] and we felt like 'this is the end of the story,'" the woman said. Turning to the assisted fertilization clinic, the first step was the hormone therapy to enhance ovulation. The woman said she had a "terrible anxiety" regarding the therapy after hearing "horror stories" regarding the uses of hormones: "January was a black month, not because I was possibly becoming pregnant but because I feared becoming ill … You always hear these horror stories about what happens during the hormone therapy" (Female IVF patient, Couple 2). She continued: "I called them [the clinic] totally messed up and told them about my concerns. I wanted them to say something like 'one in three million suffer from such side-effects,' but instead they told me that 'this is your decision.' Well, they told me so, but I was so frustrated and even more stressed by not getting any advice or counseling" (Female IVF patient, Couple 2).

When telling her husband about her concerns, he said that he was willing to drop the entire idea of assisted fertilization if the cost would be a constant ongoing anxiety for his wife. The woman declined all such ideas:

> *We were almost beginning to fight, because he said that "well, we don't need to do this if you are suffering this much," but I said no! (Female IVF patient, Couple 2)*

> *I just wanted to emphasize that this was not a life-or-death matter for us, that we needed to have a child regardless of the costs … In that case, we could terminate the process. (Male IVF patient, Couple 2)*

After some time, the woman managed to handle her fears and experienced relatively little side effects. The next unpleasant experience was the egg retrieval, perhaps the single most unnerving experience:

> *And then they retrieved the eggs and that was probably the most horrible thing in the entire process. It was no walk in the park, I can tell you. You're like lying down in this gynecology chair and you get loads of morphine but that is the only good part about it … I had to ask them all the time, "more morphine, please" because it was really painful. (Female IVF patient, Couple 2)*

Using a needle to enter the ovaries through the vagina, the egg retrieval is a most advanced procedure that safely retrieves a number of oocytes, unfertilized egg cells, to be fertilized in the laboratory. After 36 hours, the couple returned to the clinic for the embryo transfer. After the transfer, a short period of waiting for results led to a disastrous outcome:

> *Female IVF patient, Couple 2: And then on the Sunday we returned to make the first transfer. They had six eggs all being fertilized. Four of them were accepted because they need to be perfectly divided and everything … Then came the two most dreadful weeks. Even before I had made the pregnancy test, I woke up this morning bleeding … it was terrible … I just cried … I was "the world's least successful woman" … Everything was totally black and I felt this is not going to end as we planned for.*

> *Researcher: So it felt like a personal failure?*

Female IVF patient, Couple 2: Yes, it was very dramatic. I think I cried for three straight hours.

The woman strongly felt the miscarriage was a personal failure and responded very emotionally. Her husband, having friends successfully undergoing the treatment and becoming parents, knew that it is not very common to succeed in the first attempt and kept calm. His wife was at times annoyed by this attitude: "At times, I thought he was just so insensitive when telling me [to relax and calm down] but at the same time it felt very good to have someone standing firmly on the ground" (Female IVF patient, Couple 2). Unlike the first couple, the second couple decided to share their predicament with friends and families so they could get their support: "Some people tell no one but I felt, and [the husband] did the same, that … unless I tell anyone, there is no one to help me when I am sad because things may go terribly wrong. That's me, anyway, rather speaking freely so people are informed" (Female IVF patient, Couple 2).

The couple continued the therapy, using one of the embryos in the freezer, and this time the outcome was different. The woman could account for the details when she realized she was pregnant:

> It was ten to five in the morning when I did the pregnancy test. I was sitting there, half asleep and just all of a sudden, What!? I just bounced up to the second floor where [the husband] was sleeping, telling him "I'm pregnant." And he's like "Great!" I was lying there, eyes wide open, not a bit tired and waiting for the morning to come. When he woke up I told him again, and he said like "Yes, I heard you the first time. Brilliant!" (Female IVF patient, Couple 2)

This time, the pregnancy ended with the birth of a healthy son in 2009 and today they live a family life similar to that of millions of other families. Especially the woman expressed her fascination over the fact that the once frozen embryo could be transformed to a living baby: "He [the son] was frozen for like two months. Only that is a miracle! It is so wonderful … I am so fascinated by the fact that the embryo has been in the freezer" (Female IVF patient, Couple 2). The other side of coin is that the embryos still in the freezer in the clinic become a concern, an issue to be eventually dealt with:

> It [the embryos] can stay in the freezer until 2013, a five year period I believe … If we have not made the second transfer, I think it will be hard to have it destroyed since we know what came out of it … But we'll cope with that in due time … We have decided since long that there will be no more [children]. But

it is haunting us, being there in the freezer ... That is the case. (Female IVF patient, Couple 2)

For instance, during the therapy, the couple were asked if they would agree to donate embryos to stem cell research after their embryos had passed their five years in the freezer—the maximum period for embryo storage according to Swedish law—but, after long discussions, they decided that they did not want to donate their embryos. "We were not willing to donate to stem cell research ... but we agreed on something else—but not stem cell research. We didn't want that ... We were talking quite a bit about it. It felt like some kind of violation of the personal integrity" (Female IVF patient, Couple 2). While embryos are destroyed after five years, the couple felt there were too close connections between the embryos in the freezer and their son, leading to their joint decision.

When being asked about their experience from the assisted fertilization clinics, the second couple, just like the first couple, did not develop any personal contacts in the clinics but were rather treated as patients in an anonymous healthcare process: "What is missing are the personal contacts. I know the system is based on standardization ... [But] in assisted fertilization it is so important to have this kind of continuity. And I cannot say we saw much of that," the man argued. "It is a 'disruptive relationship' [with the clinic staff] you may say," the woman added. Despite this sense of lack of personal relations in the healthcare work, the outcome from the therapy was what was hoped for, a child to care for.

The experiences of these two couples may or may not be typical or representative of how assisted fertilization therapies work or unfold. Some become parents, but many don't; hopes and expectations accompany the physical ordeals or even sufferings of the female patient; limited theoretical and practical understanding of the human reproductive processes and organs prevents credible explanations for both failures and successful pregnancies; ethical and practical issues needs to be addressed *en route*. The assisted fertilization clinic is a site where human hopes and "biological instincts" (used here for the lack of a better term) are bound up with advanced technoscientific apparatuses and procedures. The assisted fertilization clinics are no "wonder factories" managing to accomplish anything but every time they succeed in producing new babies it is regarded as the wonder of life by the lucky parents. Assisted fertilization clinics are both deeply seated in human needs and aspirations at the same time as they are advanced technological sites. This venturing into the secrets of human reproduction is a fascinating endeavor, and numerous couples and single women have been able to take advantage of this clinical expertise. At the same time, failure and despair accompany the clinical work, leaving many couples, like the first couple above, in a situation where they gradually reach the painful insight that even the state-of-the-art technosciences may not be able to overcome the hurdles put up by nature.

In the contemporary era, childlessness is not only an unfortunate predicament beyond human influence but is also transformed into a "medical condition" that may be corrected and modified in clinical procedures. Reproductive medicine gives hope to sub-fertile couples but also leads to a variety of social concerns and ethical issues to be handled and debated. In addition, assisted fertilization work is organized on basis of certain principles and rationales that have been subject to relatively little scholarly attention. In the following, this technoscientific domain of work and economizing will be explored in greater detail.

The Baby Business

In 1932, Aldous Huxley published his dystopian vision of the future world, the emblematic novel *Brave New World*. Unlike George Orwell's equally famous *1984*, Huxley's image of the future is not a totalitarian society in the tradition of Nazi Germany or Stalin Soviet Union wherein people are oppressed on basis of an intricate system of surveillance, control and penal practices. For Orwell, the future in the 1980s would merely be a continuation and amplification of what was already observable in the 1930s in fascist and communist countries in Europe.

Huxley was more visionary. In his brave new world, people are no longer oppressed in the traditional sense of the term because they do not experience any oppression. Instead, Huxley portrays a society wherein science and technology have acquired a hegemonic position and where human happiness is accomplished on the basis of pharmaceutical substances, a widely used drug called soma. Perhaps the most spectacular accomplishment of this future society is that rather than resting on "natural" human reproduction, all reproduction is organized as an industrial process wherein five distinct classes of human beings are created, each equipped with the adequate intelligence for the role they serve in society. The Alpha humans are highly intelligent and are developed to conduct qualified and intellectually demanding work while, on the lower end, the feckless Epsilon humans are designed to conduct menial tasks and have little ambition besides doing what is expected from them. Huxley's future society is thus a far-driven class society wherein there is no need for social selection or social migration because such concerns are already resolved in the industrial process of human reproduction. While *1984* offers a few possibilities for resistance and hope, *Brave New World* is in many ways a more chilling scenario for the future.

Among the key terms that Huxley proposed is the concept "test-tube babies," a concept that in many ways effectively exploits the common-sense binary separations between nature and artifice, life and inert matter, natural reproduction through intimacy and intercourse and cold, disembodied laboratory procedures. Huxley's term test-tube baby has been consistently used in the discourse on assisted fertilization. No matter how many stories of despairing parents facing fertility problems but successfully becoming parents through the help of assisted fertilization procedures, Huxley's *Brave New World* still haunts the domain of reproductive medicine and assisted fertilization. In fact, the term test-tube baby is one of the first terms that one tends to associate with assisted fertilization. Also the very term in vitro fertilization (IVF), a common term to denote assisted fertilization, means literally "in the test-tube fertilization."

While other areas of advanced medical practice, ranging from molecular biology to organ transplantation, are commonly admired for their capacity to intervene in the human body and to restore functions and to eliminate injured or poorly functioning organs and tissues, reproductive medicine and assisted fertilization is not only combating scientific, technical and financial difficulties but also something potentially much worse—common-sense thinking. Human reproduction and parenthood are undoubtedly deep-seated emotional, social and cultural events in any society (Ginsburg and Rapp, 1991). Virtually any human society appears to have instituted rituals, ceremonies, taboos and institutions pertaining to the domain of human reproduction. In the Greco-Roman or Judeo-Christian cultural tradition dominating in Europe, the marriage between a man and a woman is instituted as the only legitimate social arrangement wherein human reproduction is socially sanctioned. Only recently has the legislation been liberalized, making lesbian couples, for example, eligible for the assisted fertilization therapies. For centuries, out-of-wedlock births have been a source of social scandals and controversies, and many women have been ostracized if they have been unfortunate to become pregnant prior to their marriage. To avoid such social stigma, at times lasting for the rest of their lives, illegal abortions have been widely used leading to much suffering and even deaths of women.

In addition to the culturally embedded regulation of human reproduction, a more recent social concern, the issue of overpopulation, a standing theme since at least the mid-twentieth century, has been a burden for reproductive medicine and assisted fertilization. For decades, much research effort was dedicated to understanding the endocrinology of human reproduction in order to curb rather than to enhance human fertility. As has been accounted for by Watkins (2001) and Oudshoorn (2003), reproductive medicine set up a research agenda to enable human sexual practices without human reproduction. Reproductive medicine is indebted to a long series of advancements in a number of disciplines including veterinary medicine, endocrinology, cytology and molecular chemistry, and in many cases animal models were used to theorize the nature of human reproduction (Friese and Clarke, 2012).

In veterinary medicine, understanding inheritance was of great interest in, for example, cattle breeding, but when research in this field was applied in the study of humans, the interest shifted from how to accomplish the most viable breed to how to avoid unwanted pregnancies. The first generation of pioneers in reproductive medicine was trained in this research program aimed at identifying effective, safe and convenient contraceptives. However, a few of these researchers realized at some point in time that the principal concern for humanity was not overpopulation per se but the birth of *unwanted* children.

Overpopulation is a terribly imprecise term as it points at a concern for the whole of the planet while ignoring the fact that one family may have 10 children to support while the family next door may suffer from their inability to conceive one single child, leading to social stigma, and, in many parts of the world, an uncertain future for the elderly having no family to support them. The generation of researchers of reproductive medicine that managed to shift the focus from how to discipline and control human fertility to how to manage and monitor human fertility in more detail understood that not only excessive human reproduction—if there is such a thing—is a social problem but also the absence of human reproductive capacities.

Just as women—men's role in conceiving a baby has for various reasons been surprisingly downplayed—have suffered a social stigma from becoming pregnant prior to marriage, involuntary childlessness is causing much concern for both women and men. In addition to the disappointment and despair experienced during the years when couples become parents, in many parts of the world wherein no welfare state arrangements support the elderly, children are expected to care for their parents. Without children, the last years of the life are in many cases difficult for older people. Human reproduction is thus playing a key role in local economic systems in many parts of the world.

During the last 35–40 year period, human reproduction has undergone a revolution. First, reproductive medicine has been further developed to map and understand the generic mechanisms and processes of human reproduction, ranging from endocrinology and the cellular mechanisms to the molecular and genetic processes. In addition, reproductive medicine as a scientific field or research program has been accompanied by the development of a clinical branch, *assisted fertilization* or *in vitro fertilization*. Reproductive medicine and assisted fertilization are intimately connected and advanced scientific know-how is applied in the clinical practice, while much clinical research work further propels the research agenda.

By and large, the development of assisted fertilization as a clinical practice is a success story, helping millions of couples and single women previously failing to become parents finally fulfilling their dreams of having children of their own to care for. At the same time, notwithstanding all these stories being told of how the "miracle of life" was created in the laboratory, human fertility is a relatively delicate matter. While less advanced—the anthropocentric smugness hopefully to be excused—mammals such as rodents may create numerous offspring in short times, humans are unfortunately not very fertile by nature. As a consequence, between 40 and 50 percent of all couples seeking assistance to become parents fail to become parents. As some of the representatives of the assisted fertilization clinics remarked, any medical practice having no more than a 50/50 success rate would have been questioned, but when it comes to assisted fertilization this is still a remarkable accomplishment.

Since assisted fertilization deals with "patients" that are in many cases otherwise healthy, there is little downside risk of undergoing a treatment; most women may experience the hormone therapy as unpleasant and stressful and the egg retrieval is a painful experience but once they finish it most won't experience any negative effects. Only in a few cases ovarial hyperstimulation syndrome or deep vein thrombosis might be caused by the treatment, which is potentially dangerous for the women. The more common worst-case scenario is that the couples seeking assistance walk away from the clinics with their dreams unfulfilled.

Even though the case of assisted fertilization is in many ways an exemplary case of how human ingenuity and intellectual efforts to understand and to dominate nature has led to clinical procedures for assisting otherwise naturally occurring biological processes, reproductive medicine and assisted fertilization is still located in a particular society and culture. In the Western world, both men and women tend to become parents at a later age. Younger people spend years studying, making careers, having a good time with friends and family, and work or study abroad for periods of time. In addition, they may spend longer periods of time as singles because they have the economic possibilities—especially women—for supporting themselves and are not yet ready to settle with one partner for the rest of their life. All these social, economic and cultural traits of the late modern society tend to work against the biology of human reproduction. The fertility of women reaches its peak in the early twenties, starts to decline around the age of 30, and after 35s starts to drop significantly. By the age of 40, the chances of becoming pregnant are substantially lower than 10 years earlier. For men, there is a decline in fertility but at a slower pace and higher age.

In addition to social influences, environmental effects are arguably influencing human reproductive capacities. Sperm motility and sperm concentration is being lowered in men's semen, potentially related to the presence of chemical substances in water and groceries. While much attention has been given to the issue of global warming in the public debates, the next big issue to deal with may be the pollution of natural resources by chemical substances such as hormones or synthetic molecules disrupting ecological systems on the molecular level (Serres, 2011). Reproductive medicine and assisted fertilization are then not to be understood as strictly scientific procedures but are better understood as a form of what Jasanoff (2005) calls the "co-production" of science and society; social changes and technoscientific advancement are not isolated processes but instead they are folded into one another, being mutually supporting or "imbricated" (Introna and Hayes, 2011). That is, scientific programs and their clinical applications never exist outside of society but are rather constitutive of society.

In addition, there is no society preceding such activities and resources but "society" is instead what is constituted by the totality of activities and processes in a specific time and place. That is, reproductive medicine and assisted fertilization are not developed in isolation from wider social interests and concerns but are instead, to some extent, mirroring, accommodating and creating social concerns and perceived problems (Shostak and Conrad, 2008).

Societies like ours are concerned with both unwanted pregnancies and absent desired pregnancies and consequently technoscientific resources are dedicated to the handling of these concerns.

Debora Spar (2006) uses the term "the baby business" to provoke a debate over the totality of technoscientific and economic activities pertaining to human reproduction. According to Spar, the baby business includes three basic domains wherein babies are being subject to both technoscientific manipulation and economic interests, namely assisted fertilization, adoption and gestational surrogacy. Assisted fertilization and gestational surrogacy rests on the same know-how basis, that of reproductive medicine, but while assisted fertilization is based on the idea of the biological mother carrying the fetus and giving birth to the baby, gestational surrogacy separated the pregnancy from the mothering. Consequently, in many countries including Sweden, surrogacy is illegal and in most countries the use of surrogate mothers is accompanied by controversy and animated debate. Following Zelizer's (2005) emphasis on the incommensurability between financial compensation and intimacy, one may propose that many people are concerned about or even abhorred by the selling of gestational surrogacy services because it violates the very norms of parenthood and mothering as it transforms pregnancies into a form of professional service. As a consequence, the international legislation is highly diverse and largely uncoordinated.

In contrast, adoption is the domain of the baby business wherein already existing children are distributed into new homes. Traditionally, developing countries have served as the pool of children for relatively wealthy families from the developed world, but there is a tendency today that many countries have enacted more strict policies regarding adoption, thus putting higher pressure on other sectors of the baby business. Moreover, the adoption industry offers children that have no parents or that are unwanted, and many suffer from mental or physical handicaps. Such children have fewer opportunities for finding a loving home and the tendency to use children as commodities with different degrees of attractiveness is an alarming feature of the practice that most people strongly respond to emotionally. The world literature and popular culture includes many stories of children spending their lives in orphanages hoping that someone to care for them and love them will show up but are bitterly experiencing that no one is ever willing to take on such responsibilities.

In other words, adoption is a social practice surrounded by strong emotions and a sense of collective guilt for the fate of children being left behind or losing their parents. At the same time, the adoption industry is a regulated and monitored practice and it is instrumental in helping parents and children create new lives for themselves. Still, all practices in what Spar (2006) refers to as the baby business are accompanied by strong moral beliefs, controversies and the possibilities for despair at the fringes. Since human reproduction is considered a sacred thing, all economic and social practices pertaining to its organization and control will inevitably be accompanied by critique and concerns. Still, both adoption and assisted fertilization are today widely used, legitimate and carefully regulated practices supporting women and men failing to conceive a child on their own. Studying such practices is an important assignment for social theorists and organization theory researchers. Human reproduction is today, whether we like it or not, part of the wider social economy and must therefore be studied as such.

On Theorizing Assisted Fertilization

This book reports an empirical study of the organization of assisted fertilization clinics in Sweden. The study of the clinics and the professionals populating the clinics and conducting the day-to-day work to counsel and inform clients, to handle the technical and clinical procedures, and to collect, retrieve, manipulate and store human reproductive material is anchored in social theory, and more specifically, an organization theory framework. However, there is no one single unified theory or analytical model being used to study assisted fertilization clinics. Instead, this clinical work is conceived as being closely related to reproductive medicine which in turn is part of experimental medicine as a professional field of expertise within the technosciences, devoted to the pursuit to explore and understand nature through a combination of technologies and research methods.

All scholarly empirical work is embedded in the fruitful relationship between empirics and data; researchers *represent* the object of study and they *intervene* in the object of study (Hacking, 1983). *Representing* is the domain of theory, the conceptual framework, a theory, which is used to understand what is observed; *intervention* is the empirical work to further refine and modify the theoretical framework. Neither theory nor empirical data can be assumed to be unproblematic. Instead, theory and empirics are parts of an experimental model and are thus mutually constitutive; the one presupposes the other and cannot be understood in isolation. Such a view of research assumes a new role for theory, a role wherein theories are resources used for enacting the world —

for modeling it. Vilém Flusser (2002: 86) says: "[T]he word theory … changes its meaning. It no longer denotes the contemplating of fixed, unchanging ideas but active modelling." The theorist uses theories to impose a specific perspective on the empirical object, to be able to perceive certain qualities in what is observed.[2] Consequently, theories play a key role in shaping the object of investigation. Favoured theories to some extent shape the empirical object. This makes theories a rather complicated resource in any research work. Says Canguilhem:

> *Theories only proceed from previous theories, often very old ones. Facts are only the route (rarely direct) by which theories proceed from one to another. Such a filiation of theories from theories along was brought to light very well by Comte when he remarked that, since a fact of observation presupposes an idea that orients the attention, it is logically inevitable that false theories precede true ones. (Canguilhem, 2008: 32)*

If theories guide and structure the analyst's perception, they are not, logically speaking, *false* but they may be *inaccurate* inasmuch as they may not be shared by others or enable an understanding of what is observed. In this view, theories are on the one hand loosely coupled with empirics while on the other hand they are bound up with the empirical object inasmuch as research work presupposes a theoretical gaze; in the sciences, there is no "view from nowhere." Moreover, perceived problems or puzzles are preceding this assemblage of theories and empirical objects. What is problematic and what is not is a social and cultural matter, anchored in worldviews and power relations. Problems and puzzles are bound up with preferences, norms and beliefs, i.e. emotional sentiments favouring certain conditions or relations. Problems are therefore never fully independent from the social community wherein they are articulated; things per se are never problematic but are considered so given certain preferences, morals, available resources and alternative choices. "[P]roblems have no independent existence; we are not interested in how problems are 'discovered,' but rather how they are constituted," Bloomfield and Danieli (1995: 32) write in their study of IT consultants.

---

2   No perceiving eye is devoid of theoretical assumptions or beliefs; observations are *theory-laden* in every sense of the term (Hanson, 1958). In the same vein, Karen Barad (2011: 451) says: "Theories are not mere metaphysical pronouncements on the world from some presumed position of exteriority. Theories are living and breathing reconfiguring of the world." Also: "[T]heories are not born from the facts they coordinate, which are supposed to have given rise to them. Or, more exactly: facts give rise to theories, but they engender neither the concepts that unite them internally nor the intellectual intentions they develop" (Canguilhem, 2008: 55–56).

The constitution of problems precedes research activities which in turn are composed of theoretical and empirical practices, the uses of theories to understand empirical objects. The scholarly pursuit to understand social practices such as reproductive medicine or assisted fertilization is thus to be conceived of as layers of meaning constituting a research problem; socially legitimate problems are translated into research programs that are further anchored in the recursive relationship between theories and empirical studies. Over time, as research work is reported, the social problem is at times (but not always) further legitimized and understood in more detail, leading to refined research problems and research programs, and eventually certain research programs are becoming prestigious or useful in commanding or predicting social or natural processes while others may be abandoned or fall from grace (Lakatos, 1970; Gieryn, 1993; Shostak and Conrad, 2008). The research work is in other words constituted as an assemblage of resources that are mutually dependent and co-produced at the same time as it is propelled by socially legitimate interests.

As being part of clinical medicine, part of the public healthcare sector in Sweden, assisted fertilization is constituted as a heterogeneous field including many professional groups and domains of expertise. In addition, assisted fertilization is part of what has been called a *moral economy*, "a system of transactions which are defined as socially desirable (i.e., moral), because through them social ties are recognized, and balanced social relationships are maintained" (Cheal, 1988: 15). Daston (1995) stresses that the sciences are moral economies in their own right:

> *What I mean by a moral economy is a web of affect-saturated values that stand and function in well-defined relationship to one another. In this usage, "moral" carries its full complement of eighteenth- and nineteenth century resonances: it refers at once to the psychological and to the normative. (Daston, 1995: 4)*

Economy here means, Daston (1995: 4) writes, "[a]n organized system that displays certain regularities, regularities that are explicable but not always predictable in their details." A moral economy is anchored in shared beliefs regarding what is right and what is wrong. Of course, there are few possibilities for including every single individual in a shared moral belief and assisted fertilization has for instance been criticized by religious groups for intervening in the elementary processes of life. Moral economies are instead resting on the capacity of reconciling various beliefs, worldviews and interests to accomplish a policy or a set of rules guiding a specific field and its social practices. For instance, in the case of Sweden, heterosexual couples and lesbian couples are eligible for assisted fertilization treatment while single women are not. Until quite recently, in 2005, lesbian couples were not eligible for the therapy but lesbian and gay activists and political groups argued in favour of a change in policy, leading to the enactment of new regulatory guidelines.

The moral economy is here becoming more liberal inasmuch as new categories of clients are permitted but not liberal to the extent that single women are made eligible for the therapy. In nearby Denmark, sharing many social, cultural and economic conditions with Sweden, single women may take advantage of assisted fertilization clinics and consequently single women being excluded from what is part of the public healthcare services in Sweden travel to Denmark to be inseminated. Various moral beliefs, primarily related to the interests of the unborn child having just one single parent, serve to exclude these single women from the therapy in Sweden. In the emerging bioeconomy, some services are provided by the public healthcare services in many welfare states, but there are still domains that are regarded to be outside of the public healthcare system's responsibilities — assisted fertilization for single women in Sweden being an illustrative case — thereby opening up for private alternatives. This balancing of public and private healthcare is one of the key challenges for healthcare politics in many parts of the world, and are examples of morally loaded matters. Assisted fertilization work is thus pervaded by various moral and normative beliefs, inscribed into policies and regulatory frameworks for clinical practices guiding and monitoring the day-to-day work.

At times, research work or social practices are treated as if they have no underlying particular interests or are pursued from any specific perspective — think for instance of theoretical physics or astronomy — while in other cases research work is highly contested for social (e.g. some domains of feminist research, psychoanalysis) or ethical reasons (e.g. stem cell research in certain countries including the United States under the Bush administration). Reproductive medicine and assisted fertilization are of central concern in any modern culture or human society relying on modern medicine (Ginsburg and Rapp, 1991). Consequently, morals and ethics are always already present in the clinical work, both in the very monitoring practices and regulations and in the interaction between staff and clients, and therefore the study of assisted fertilization is by no means a strictly scholarly pursuit, aiming at inscribing theories into practices, but it is also part of the reproduction of the moral economy of assisted fertilization.

As organization theory researchers, as members of a particular culture and society, as parents or aspiring parents, the analyst is by no means detached or standing apart from the social practices of the assisted fertilization clinics. Instead, the shared morals and ethical norms are already present in the theoretical gaze of the analyst, both helping him or her to see what may be problematic, interesting and worthy of further attention, and what is not, and restraining this gaze to certain topics. For instance, critiques of reproductive medicine and assisted fertilization on the basis of theological concerns are acquiring relatively little attention in basically secular countries like Sweden. When the Pope declares that contraceptives are prohibited even though there is ample evidence of how the use of condoms has positive effects on sexual health and prevents the spread of sexually transmitted diseases in developing countries, such statements are often treated as evidence of the stodgy and backward conservatism of the Catholic Church. That is, religious leaders may be permitted to play ceremonial roles in contemporary society but their ambition to inform and guide humans in other matters is commonly frowned upon in de-traditionalized societies increasingly governed on the basis of scientific evidence and reason rather than religious teachings.

In other words, the moral economy underlying assisted fertilization is what may be called *infra-theoretical* inasmuch as it is rarely surfacing in the research work while it is always already present in the analyst's gaze, in his or her capacity for seeing elements of the empirical material. As Daston (1995: 6) reminds us, "[t]he moral economy of science is more about self-discipline than coercion." The self-discipline and infra-theoretical perspectives elicited in this study are difficult to explicate exactly. However, as researchers and authors of this book, the factors in our context that we have identified as important are that we are part of a society in which the practice has become accepted, shown for example by the fact that in Sweden it has become partially integrated into the public healthcare system. Also, we have no political affiliations, religious views or other similar reasons to be fundamentally skeptical of assisted fertilization. We both have friends and acquaintances who have become parents following assisted fertilization. Though these treatments have sometimes been trying, we also know of people who have gone through the difficult processes of adoption. Thus, prior to the study, we were likely predisposed to a more accepting or positive than negative attitude toward the existence and development of the treatments. The social science theories used in the study have predispositions of both positive and critical standpoints in relation to technoscientific developments, the life sciences and the institutionalization of new organizational practices in general, as the next chapter will show.

In summary, the study of assisted fertilization is a matter of inscribing a particular clinical practice within a wider organization theory framework that already contains certain moralist beliefs and ethical standpoints. There are thus limited possibilities for a "value-neutral" or disinterested view of this social practice but the analyst's view of the matter is already shaped and informed by predominant social beliefs. Still, it is one of the foremost assignments of the practicing researcher to try his or her best to transcend and overcome such institutionalized ways of seeing and believing in order to accomplish new and interesting perspectives on social practices. The capacity to think against the grain is the marker of the creative and innovative scholar, the blessing of the thinker having the ability to transcend his or her immediate life world.

Outline of the Book

The book is composed of three parts. The first part includes two chapters, the Chapter 1 introducing the theoretical framework used to understand assisted fertilization work, and the Chapter 2 reviewing the literature on reproductive medicine and assisted fertilization. The second part includes four empirical chapters. In Chapter 3, the development of assisted fertilization practice and the clinics in Sweden is accounted for, paying specific attention to the institutional and political setting of the 1960s, 1970s and 1980s, wherein the new possibilities in reproductive medicine were transformed into both clinical work but also new legislations and regulatory frameworks. In Chapter 4, the work conducted in the front-office, the domain wherein the clients or patients are encountering the clinicians including gynecologists, midwives, nurses and psychologists, is examined. In this domain, all activities involving the client are located. The work thus both includes medical investigations regarding fertility, the sharing of information regarding, e.g., hormone therapies, and all sorts of counseling activities aimed at supporting the clients or patients emotionally and socially during the therapy.

In Chapter 5, the focus shifts from the front-office to the back-office, the laboratory where all the reproductive materials—gametes such as egg and sperm and embryos—are handled, manipulated, stored and examined. While the front-office work in various ways involves the clients or patients and demands their participation, the work in the laboratory is more technical and analytical and in general the clients or patients are separated from these activities. Also, professionally, the two domains differ inasmuch as the laboratory work is primarily conducted by embryologists, biomedical scientists, biochemists, and so forth, having professional expertise in examining and manipulating human reproductive materials at the cytological, and at times even the molecular, level. Besides the professional expertise and experience demanded to operate in this domain, the laboratories are filled with technologies and other material resources that constitute the laboratory work. In Chapter 6, the final empirical chapter, issues pertaining to the regulatory framework and legislation structuring the work in the clinics are addressed. Rather than being a one-sided process wherein the political and regulatory bodies dictate the regulatory framework, the case of Sweden shows that representatives of reproductive medicine and assisted fertilization clinics are actively informing and negotiating with the political system in order to make assisted fertilization therapies available for as large groups as possible. In addition, the storage and use of human reproductive materials is another domain wherein ongoing discussions across the institutional boundaries have led to new regulatory bodies.

The third part includes Chapter 7 wherein some of the implications for organization theory and management studies are addressed. In addition, the wider question of the role of biopolitics and what could be called "the management of life" are addressed. Reproductive medicine and assisted fertilization practice are interesting because they represent the field of medicine for people that are otherwise healthy and therefore the jurisdictional domain of medicine is extended to not only cure illness but also to deal with impaired or absent biological capacities. Perhaps this is part of the explanation for why assisted fertilization has been received with some skepticism in various quarters over the years, that it is assumed to channel resources away from more pressing medical concerns in, for example, the healthcare and research on terminal diseases. Chapter 7 addresses such issues and seeks to locate assisted fertilization within a wider social and organizational framework and the contemporary bioeconomy. Finally, an appendix accounts for the methodology of the study, its data collection and data analysis methods.

Summary and Conclusion

Reproductive medicine and assisted fertilization is a deeply fascinating domain of the technosciences. Since human reproduction is, biologically speaking, the most central human activity, the key to the reproduction of the species safeguarding that the genome is carried into the future, reproduction is embedded in significant cultural and social beliefs and norms, institutions and taboos. Throughout the history of the human species, reproduction has been mystically concealed within the human body, in the female uterus, and there has been only limited insight into the endocrinology and cytology of the cell division and cell growth taking place after the egg has been fertilized by the sperm. Only during the last 50 years or so have humans been able to actively intervene into the process, and consequently there have been some concerns raised regarding the legitimacy and risks in such endeavors.

The history of reproductive medicine and assisted fertilization practice is in many ways a success story even though representatives of the field are persistently emphasizing that they are failing in about half of the cases. The advancement of new know-how, new technologies, new tools and materials, and policies and regulatory frameworks have all contributed to the gradual stabilization of a technoscientific and medical practice that is both safe and — given the still limited understanding of human infertility — effective. However, describing assisted fertilization as just a technoscientific success story is concealing the expertise and day-to-day accomplishments needed to make the clinics work as well as they do, and consequently it is of interest not only for the field of medical research or the broader social sciences to study assisted fertilization clinics. Also the field of organization theory and management studies needs to pay attention to the advancement and commercialization of the life sciences in order to understand that the contemporary economy is not only a matter of the production and consumption of commodities or services but also that the life sciences make their contributions. For instance, reproductive medicine and cosmetic or aesthetic surgery are two branches of medicine which today are offering clinical services. While the differences between these two domains of expertise are substantial, they are nevertheless derived from research made in experimental medicine and brought to the market as advanced medical services.

At the same time as assisted fertilization clinics need to be studied from an organization theory perspective, such a view can never be taken in isolation from wider social changes and interests. In the contemporary period, biopolitical programs are not only targeting human health and sanitation but are also starting to include new medical and technoscientific possibilities derived from the life sciences. In the emerging bioeconomy, characterized by the commercialization and commodification of the life sciences, some services are accommodated by and provided by the public healthcare services in many welfare states, but there are still domains that are regarded to be outside of the public healthcare system's responsibilities — cosmetic surgery being once again an illustrative case—thereby opening up for private alternatives. This balancing of public and private healthcare is one of the key challenges for healthcare politics in many parts of the world, and deciding what should be included in the public health offering and what should be excluded are not trivial matters. Recently, debates such as whether erectile dysfunction therapies such as Viagra should be sponsored by the state or not have again emphasized the porous and fluid line of demarcation between what could be regarded a public responsibility and a private concern, related to moral economies.

In the bioeconomy, fueled by new possibilities derived from the life sciences, such issues are surfacing all the time, potentially leaving policy makers and politicians with a growing number of controversies to be resolved. However, it is one of the intentions of this book to show that it is possible to strike a balance between public responsibilities and private and enterprising initiatives when translating medical know-how and clinical expertise into marketable commodities. In the contemporary society, there is no strict separation between markets and hierarchies but quite often the two blend without any major controversies. Expressed differently, in the general liberalization of the markets, opening up for private initiatives, there is still a role to be played by the state and the public sector and such positions are not undermining the role of enterprising and entrepreneurial actors. If there is a still something like a "third way" in politics, it is this capacity to organize the bioeconomy as what is balancing the public healthcare and private alternatives.

1

Materiality, Technoscience and Organizing

Introduction

The field of reproductive medicine and its clinical branch, assisted fertilization, needs to be understood within a broader socioeconomic and cultural framework including the emergence of the modern welfare state and what Michel Foucault speaks of as biopolitics and what more recent scholars such as Rose (2007) have referred to as the bioeconomy. In addition, reproductive medicine is part of the technoscientific field of the life sciences, aiming at understanding biological systems and ultimately life per se.

The field of medicine has its roots in ancient thinking, and major contributors to the field of medicine in the ancient period, such as Hippocrates and Galen, are invoked as forerunners to modern-day medicine (Bynum, 1994). Medicine has been an academic discipline from the very beginning, siding with theology and law as the classic disciplines. In places such as Padua and Paris, medical schools were established as part of the university system already in the thirteenth century but, to be fair, medieval medicine was nothing like contemporary advanced healthcare science. When, for instance, the plague, the Black Death, swept through Europe in the middle of the fourteenth century, leaving entire regions devastated, the physicians of the day had few cures to offer. The curious thing with medicine is that while doctors were unable to provide many advanced therapies until at least the end of the eighteenth century when the smallpox vaccine was developed by Edward Jenner, it has always been a highly prestigious profession:

> What is striking about the traditionally high status of medicine is the fact that it was based on virtually no valid expertise at all. The training on which physicians prided themselves consisted of ancient works like Galen, containing

> *physiological theories whose practical application were not merely wrong but positively harmful. Prevailing theories of disease led to practices such as bleeding and purging as major cures ... In general, with the exception of Jenner's smallpox vaccination developed in 1798, there were no valid medical treatments at all until 1850. (Collins, 1979: 139)*

Potentially because physicians operate in the intersection between life and death and patients have little hope other than to trust the physician's advice, medicine has been a status profession for centuries (Attewell, 1990). However, incompetent and unqualified physicians have received their fair share of ridicule. According to Voltaire, "the art of the medical profession consists in amusing the patient for as long as it takes nature to cure him or her" (Voltaire, cited by Blech, 2006: ix), and no less than four comedies written by Molière feature incompetent physicians. However, from the end of the eighteenth century and the first half of the nineteenth century, medicine shifted from being a speculative practice rooted in ancient thinking, most noteworthy Galen's doctrine of how the "fluids" of the human body regulated health, to being an experimental field of research.

While early pioneers such as Tomas Sydenham in the UK and Xavier Bichat in France made major contributions to the advancement of clinical medicine (Bynum, 1994, 2008), Claude Bernard's *An introduction to the study of experimental medicine*, first published in 1865, is often regarded as the starting point for modern medicine. Throughout the nineteenth century, the sciences were transformed from being "amateur sciences" or activities funded by the European courts to modern disciplines located in the institution of the research university (Lenoir, 1994; Bynum, 1994). Unlike the natural sciences such as chemistry and physics—biology was not yet an independent discipline—medicine was not thriving in the university system wherein old doctrines were dogmatically debated, effectively preventing the development of experimental practices. Instead, the medical schools, located in the very domain of practice, became the principal site for the advancement of medicine as a scientific discipline. As a consequence, medicine was from the very beginning instituted as a professional practice standing with one foot in scholarly pursuits and theorizing and with one foot in the practical work to diagnose and cure the sick. Ever since this dual model has been established, it has served as the guiding principle and a predominant institutional logic for the medical school.

The marrying of the experimental sciences and medicine as a professional practice has been an ongoing pursuit and still today there is a debate whether, for example, medical school students should be trained in the experimental sciences by, for example, biochemists or if their education should be more exclusively focused on the clinical work of the profession (Dunn and Jones, 2010). Such debates and controversies reflect the history of the discipline as being constituted by converging paths. At the same time, in the university setting, advancement of biochemistry and related disciplines provided new inroads to the study of the biological systems, and gradually biology became an individual discipline operating within its own institutional boundaries. In addition, while the period between 1730 and 1790 was dominated by mechanistic theories of biological systems (Riskin, 2003: 118), from the beginning of the nineteenth century, mechanist thinking was gradually replaced by vitalist theories.[1]

Undoubtedly, the history of modern medicine is by and large a success story. The capacity to cure disease and to use surgery to save life and human suffering is for most people one of the finest contributions of mankind. However, increased life expectancy is not only an accomplishment of medicine but is equally an effect of various political decisions leading to better housing, better nutrition, fewer people dying from war and armed conflicts, and so forth. In many cases, commentators have argued, such improvements derived from the democratization of society and a more equal distribution of economic resources have been of greater importance than advanced medicine. Regardless of such discussions, modern-day medicine is in many ways a remarkable accomplishment and almost daily news regarding the advancement of the discipline is reported.

In the late modern period, characterized by the influence of the advancement of the technosciences in virtually any domain of human lives and the political concern for managing not only health but also "life at large" (Rose, 2007), medicine is brought to the fore. Today, the life sciences and medicine are commercialized in various ways and for instance cosmetic, plastic or aesthetic surgery, a branch of experimental medicine and surgery, is a booming industry in the intersection between medicine, and more specifically surgery, the beauty industry and celebrity culture.

While the manufacturing of goods and the service industries may have diminishing return on utility—there may be a limitation on, for example, how many television sets one may need—the life sciences are today in a position

---

1 The vitalist theories were partially derived from the writings of Kant on the concepts of *Bildungstrieb*, a form of self-perpetuating force of biological organisms and *anlagen*, the "purposive dispositions" of biological organisms (Bennett, 2010: 65; Lenoir, 1980).

to offer services and therapies that are claimed to curb the natural effects of ageing or increasing the well-being of humans. Such effects may have less diminishing return on utility and as the population in the Western part of the world is becoming older yet economically well endowed, there are ample opportunities for commercial products and therapies resting on life science know-how. What Rose (2007) calls the bioeconomy is thus characterized by an ongoing commercialization and commodification of the life sciences. Terms such as "biovalue" (Mitchell and Waldby, 2001; Waldby, 2002) and "biocapital" (Sunder Rajan, 2006; Helmreich, 2008) have been introduced—in general, the prefix "bio" tends to be used *ad nauseam* in some scholarly literature (see, e.g., Oliver, 2000)—to capture how know-how pertaining to the mechanisms and regulation of biological systems is generating economic value when being transformed into commodities and therapies. In the contemporary period, the life sciences are brought to the forefront of both political and commercial interests.

Living in Material Worlds

MODERNITY AND MATERIALITY

One of the key terms in denoting historical eras in the social science vocabulary is the concept of modernity and combinations thereof. Understanding the broader socioeconomic and cultural context of the emergence and organization of assisted fertilization is also related to the unique characteristics of the modern era, as it relates to materiality. Modernity, Gunning (1995: 15) argues, is less of a "demarcated historical period" as it is a "change in experience." These experiences were clearly marked by the change in production during the industrial revolution of the nineteenth century and the swift technological advances of the century leading to "the growth of urban traffic, the distribution of mass-produced goods, and successive new technologies of transportation and communication" (Gunning, 1995: 15). Especially the period from the late 1840s to the end of the 1870s saw the take-off of mass-production capitalism. Between 1830 and 1870 foreign trade in Germany, Scandinavia, Britain, Austria and France increased between four and five times (Hobsbawm, 1975: 50). The railway mileage increased in Europe from 1,700 miles in 1850 to 101,700 miles in 1880; in North America the growth was from 2,800 miles to 100,600 miles of railway (Hobsbawm, 1975: 54). In addition, between 1850 and 1880 British steam tonnage increased by 1,600 percent and in the rest of the world it increased by 400 percent (Hobsbawm, 1975: 58). In the 1840s and 1850s, the telegraph spread across Europe and North America, from 2,000 miles in 1849 to 111,000 miles in 1869 (Hobsbawm, 1975: 69).

All these economic and technical advancements helped produce an entirely different society even though the speed of industrialization varied greatly between countries and regions. The mass-production capitalist economic regime dominated in most of Europe and North America, periods of economic decline during, for example, the great depression in the 1870s and the 1930s aside, until the early 1970s. This period, starting arguably as suggested by Hobsbawm (1975) after the revolutionary year of 1848, and finishing around the first oil crisis in 1973, has been called the modern period. These 12 decades of swift economic growth and increased welfare and consumption were characterized by a significant modification of the urban space as railways, skyscrapers, factories and transportation systems were constructed and laid out on the land. This modernity was concrete and immutable, manifested in bricks, cement and metal.

The period after 1973 looks somewhat different, especially from the middle of the last decade of the twentieth century when the Internet and digital media start to influence social interactions. While the modern period was characterized by conspicuous and solid forms of materiality, the so-called late modern period (a phrase used by Anthony Giddens) is defined on basis of the flow of information. "The system's 'matter' has changed 'phase,' at least since Bergson. It is more liquid than solid, more air like than liquid, more informational than material," Serres and Latour (1995: 121) say, pointing at the shift in focus from goods to services, from commodities to information, as the principal driver of the economy in the late modern period.

The influence of the manufacturing industry is shrinking in the Western world and instead knowledge-intensive industries and the service sector grow in proportion. Unemployment rates are stuck at around the 10 percent level or even higher in most parts of the Western world. While the modern period was characterized by its immediacy, its direct and highly visible consequences, the late modern period is more elusive and fluid, bound up with abstract social and technical systems that are far from transparent for the outsider. For instance, the growth of a finance industry operating on the basis of the trade of sophisticated derivative instruments whose function outsiders barely understand is indicative of how some industries are more or less obscure for the layperson. Between 1997 and 2007, the global market for derivatives rose from $41 trillion to $677 trillion (Callinicos, 2009: 74), testifying to the increased importance of the finance industry.

Lipovetsky (2005: 40) uses the term "hypermodernity" to capture some of the *Zeitgeist* of the contemporary period, suggesting that this period of time demonstrates a "paradoxical combination of frivolity and anxiety, euphoria and vulnerability, playfulness and dread." While the modern period, as emphasized by Lyotard (1984) in his influential essay, was characterized by the grand narrative of progress and liberation, such "narratives of progress" (Lipovetsky, 2005: 35) are displaced by "an anxiety about the future." Lipovetsky (2005) even suggests that the contemporary period is characterized by an increased focus on the present, on immediate consumption and need satisfaction:

> *A whole hedonistic and psychologistic culture has come into being; it incites everyone to satisfy their needs immediately, it stimulates their clamour for pleasure, idolizes self-fulfilment, and sets the earthy paradise of well-being, comfort and leisure on a pedestal. Consume without delay, travel, enjoy yourself, renounce nothing: the politics of a radiant future have been replaced by consumption as the promise of a euphoric present. (Lipovetsky, 2005: 37)*

Stiegler (2011) makes a similar argument, speaking about stability as an "exception" in the modern mindset:

> *Before the Industrial Revolution, adoption occurred according to traditional rhythms and rituals that framed change within the horizon of a primordial, eternal stability: change was seen as an accident. Modernity has reversed this point of view: stability had become the accident, the exception, and change the rule. (Stiegler, 2011: 92)*

In this perspective, there is an "accelerated obsolescence" in the present period (Lipovetsky, 2005: 36), an emphasis on consuming new products and abandoning the old regardless of their functionality. Like in perhaps no previous period, commodities become obsolete at a faster rate. Lipovetsky (2005) thus portrays the contemporary period as being a composite of essentially opposing forces and emotions, a blend of frivolity and anxiety, a consumerist ideology devoid of meaning as work opportunities recede. In the late modern or hypermodern period, a socially constructed culture of worry and concern is blending with a consumerist ethos enabling the circulation of capital; humans worry about their future, about work opportunities, interest rate levels, and property values, at the same time as they are expanding their consumption. "In the US in 1980 the average household owed around $40,000 (in constant dollars) but now it's about $130,000 for every household, including mortgages," Harvey (2010: 17) reports. Private consumption is apparently the driving force behind the capitalist regime of accumulation but at the costs of concerns regarding payment schedules and interest rates.

The institutional structure of the economy is accompanied by technological changes. Modernity operated on the basis of tangible technologies but the late modern society is by and large defined on the basis of the information and communication technologies, the digital media, constituting everyday life. If the railroad (in the nineteenth century) and eventually the automobile (in the twentieth century) producing new transformation networks defined the modern era, digital media (e.g. the computer) shape the late modern period. Much has been written and said about the computer by social theorists, philosophers, historians and media pundits and it is beyond doubt that the computer has enabled a swift circulation of information and new forms of simulation and computation. Digital media are thus the infrastructure par excellence in the contemporary period. This shift to digital media as the principal dominant technology does not imply that the modernist technologies become irrelevant; on the contrary, the railroads and the freeways still serve an important purpose in constituting society but they are receiving less thought and reflection as they primarily sustain rather than overturn social formations in the contemporary period. The modernist space of buildings and roads are still further developed but their cultural significance is lowered in comparison to, for example, digital media. Under all conditions, the late modern society is inextricably bound up with various forms of materiality, with the tools, technologies and materials mobilized in the day-to-day work to reproduce society. Such materiality is part of the context of the emergence and enactment of assisted fertilization, as the case studies presented in this volume will demonstrate.

THE NEW MATERIALISM

The influential role of materiality in the modern period and the relationship to social patterns has consequences for different groups in society. In the field of gender theory and feminist studies, the concept of materiality has been heavily debated (Fraser, 2002), especially in what has been referred to as the third wave of feminist thinking (Mann and Huffman, 2005). Feminist scholars have demonstrated a long-standing skepticism regarding biological explanations of gender differences and inequalities and in many cases this has left them with a social constructionist epistemology (Ahmed, 2010).

The work of post-structrualist feminist philosphers such as Judith Butler (1993, 1999), Elizabeth Grosz (2004, 2005) and Rosi Braidotti (1994, 2002, 2006), and work in the field of feminist studies of technoscience (Johnson, 2007, 2008; Fraser et al., 2005; Fraser, 2003), embodiment (Sharp, 2011; Gimlin, 2010; Heyes, 2009; Pitts-Taylor, 2007; Blum, 2005; Witz, 2000; Broadhurst, 1999) and feminist epistemology (Barad, 1998, 2003, 2007) have aimed at rehabilitating a feminist enactment of matter. As Ahmed (2010: 32) remarks in her review paper on what has been called the "new materialism" (Hird, 2004; Coole and Frost, 2010) "feminism it seems has forgotten how matter matters." Lykke (2010) proposes the term "post-constructionism" to capture the recent work to reconcile materiality and feminist thinking, a term emphasizing that constructionist epistemology no longer needs to be the sole alternative to "naïve" biologism and other forms of crude material epistemologies. This new materialism is indebted to a series of philosophical programs aiming at theorizing matter not as an inert and passive entity but as what is changeable and fluid.[2]

The literature on new materialism in the feminist literature is quite diverse and is characterized by polemics. The work of Karen Barad (1998, 2003, 2007), fueled by the epistemological writings of quantum physicist Niels Bohr, one of the true heroes of twentieth-century technoscience, is one such recent comprehensive ontological and epistemological framework taking a firm stance vis-à-vis relativist epistemologies while avoiding naïve realist positions. In Barad's feminist epistemology (Rouse, 2004; Pinch, 2011), matter is to be examined within specific experimental systems and since all matter is situated and context-dependent, it is also objectively true that certain materiality exists. Barad suggests that the experimental system and the matter produced therein (molecules, neutrines, etc.) cannot be isolated and examined as individual entities; the experimental system and its materiality are always of necessity co-produced. This renders matter as a fabricated and engineered resource, not a "brute" indisputable fact that is always already given "by nature." For feminist theorists, this distinction between what is "natural" and "encultured" or "fabricated" is a cumbersome line of demarcation, but Barad suggests that matter as we know it is primarily produced within an engineered technoscientific system.

Also outside of the gender theory and feminist studies circles, the issue of materiality has been addressed by, for example, Manuel DeLanda (1997, 2002, 2006) and Brian Massumi (2002), a corpus of texts that are thoroughly influenced

---

2   This epistemological line of thinking perhaps begins with Spinoza (Giancotti, 1997) and includes philosopher such as Nietzsche, Bergson, William James, Whitehead and Deleuze.

by the work of Gilles Deleuze. In the social science literature, there is an interest in conceptualizing and studying the materiality of everyday life (Miller, 2005, 2010) and the concept of *object* has been much theorized in both the social science literature (Brown, 2010; Daston, 2008; Henare et al., 2007; Turkle, 2007; Law and Singleton, 2005; Harré, 2002; Pels et al., 2002; Knorr Cetina, 1997) and in management studies (Suchman, 2005; Adler, 2005; Fleming and Spicer, 2005; Lowe, 2004). There is a growing interest, not only in feminist circles, in the need for appropriating new forms of materialism escaping determinst biologism, in all things material, tangible and physical constituting everyday life.

In technoscience, researchers rarely if ever encounter nature "in the raw" but rather develop and fine-tune experimental systems capable of recreating controlled specimens of nature. The concept of new materialism—despite all its polemical shortcomings, most noteworthy the claim of novelty and epochality (consider the small but important linguistic marker "new")—is useful when examining and studying the commercialization of life science know-how and assisted fertilization work more specifically. The term also testifies to a newly awakened interest for materiality and matter at large. In the social sciences and the field of organization theory and management studies, the "linguistic turn" has dominated for a significant period of time, rendering narratives and forms of communication and symbolism the principal resources for the study of social systems. But social systems are not only a matter of storytelling and symbols but are equally sites where material resources are mobilized and put to work; overlooking and ignoring materiality is thus to fail to understand how social systems are constituted and work. Consequently, the literature on new materialism is of great importance for the research program presented in this volume since it involves social humans who organize, offer and receive technoscientific interventions into material bodies.

Materiality Put to Work: Technoscientific Practices

CONSTRUCTING EXPERIMENTAL SYSTEMS

The development and emergence of the life sciences and assisted fertilization is part of a general development of experimental sciences. This development is in turn related to a fundamental shift in the role of theory in science in general. Rheinberger (1999) speaks of a shift in the philosophy of science from a Kuhnian view (after Thomas S. Kuhn) of "science as theory" to a Fleckian or Bachelardian view (after Ludwik Fleck and Gaston Bachelard) of "science as experimentation and practice." In this latter view, theories are indispensable products from scientific work but they are still part of a larger experimental setup including technologies, tools, laboratory specimens such as tissue or genetically modified animals, and so forth. Kuhn (1962) rendered scientific work as what is essentially a struggle over what theoretical framework had the highest explanatory potential, and, *ipso facto*, the highest legitimacy, but Fleck and Bachelard conceived of technoscience as what is bound up with the very materiality put to use—a materiality that is always in peril, always at stake, always at risk in terms of malfunctioning. At the same time, Ludwik Fleck regarded science as being based on the work of a *Fachleute*, a "community of experts" (Rheinberger, 2010a: 170) being in the position to create their own rules of engagement. Says Fleck:

> For the natural sciences is the art to shape a democratic reality and to orient oneself accordingly—therefore to become transformed by it. It is a permanent, much more synthetic than analytic, never ending work, like the work of a river which forms its own bed. This is true, living natural science. We never must forget its creative-synthetic and social-historical aspects. (Ludwik Fleck cited by Rheinberger, 2010a: 170)

Scientists are inventors of worlds, populated by tools, machines, specimens and theoretical frameworks, wherein "the acquisition of knowledge, especially of scientific knowledge, becomes an iterative procedure, out of which the possibilities for the next round emerge only gradually and depend on the actual state of epistemic affairs" (Rheinberger, 2010a: 172).

In addition, Gaston Bachelard emphasizes the role of what he calls *phenomenotechnologies*, "[e]nterprises addressing and shaping their objects of investigation in the laboratory in a technical horizon," in Rheinberger's (2010a: 172) formulation. Bachelard suggests that the technologies used in scientific work are not freestanding entities capable of mirroring underlying and external realities. Instead, the technologies used always already contain the working hypotheses of the practicing scientists; they are what Bachelard referred to as a *théoreme reifiée*, a "reified theorem"—a theory translated into a technological apparatus. "Phenomena must be selected, filtered, purified, shaped by instruments; indeed, it may well be the instruments that produce the phenomenon in the first place. And instruments are nothing but theories materialized," Bachelard (1984: 13) says.

Fleck suggests that scientific communities are "thought collectives" sharing a basic "thought style" (German, *Denkstile*) and Bachelard proposes that the very thought style is already manifested in the experimental system being developed within a field of technoscientific investigation. Based on these two "post-Kuhnian" epistemological frameworks—which in fact are better described as "pre-Kuhnian frameworks" in terms of not only preceding the works of Thomas S. Kuhn but also, as in the case of Ludwik Fleck, shaping Kuhn's epistemology—Rheinberger constructs his theory of technoscience on the basis of two central concepts, that of the *experimental system* and the *epistemic object*.

Rheinberger (1999: 288) reserves the term *experimental system* for "a unit of research, designed to give answers to questions we are not yet capable to ask clearly," i.e. it is a "device" that "not only generates answers" but also "shapes the questions to be answered." Rheinberger (1997) clarifies how an experimental system is constituted:

> *Experimental systems are to be seen as the smallest integral working units of research. As such, they are systems of manipulations designed to give unknown answers to questions that the experimenters themselves are not yet able clearly to ask ... They [laboratory machinery] are not simply experimental devices that generate answers; experimental systems are vehicles for materializing questions. They inextricably cogenerate the phenomena of material entities and the concepts they come to embody. (Rheinberger, 1997: 28)*

Rheinberger (1997, 1999) thus uses the concept of experimental system to denote the entire technoscientfic apparatus that are put to use to explore any natural (e.g. physical, chemical, biological) system. Experimental systems include tools, technologies, specimens, regimes for inscriptions, analytical procedures and theories, all making their own idiosyncratic contribution to the constitution of an understanding of an object of inquiry. An experimental system is commonly assembled in a laboratory but is not reducible to the local site as the experimental system is ultimately distributed across the community of researchers.[3]

---

3   Rheinberger's concept of experimental system is Fleckian in emphasizing the importance of communal resources (theoretical frameworks, technological skills, analytical procedures, and narrative competencies) and Bachelardian in stressing that the technologies and tools mobilized in the work already contain the operative hypotheses of the research community.

Just like Fleck used the metaphor of a river shaping its river bed to illustrate how the scientific community is recursively both constituting and constituted by the research work, so too does Rheinberger suggest that the experimental system is shaped and modified as new empirical data is being produced; new theories and ad hoc hypotheses are added to the analytical framework to accommodate the new findings, new laboratory practices serve to handle specific concerns. "An experimental system can be compared to a labyrinth whose walls, in the course of being erected, simultaneously blind and guide the experimenter," Rheinberger (1999: 291) says. The experimental system thus constitutes the life world of the scientist, the domain or *topos* wherein he or she is pursuing certain goals and constituting the horizon of possible explanations to identify phenomena. Alluding to Niklas Luhmann (1995), the experimental system is in Rheinberger's view something like an autopoetic system, capable of both producing and accommodating new communication. This brings us to the second important concept in Rheinberger's analytical framework, that of the *epistemic object*.

While the experimental system is the totality of tangible and intangible resources put to work in technoscientific practice, ranging from the prestigious and spectacular new technologies located at the center of the research activities—what Hackman (1989: 32) calls "heroic devices"—to the small and seemingly insignificant (i.e. the notepads wherein the researcher jots down observations, scattered thoughts, what Rheinberger [2010b] refers to as the "notes and scribbling" of the research work), the epistemic objects are the principal "output" from the experimental system. This does not make epistemic objects wholly unified and tangible "objects" in the conventional sense but they may be fluid and malleable entities whose very existence is at times disputed (as in the case of elementary particles in high-energy physics) or whose status as entity or process may be debated. Says Rheinberger (1997):

> [Epistemic things] are material entities or processes—physical structures, chemical reactions, biological functions—that constitute the objects of inquiry. As epistemic objects, they present themselves in a characteristic, irreducible vagueness. This vagueness is inevitably because, paradoxically, epistemic things embody what one does not yet know. Scientific objects have the precarious status of being absent in their experimental presence; they are not simply hidden things to be brought into light through sophisticated manipulations. (Rheinberger, 1997: 28)

Experimental systems are thus structured around the study of certain elementary epistemic objects, for instance, in the case of the life sciences, a gene sequence, a protein or a group of proteins, a certain metabolic process and the metabolites produced. Epistemic objects are thus analytical entities that to some extent embody—similar to the technologies used—the underlying theoretical assumptions.

Rheinberger (2010b) spends some time explaining how epistemic objects can be quite vague and flexible without de-stabilizing the experimental system producing the epistemic object. "Imprecise epistemic objects and concepts work because they are malleable and can be integrated into different contexts in accordance with changing needs," Rheinberger (2010b: 157) remarks, underlining how experimental systems may work with relatively fluid and changeable epistemic objects. For instance, the epistemic object of the "gene," of key importance for the life sciences since the rediscovery of Mendel's research on the hereditary material in the first years of the twentieth century by German biologists, is an example of an epistemic object demonstrating such shifting meanings:

> The epistemic object known as a "gene" was and remains influential in the history of heredity, not least because it displays the imprecision typical of such entities. Yet this situation should not lead us to make blanket generalization: not all fertile scientific concepts must be polysemic. My aim is not to strike precision from the list of scientific values. What people understand by precision is, however, historically variable. Moreover, arriving at a more precise understanding of what imprecision means in science—that is, treating it as an epistemic possibility rather than rejecting it out of hand—is one of the main objectives. (Rheinberger, 2010b: 168)

By being "polysemic," an epistemic object can serve many purposes and maintain and uphold many experimental activities. As technosciences are moving toward more complex research problems (i.e. the exploration of the biological pathways involved in neurodegenerate diseases), it is becoming more complicated to formulate theories about entities that are freestanding and are located in quite simple cause-and-effects schemes. Instead, scientists work with complex analytical models wherein a range of epistemic objects are interrelated, yet analytically separated to be able to pursue their research work. "As the complexity of a system increases, our ability to make precise and yet-not trivial assertions about its behaviour diminishes," Lofti Zadeh (1987, cited in Rheinberger, 2010b: 169) argues. In other words, the very term "epistemic objects" is something like a misnomer because there may not be a distinct "object" that is being studied but instead entire processes or cycles (e.g. the production of protein on the basis of specific gene sequences, so-called *Single Nucleotide Polymorphisms* or SNPs) are examined.

Regardless of such analytical difficulties facing scientists, Rheinberger's analytical model separating experimental system and epistemic objects is useful because it emphasizes the gradual and ongoing stabilization and modification of the experimental system and its output (notes and scribbles, data, epistemic objects, propositions and theories, etc.). Using Simondon's (1980) vocabulary, one may argue that experimental systems are individuating and transducing as they respond to new information and new conditions. Rather than being once and for all settled, experimental systems unfold in the course of practical research work. In this view, the experimental system is not what is constructed "in the heads" of scientists in their theoretical models and analytical procedures, nor is it what is simply laid down in the technologies, but experimental systems are constituted at the very intersection of a range of resources, tangible as well as abstract, advanced as well as mundane. However, at the bottom line, the scientists, in the life sciences and otherwise, are dependent on the materiality they are mobilizing—the technologies, the specimens, the laboratory animals, and the preparations.

INSTRUMENTAL TECHNOLOGIES AND MODEL ORGANISMS

It is here possible to make a distinction in, for example, the life sciences between the *instrumental technologies* being part of the infrastructure of the experimental system and the *model organisms*, the particular biological system (e.g. a genetically modified mouse or a yeast cell) used to represent an entire category of biological organisms. In the research work, these two categories of materiality are constantly interrelated. Jasanoff (2005: 3) uses the term *co-production* when addressing how science and society are always bound up and produced in tandem; society is always already present in the research work and scientific contributions shape and inform society (Shostak and Conrad, 2008). Social beliefs about, for example, obesity as being a health concern and potentially dangerous leads to research activities (Monaghan et al., 2010; Throsby, 2009; Jonvallen, 2006) and once research is reported, often in the case of popular science journalism, it produces social consequences. Jasanoff (2005) explicates her position:

Science, in the co-productionist framework, is understood as neither the simple reflections of the truth about nature nor an epiphenomenon of social and political interests. Rather, co-production is symmetrical in that it calls attention to the social dimensions of cognitive commitments and understandings, while at the same time underscoring the epistemic and material correlates of social formation. Co-production can therefore be seen as a critique of the realist ideology that persistently separates the domain of nature, facts, objectivity, reason and policy from those of culture, values, subjectivity, emotions and politics. (Jasanoff, 2005: 3)

Adhering to a line of demarcation between, on the one hand, instrumental technologies and, on the other, model organisms, these two groups of resources play distinct roles in "co-producing" technoscience and society. Hacking (1992: 58) argues that "instruments" serve a central role in maintaining and reproducing science: "The process of modifying the workings of instruments—both materially (we fix them up) and intellectually (we re-describe what they do)—furnishes the glue that keeps the intellectual and material world together. It is what stabilizes science." Speaking of the *matériel* of the research work, a term denoting the "apparatus, the instruments, the substances or objects investigated," Hacking (1992: 32) argues that the material resources are "flanked on the one side by ideas (theories, questions, hypotheses, intellectual models of apparatuses) and on the other by marks and manipulations of marks (inscriptions, data, calculations, data reduction, interpretation)."

Schickore's (2007) study of the development of the microscope, a technology examined in detail in Robert Hooke's monograph *Micrographia* published in 1665, demonstrates how instruments, theories and data are co-produced and folded into one another. "[T]o understand microscopy, one needs to look beyond technical, theoretical, and institutional developments and take into consideration the microscopists' methodological and epistemological reflection and practices," Schickore (2007: 3) says. As the microscopes were technically refined, the "precision" of the observations was enhanced and consequently the community of scientists using visual inspection and microscopes became aware of the need for accuracy in the measuring devices (Schickore, 2007: 68–69).

Consequently, *precision* became a central epistemic category in scientific ideologies. At the same time, the microscope was used differently by various scientific communities; mathematical surveyors greeted the microscope as a tool that extended their technical possibilities while anatomists in experimental medicine used the microscope to validate concrete research results—the cell theory developed in the nineteenth century in experimental medicine and biology is for instance indebted to visual media (Harris, 1999). The microscope was thus enacted within pre-existing scholarly communities exploring different domains. Schickore (2007) demonstrates that the instruments of visual inspection were both expanding the domain of scientific possibilities (leading to, for example, increased precision in visual observation and the verification of theories) at the same time as the microscope was shaped by the predominant beliefs, norms and scientific ideologies of its users.

For Pickering (1995: 7), proposing what he calls a *pragmatic realism* epistemology refusing any correspondence theories, theories suggesting that scientific vocabularies and theorems are capable of "corresponding to" underlying matter,[4] suggests that instruments such as machines are "balance points" occupying liminal positions between "the human and nonhuman worlds." In this view, instruments and machines are capable of anchoring and aligning various resources, serving as manifestations of technoscientific expertise and authority. Griesemer (1992: 55) makes a distinction between what he calls *instruments* and *detectors* wherein the former are "objects designed to measure," offering some kind of frequency or ratio or other numerical data serving as the input for further analysis, while the latter are "devices constructed according to known processes that demonstrate the occurrences of phenomena, as, for example, ammeters use known properties of electricity and magnetism to detect electronic currents." Instruments thus measure the magnitude of qualities examined and detectors identify occurrences. Griesemer (1992) is adding that in many cases detectors are functioning as instruments and therefore the two categories are overlapping. Griesemer (1992) shows how difficult it is to establish mutually excluding taxonomies in the analysis of technoscientific practices as experimental systems are operating on basis of a patchwork of mutually constitutive resources (e.g. theories and instruments).

In addition to instrumental technologies, model organisms are technologies in the sense that they are technoscientific tools, fabricated nature, developed as an ersatz resource for nature "in the raw." Rheinberger (2010b: 224) speaks of the model organism as "one of the technical conditions of an experimental system in which the epistemic object acquires its characteristic contours."

4   In an interview published in 2003, Pickering (2003: 90) clarified this position: "I am not a correspondence realist. I think that contemplating such structures is at best an aid to the imagination, a kind of mental gymnastics that can help some people to think becoming. And I think imagination is important because how we imagine the world to be and how we act in it hang together. That goes with my performative story of knowledge in relation to practice."

Rheinberger (2010b: 7) defines the term accordingly: "A model organism is a living thing from the plant, animal, or bacterial kingdom that has been tailored to experimental purposes: manipulating it can generate insights into the constitution, development, or evolution of an entire class of organisms." Being a variety of biological systems including laboratory animals such as genetically modified mice (Rader, 2004) or standard, relatively simple biological systems such as the Drosophila, the fruit-fly or banana-fly (Kohler, 1994), a yeast cell, or a virus, the model organism "stands in" for biological systems *in general*. Serving this role and being located in-between "technology" and "life," the model organism oscillates between representing a class and being a singularity.

The model organism creates the possibility for producing what Fujimura (1996) calls "doable problems," providing the scientists with a fully equipped experimental system, but leaves the scientific community with the question whether one can make inferential statements regarding for instance how the metabolism of a particular yeast cell corresponds to the human metabolism in type 2 diabetes patients. Does the yeast cell metabolism merely represent itself or can broader and more general statements regarding the process of metabolism be made on basis of observations made in the model organism? One of the standing phrases in popular science journalism is that certain observations have been done in a specific group of model organisms (e.g. mice) but that "there is a need for further research prior to any therapies being produced," testifying both to the widespread use of the model organism in the life sciences and that there are major epistemological leaps involved in moving from one model organism to the clinic.

Under all circumstances, the model organism is truly a balance point in Pickering's (1995) sense of the term as being the nexus where technology and life meet: "[In biological experiments] life and technology meet; since in general the living entity is wet and soft and the technological one is dry and hard special precautions have been taken to ensure their compatibility," Rheinberger (2010b: 218) writes. While the experimental system is largely composed of technologies and tools, the model organism is a living entity that is given the status of capturing "the living" in its totality: "Model organisms are *organic* tools and for that very reason are all the more valuable since the instrument is made of the same organic stuff as the object under investigation" (Rheinberger, 2010b: 224).

In Rheinberger's view, the widespread use of the model organism is making the distinction between culture and nature less meaningful, even to the point where it "may begin to disappear altogether." Since technoscience operates on the basis of fabricated species of nature such as genetically modified mice, for example the famous oncomouse (see, for example, Murray, 2010), nature and culture are no longer separated by some epistemological iron curtain but culture is already laid down in the scientific practices and culture (i.e. society) is accommodating the advances of the sciences and leading to new social practices and desires (as in the case of cosmetic surgery, derived from the advancement of sophisticated surgery know-how and biomaterials. See, for example, Davis, 2002; Brooks, 2004; Blum, 2005; Pitts-Taylor, 2007; Holliday and Cairnie, 2007; Gimlin, 2007; Heyes, 2009; Heyes and Jones, 2009). Jasanoff's (2004) idea of co-production applies to the analysis of model organisms.

In summary, Rheinberger (1997, 1999, 2010a, 2010b) proposes a materialist theory of technoscience, speaking of experimental systems and epistemic objects as being interrelated and co-produced as a collective social practice embedded in the informed use of material resources such as instrumental technologies and model organisms.

THE USE OF VISUAL MEDIA IN THE LIFE SCIENCES

The history of the sciences and experimental medicine is also a history of the various technologies, tools and media used in the pursuit of exploring biological matter. In the nineteenth century, the great breakthrough of the empirical sciences such as experimental medicine (Bernard, 1957; Bynum, 1994; Foucault, 1973), new instruments were developed using both visual (Schickore, 2007; Pasveer, 2006; Warwick, 2005; Golan, 2004; Cartwright, 1995) and audible perception (Sterne, 2003) to guide and support the diagnosis of the patient and the examination of biological specimens:

> [M]odern medicine embodies in its development a movement from the theoretical to the perceptual. This rise of empiricism is key here, but more important than the approach is the construction of a new object ... Hearing would play a tremendous role in this new medical epistemology. (Sterne, 2003: 192)

In Victorian England, precision was a fashionable term and the new technologies and media such as the microscope, a technology developed during the scientific revolution of the seventeenth century, both drew on and reinforced this norm of precision. Porter (1995) argues that the concern for precision was embedded in the comprehensive social reorganization of nineteenth-century society, characterized by urbanization and quick economic growth by the mid-century. The very idea of precision was thus produced both outside of and within scientific communities:

> *Exact measures were the product of reorganizations of working practices … The criteria which such measures had to meet were not to be stipulated in advance, but were established in the course of the project. The label of precision attached to any measure hinged on cultures of communal trust and was a consequence of the strength of the social relations between these separate and complex institutions. (Schaffer, 1995: 164)*

Schickore (2007: 68–69) suggests that the development and refining of the microscope occurred in the mutual reinforcement of empirical demands for precision and the technical possibilities provided by the new instruments: "The increased precision of instruments made it possible to notice imprecision. The microscope was a key driving force behind these developments because it was used to assess and enhance the degree of accuracy of measuring devices." In addition, the microscope established an "epistemology of the eye" rendering visual perception a legitimate source for knowing the world; the sciences became empirical and not only a matter of cognition, of thinking. The scientist's gaze was merely extended and refined through the use of the microscope and increasingly more detailed observations could be made, further calling attention to the limitations of the technology, in turn producing new generations of microscopes. Communal scientific doctrines regarding the value of precision, technologies and visual practices were developed in tandem and mutually constitutive. The visual technologies thus helped establishing new methodologies and new standards for qualified research work:

> *Practical ability breeds conviction … the microscopists' preoccupations with their practical abilities and means stabilized the debates about microscopic objects. The debates about and experiments on practical procedures refined the methods and sorted them into correct and wrong ones, thereby gradually channeling the divergent accounts of organic tissue. If the practitioners of microscopy reached a consensus, it was first of all the consensus about methodological standards. The applications of these standards made microscopic findings epistemologically well grounded. (Schickore, 2007: 255–256)*

As a consequence of the new visual and audible media (e.g. the stethoscope), there was a new demand for technical training to master the technologies and gradually new professional communities such as the radiologists working with x-ray, the latest advanced visual technology by the turn of the twentieth century, evolved and established themselves (Pasveer, 2006; Warwick, 2005; Golan, 2004). Visual and audible media were firmly established in scientific and medical practice by the end of the nineteenth century, all helping to advance the sciences as legitimate and respected social practices.

Uses of biomedia

One of the key domains using visual media is the technosciences. Being a combination of the use of advanced technologies and equipment (including "technobiological systems" such as genetically modified laboratory animals, see Kohler [1994] and Rader [2004]) and theoretical know-how, embedded in clinical research and theoretical work, there is a somewhat problematic recursive relationship between the technologies used and the theories used to explain the output from the use of the technologies. In Roth's view (2009: 213), scientists have set themselves a difficult task in terms of not having the criteria to evaluate the outcomes independently from their actions. They are placed in what Roth calls a chicken-and-egg situation (i.e. one of "radical uncertainty") wherein, in order to evaluate their actions, they have to draw on the outcomes of these actions; however, to evaluate the outcomes, they have to rely on their actions. Facing this dilemma—questioning either the outcomes or the actions (including the experimental system wherein they operate)—scientists tend to choose the output as the principal source of concern:

> *Experienced practitioners may question their observational actions, doubting what they see, but they normally take actions for granted in the sense that they take them as aligned with the goal intentions that had brought them forth. If an action has not realized its goals, it is reproduced often with a slight modification (researchers try again, implying it will work this time). (Roth, 2009: 329)*

For instance, in Barley and Bechky's (1994) study of laboratory technicians, failure was perceived as deriving from *mistakes, malfunctions* or *enigmas*. Mistakes, often derived from inadequate training or experience, could be corrected while malfunctioning technologies or equipment could be handled; however, the residual category, the enigmas, puzzled the laboratory technicians. Roth (2009) suggests that research projects may continue for a significant period of time until researchers find themselves in a situation where they no longer fully know whether the actions taken produce the outcomes they anticipate:

> *Tools and instruments mediate practical action. Uncertainty therefore pertains not only to the things created in scientists' action but also to the means of*

production (tools, instruments) that are used in, enable, and therefore mediate
individual actions and the activity as a whole. Thus, uncertainty can be ascribed
to a tool or instrument of a scientific production. (Roth, 2009: 331–332)

While such situations are rare, there are certain methodologies or even research programs that evaporate as these dilemmas cannot be resolved. In most cases, where research programs are not abandoned, the researchers choose to believe in the technologies' capacity to produce meaningful images of the object under investigation (see, for example, Coopmans [2011] and what she calls "imaging practices" and empirical studies reported by, for example, Simakova [2010] and Smith [2009]).

Alac (2008), studying functional magnetic resonance imaging (fMRI) (Joyce, 2008; Prasad, 2005; Beaulieu, 2002), a medical visualization technology producing images of brain activity, is a good example of how some aspects of the biological system are provided with a visual form: "fMRI images are 'visual' and 'visible' versions of what previously was not visual, inasmuch as they allow the practitioners to deal with the invisible in a practical manner," Alac (2008: 504) claims. However, this visuality is limited to professional groups that have long-term training and experience of understanding the images and what they indicate, as well as what therapies or actions to prescribe. It is a professional domain of jurisdiction to be able to be visually literate regarding fMRI plates, namely that of radiologists. Being able to establish what is called *disciplinary objectivity* (Timmermans, 2008; Megill, 1994), radiologists share the capacity not only to use the advanced technoscientific instruments but also to decode the images produced and to articulate adequate therapies. The communal vision of the radiologist is thus a highly distributed capacity, acquired during significant periods of training. In Alac's (2008: 503) view, seeing is

> *[a] process situated at the intersection between instruments and technology,*
> *practices, settings, and the practitioners' embodied accounts. It describes how*
> *the local management of seeing involves previous dealings and cumulative*
> *practices of know-how, and how it receives its rhetorical force by reference to the*
> *usual procedures of laboratory members. These procedures are nested in larger,*
> *historically evolving, socio-technical networks whose specifications are bound*
> *to the locally instantiated assemblages of instruments, embodied techniques,*
> *and everyday discourses in the laboratory.*

The radiologist's gaze is thus bound up with visual media, historical trajectories, professional projects, and so forth. Yet, the question of what the radiologist actually sees has not yet been explained. Alac (2008) suggests that what the radiologist sees is based on collectively enacted procedures and standards but she says relatively little of what the images show. Burri and Dumit (2008) share this perspective and suggest, similar to Alac (2008), that "[v]isual representations cannot be understood in isolation from the pragmatic situation in which they are used … it is not enough to simply describe the things images depict of the meaning they reflect. We have to focus also on the textual arrangements and discursive practices within which these representations are embedded" (Burri and Dumit, 2008: 300). However, rather than nourishing naïve beliefs in the ability of images to depict *actual* natures, scientists are highly aware of the complicated epistemological status of images. Leading scientific journals like *Nature* demand that authors describe what kind of Photoshop filters and processes have been applied before the images are published (Burri and Dumit, 2008: 305). As suggested by media theorists, digital images can be endlessly manipulated and it is thus important to account for the procedures used when producing the image.

Prasad (2005) is implicitly suggesting that what the radiologist using fMRI is capable of seeing is both an image of an underlying material substratum and *the very machinery per se*. Using the concept of *cyborg vision*, Prasad says that this vision is always mediated, indeed *enframed* by the technology, while the idea of a realist depiction of the human body has not been abandoned.

In the cyborg visuality regime, images have become bits of data in cyberspace that can be, and are, manipulated by human beings. This does not mean that within this new visual regime, claims toward realism of images are disbanded. If that were so, there would be no reason to have MRI [magnetic resonance imaging] radiological analyses. Cyborg visuality produced by MRI works within different frameworks of realism that do not seek mechanical reproduction of the observed objects(s). MR images produce different reconfigurations of the body, each of which provides a partial perspective of the body and together they constitute the MR radiological gaze (Prasad, 2005: 310).

The radiologist's gaze is thus always a gaze *through* and *with* the technoscientific apparatus. This mediated and enframed vision is thus strongly entangled with the technology—without the technology, there would be no radiologist's gaze. The radiologist can choose between cyborg vision and no vision. This cyborg vision is also deeply paradoxical inasmuch as visual images invite common-sense thinking while this mode of thinking is declared incapable of explaining what is seen on the plates and images. As long as visual media remain confined to professional communities, this condition will not need to constitute a concern; however, as soon as, for instance, technoscientific images are brought into society, their status will become implicitly subject to questioning.

In Dumit's (2004) study of positron emission tomography (PET) scanning of the human brain, the trial of John Hinckley Jr., the man who shot Ronald Reagan in 1981, is addressed as a case where PET images were used to support Hinckley's case. The PET images could not, naturally, "speak for themselves" but needed to be accompanied by expert comments and explanations that drew on subjective interpretations of the images of Hinckley's brain. Since no expert can say anything particularly credible regarding the connections between the image of the brain, Hinckley's actual brain, the event of the shooting, and the legal allegations, the whole event evolved as a situation wherein complex social processes were supposed (the defense proposed) to be reduced to, and explained, on the level of a few blots on a photographic plate. Dumit (2004) explains:

> [E]ven though the brain images are produced by people, they are coproduced by scientific machines, and it is the machines, especially computers, that leave their mark. Scientists ... increasingly attempt to remove their marks from the image, even though they must still provide the text ... At the crux of this relationship between the image that (objectively) speaks for itself and the expert who (subjectively) speaks ... is a desire by the court and by everyone else to reduce ambiguity, to make things clear, and clearly acceptable. (Dumit, 2004: 119)

Consonant with Daemmrich's (1998) study of the difficulties involved in using DNA typing—a technology for the identification of unique DNA sequences in a biological specimen, e.g. a blood sample—in court and practices of display and demonstrations at large (Simakova, 2010; Smith, 2009), Dumit (2004) demonstrates that technoscientific visual media are rather complicated to make use of in legal practice because what would seem to be "objective" representations of factual conditions are always open to professional judgment and evaluation. Such professional judgment and evaluation are questionable evidence from a legal perspective and therefore their juridical value is disputed. While truth in a disciplinary objectivity perspective is a matter of professional agreement, the legal system cannot rely on such expert witness unless credible connections can be made between the image/material substratum and actual behaviors and actions. It is relatively rare that such extended claims are scientifically legitimate, i.e. are resting on undisputed, disciplinary objective evidence (see, for instance, Shostak and Conrad, 2008).

Cohn (2004) addresses what kind of knowledge claims may be made on the basis of images. Rather than recognizing the technological apparatus and technology-mediated materiality at their service, Cohn suggests that some proponents of brain scanning claim they are in the position to "see life itself." Cohn (2004: 55) says that in these quarters brain scans are not seen as presenting "bare life" but as presenting "human existence in its totality," the very essence of what makes us conscious and what is constitutive of what Cohn (2004), drawing on Agamben (1998), calls *bios*. This ambition, based on a far-driven *scopophilia*, "the pleasure of looking," is exemplified with reference to a textbook in medical visualization technologies:

> *New imaging techniques make the internal world of mind visible … As we enter the twenty-first century functional brain scanning machines are opening up the territory of the mind just as the first ocean-going ships once opened up the globe. (Carter, 1998, cited in Cohn, 2004: 56)*

In this view, the "new imaging techniques" are supposedly capable of, for the first time, presenting the human mind in broad daylight. This enthusiasm, however, rests on a series of epistemological assumptions that reduce the human mind to a matter of the brain activities and flows that can be provided with a visual form:

> *[W]hat can be witnessed among researchers at the forefront of the technology is a claim that the mind is being mapped onto and into the brain, subsumed by a complex materialist paradigm, and so doing away once and for all with any legacy of dualism. The assertion is clear: that ideas of life and the mind will now be contained, enclosed, within the emerging science of the brain. (Cohn, 2004: 59)*

The mind and human life *qua* consciousness is here confined to the visual media of this particular research programme. Not only are neurologists capable of producing evocative images of the human brain, they are also, *en passant*, claiming to be able to capture and illustrate life. The brain scanning technology is then not delimited to certain paradigmatic procedures, instead taking a leap into a far more complicated question, namely that of life per se. The visual media are unquestionably seductive in terms of enticing scientists and other experts to draw far-reaching conclusions.

The technosciences are social practices embedded in the capacity of combining abstract theoretical frameworks and concrete empirical observations, either direct or mediated. Mediated perception, visual or audible, is however not strictly a matter of using one single isolated sense but instead engages a variety of human faculties, embodied as well as cognitive. Seeing and listening to, for example, the biological processes of an organism therefore includes the capacity of moving back and forth between inherited analytical framework prescribing how, for example, the cardiac system "should sound" and actual observations potentially deviating from the "normal case" to enable a diagnosis of the patient. As in many cases of material practices, tools, perception and cognition constitute an assemblage—the diagnosing physician—that selects and filters empirical data to be able to articulate a proper diagnosis of the health condition of the patient. Modern technoscience is through and through a mediated practice.

The Organization Theory Perspective: Materiality and Organizing

TECHNOLOGY AND MATERIALITY IN ORGANIZATION STUDIES

The idea of materiality is also used and developed, as mentioned earlier, in the field of organizational studies. A number of social theorists, including Veblen (1904), Woodward (1965) and Blauner (1964), suggested early on that organizations are co-produced with the technologies, tools and other material resources mobilized. Perrow (1983: 534) suggests that the design of technological systems are not "entirely determined by technical or engineering criteria" but instead there are a significant degree of choices available and these choices matter in terms of influencing different social practices. Perrow (1983) emphasizes a recursive view of technologies and organization wherein "the mere things"—the "equipment, its layout, its ease of operation and maintenance"—are "shaped by organizational structure and top management interests, [which] in turn shape operator behavior" (Perrow, 1983: 540), and vice versa. Barley (1986: 81) has argued in a similar vein that technologies are not simply implemented into what he calls a "realm of action" but are on the contrary "incorporated into the everyday life of an organization's members."

Technologies are thus not simply "given" but are "enacted" by the organization members' uses at the same time as new technologies and other forms of materiality are influencing the organization (Leonardi and Barley,

2008, 2010; Winance, 2006). Elsewhere Barley (1990: 67) warns against an all too simplistic view of how technology is appropriated in organizations:

> Technologies are depicted as implanting or removing skills much as a surgeon would insert a pacemaker or remove a gall bladder. Rarely, however, is the process so tidy. Events subsequent to the introduction of a technology may show that reputedly obsolete skills retain their importance, that new skills surface to replace those that were made redundant, or that matters of skill remain unresolved. In any case, groups will surely jockey for the right to define their roles to their own advantage.

In organization theory, a substantial literature addressing the technological and material constitution of organization shows how social and cultural conditions are combined with technological and material resources in the day-to-day practices in organizations (Gherardi, 2010; Zammuto et al., 2007; Yates and Van Maanen, 2001; Lanzara and Patriotta, 2001; Woicehyn, 2000; Martin and Kambil, 1999; Orlikowski et al., 1993; Bloomfield, 1991).

During the last few years, there is a renewed interest in materialist theories of organizing. Such an emphasis on materiality and matter does not, however, imply a return to a naïve realist materialism wherein material conditions are essentially determining social conditions. On the contrary, terms such as *sociomaterial practices* and *imbrications* proposed in the literature underline that materiality such as technologies are socially enacted while simultaneously being constitutive of social relations. There is a recursive relationship between social and material resources and only by examining how social and material resources are folded into one another can one fully understand social practices. "Work practices are inherently sociomaterial, and so to understand work, we must understand sociomaterial (re)configurations ... these practices don't just mediate work, they perform organizational realities," Orlikowski and Scott (2008: 467) argue, defending what Orlikowski (2007) has called "sociomaterial practices," a term indebted to the work of Lucy Suchman (2007). Orlikowski and Scott's (2008) review of top-tier organization theory journal papers shows that technology is a relatively underrepresented topic in organization studies. The reason for this neglect, Orlikowski (2010: 128) suggests, is that "[t]echnology is either invisible or irrelevant to researchers trained in social, political, economic, and institutional analyses of organizations."

Lacking the theoretical and practical understanding of technology and other material resources mobilized in organizations, students of organization and managerial practice often choose to ignore or marginalize the role of technology. For Orlikowski (2010), this is an unhappy tendency as much organizational processes and activities are constituted by material resources such as technology and digital media. Orlikowski (2010: 135) even speaks of the "constitutive entanglement" of humans and technologies, that is, the "capacities for action" are determined by how well humans and technologies are co-aligned and integrated. The term constitutive entanglement is proposed by Orlikowski (2010: 128) as part of what she calls a "relational ontology," an ontological position wherein neither humans nor technologies are privileged or treated as "separate and distinct realities" (Orlikowski, 2010: 134), but wherein the social and the material are mutually constitutive. Such a relational ontology would be the opposite of what Suchman (2007: 3) calls an "ontology of separateness" — "an ontology of separate things that need to be joined together." In many studies of the use of technologies, such an ontology of separateness is assumed as humans appropriate technologies and turn them into useful artifacts suiting their interests. However, it is not only the user enacting the technology or material resource but also the user is shaped by the technology.

Both Orlikowski (2010) and Suchman (2007) thus call for a more elaborate view of how technologies and other material resources are not only passive, inert matter subject to social interests but how they actively intervene in human and social lives. This is thus relevant also to organizations in general, not only to experimental and technosciences such as the life sciences.

AGENCY AND MATERIALITY

Agency, the capacity to act within a specific field of practice, is a key term in this context. All agencies, Orlikowski (2010) and Suchman (2007) suggest, are bound up with the material resources at hand but such agencies do not need to reside in human actors. Instead, human actors are but one indispensable element in agencies constituted through the relations between heterogeneous resources. Says Orlikowski (2010):

> *Rather than attributing agency either to individual actors (designers, engineers, team members) or particular technologies (computer, algorithms, graphics engines, networks), capacities for action would be studies as relational, distributed and enacted through particular instantiations. (Orlikowski, 2010: 136)*

To loosen the concept of agency from the human actor in order to stress the relational constitution of heterogeneous agencies is a radical position derived from the relational ontology advocated by Orlikowski (2010). In such a view, in Miller's (2005: 12) formulation, agency "cannot be reduced to a mere epiphenomenon of the social." A number of studies of information systems, for example, have used the term *imbrications* to underline how social and material resources are folded into one another and mutually supportive. "To imbricate means to arrange distinct elements in overlapping patterns so that they function interdependently," Leonardi (2011: 150) writes, and Introna and Hayes (2011: 108) argue that "the term 'imbrication' literally refers to overlapping, but mutually supporting layers (as used in tilting, for example)." In this perspective, routines (as "social" arrangements) and technologies (as "material" artifacts) are no longer practically nor analytically separated but instead they are "[t]he infrastructure that the imbrications of human and material agencies produce" (Leonardi, 2011: 151). Bloomfield and Danieli's (1995) study of IT consultants illustrates how the "social" and the "technical" are always bound up in the consultants' work:

> [D]ifferentiating between the technical and the social is not some empirical or objectively given activity—we never know technology independently of the mediation of various accounts, experts and spokespersons—it is an exercise of power and therefore an expression of socio-political skills ... For example, the boundary between what is regarded as technical and what is seen as social is ... inherently flexible: a "social" or "organizational" problem may be constituted or translated as a "technical" one; or a "technical" problem may be translated into a "social" one. (Bloomfield and Danieli, 1995: 26)

Another case where the social and the material are imbricated is in the domain of scientific demonstrations or sales demonstrations wherein the demonstrator needs to balance realism and theatrical performances to let the spectators "see for themselves" while maintaining strict control of the performance (Smith, 2009; Simakova, 2010; Stark and Paravel, 2008). First developed by Robert Boyle in the seventeenth century (Shapin and Schaffer, 1985; Smith, 2009: 451–452), scientific work has been developed as a form of visual practice wherein hypotheses are tested empirically and observed by credible observers (preferably other scientists trained in the same discipline and certainly the *gentilhommes* of the privileged classes in Boyle's era). At times, such demonstrations have been used to promote, for example, a new product (Simakova, 2010) or a new imaging technology (Coopmans, 2011), and in such cases the demonstrator is struggling to strike a balance between making the technology too general and opaque and thus at risk of being misunderstood by the audience, and making it all too realistic and situated and therefore potentially failing to promote what Smith (2009) calls the *technology-in-the-practice* as a time-and-money-saving device. Smith is here using a theatrical metaphor to point at the demonstrator's dilemma: "Scientific demonstrations appear to be partial fabrications in the manner of theatre. Although spectators will know that they are not watching a literal slice of experimental life, many aspects of the reframing will be opaque. So the experiment, and indeed the encounter with nature, will be experienced as real in some ways" (Smith, 2009: 454).

Speaking in terms of imbrications, demonstrations are simultaneously determined by technological possibilities and affordances but must always be related to the social life world of the spectators to fully make sense. Balancing general technological possibilities and specific social needs and demands is thus at the very heart of any demonstration:

> To let the spectators see for themselves, and yet maintain control over what they see, the demonstrator must design a performance which appears natural but which is contrived to deliver specific information and only that information. As with theatre, this is achieved by careful scripting ... Scripting is necessary to achieve naturalness while sustaining the ongoing mapping of functions to needs that would not be evident in a slice of real life. (Smith, 2009: 468)

Since the demonstration of a new software was riddled with a series of activities that aimed "[t]o project the credibility of themselves and their organizations" (Smith, 2009: 469), in some cases in conflict with professional norms regarding transparency and the belief that a "good, professional work" should be able to stand critical scrutiny, the demonstrations and "sales pitches" were "universally disliked" among Smith's interviewees (Smith, 2009: 470). Operating under the belief that technologies are freestanding artifacts in no need of scripting and staging activities, these software demonstrations were then hybrid events where the social and the technological are mutually constitutive and entangled.

Similarly, in her study of the use of "telemedicine," a form of counseling service for cardiac patients in Italy, Gherardi (2010: 503) suggests that the technologies used (telephone systems, information technologies, procedures for how to counsel calling patients, etc.) are "[n]ot born 'usable' and 'reliable' regardless of their users; on the contrary, they become such when users institutionalize them as one 'practice' among other working practices." Gherardi (2010: 519) here speaks of the telemedicine system as a form of "material-semiotic practice" where materiality and socially embedded expertise are combined to accomplish a new form of reliable healthcare service (see also Fujimura [2006] for a more critical view of the term).

In Suchman's (2000) view, there needs to be an organizational "alignment" of social and material resources in order to accomplish organizational goals. Similar perspectives, emphasizing the role of blending the social and the material, have been advanced in the study of financial trading (Callon et al., 2007; Beunza and Stark, 2004). Sociomaterial practice is thus an analytical perspective that does not enact a strong epistemological boundary between social relations on the one hand, and materiality (technologies, artifacts, biological specimens, etc.) on the other. Instead, all uses of materiality are socially embedded and all social relations are anchored in material conditions. Social and material resources are implied in one another.

Beunza et al. (2006), being part of what they refer to as "the social study of finance program," the sociological study of how financial trading is accomplished through the combination of social, juridical and technical arrangements, propose the term *material sociology* as a general label for a series of research endeavors:

> *Material sociology pays attention to the role played in social relations by artefacts and other physical objects and entities (including human bodies viewed as material entities). Since that role is of course pervasive, all sociology should be material, yet social theory frequently abstracts away from material entities and empirical enquiry often does not focus on them. (Beunza et al., 2006: 724)*

While Suchman (2005, 2007) and Orlikowski (2007) take their starting point in the sociological term *practice*, used by a range of social theorists including Antonio Gramsci and Pierre Bourdieu, and suggest that practices involve the uses of materiality, Beunza et al. (2006) advocate a more general program locating the very term materiality as the starting point rather than as a term accompanying "social" resources. Sociomaterial practices as an analytical term are thus starting with social practices and arrive at materiality as a theoretical necessity while material sociology takes the material as the starting point. This may appear as a moot issue but it is an important distinction. In addition to these two perspectives, the actor network theory literature, derived from and closely entangled with the science and technology studies literature, advances yet another theoretical perspective that may be helpful in guiding studies of materiality in organizations.

The anthropologist Tim Ingold (2000: 372) stresses that artifacts are embedded in what he refers to as a "system of relations"; the artifact is never a freestanding entity but is on the contrary what is produced as well as put to use within a specific horizon of meaning. Even though Ingold (2000) is speaking about non-Western societies, the same observation would apply in late modern societies. Cochoy (2009: 32), for instance, studying the artifacts and technologies involved in retailing and everyday shopping activities, argues that "[the] management literature still for the most part continues to ignore objects and to focus on 'purely' social and organizational processes." Cochoy (2009: 33) continues: "The mundane, down-to-earth, functional, material and practical aspects of consumption are as important in the business game as their intellectual, ritual, cultural or anthropological approach." Mundane and all-too-familiar technologies such as the shopping cart are studied by Cochoy (2009) as having their own technological, social and cultural trajectory being developed as a balancing point between various objectives and concerns. Cochoy's study of the shopping cart is thus representative of what Preda (1999: 349) calls a "thing-centered form of sociality," a sociality that is bound up with the uses of technologies, tools and artifacts. In this view, technologies, artifacts and so forth are "socially active things" which are examined not as isolated and autonomous entities but as being part of "[t]he processes out of which order emerges" (Preda, 1999: 349). Preda explains his position by making reference to laboratory technologies and tools:

> [T]he things of the lab appear both as the fundamental resources of this specific form of sociality and as setting up the rules by which actions unfold. They are neither ready-made for scrutiny nor passive instruments. This means that they have to be practically configured, according to said conditions, to the epistemic resources of the human actors but also according to those incorporated by the other things present in the lab. (Preda, 1999: 352)

Preda (1999) here defends a truly Bachelardian view of the artifacts in saying that the artifacts embody the knowledge being developed in the lab at the same time as they are used to produce new knowledge: "The things of the laboratory incorporate a knowledge that is already there; at the same time, they are achieved as new knowledge in the process of scientific inquiry. A pipette, for example, incorporates an already available knowledge about the relationship between pressure and volumes of liquids" (Preda, 1999: 353). As a consequence, Preda (1999: 356) concludes, artifacts are "materialized knots of practical knowledge." In Preda's view, there are not technologies, tools and other material resources on the one hand, and social resources such as know-how and practices on the other, but the two resources are folded into one another, constituting an assemblage of resources that are to some extent mutually constitutive.

Even though Preda (1999) exemplifies by referring to laboratory work, Winance's (2006) study of how a disabled person named Mrs. Atti is trying out a wheelchair illustrates Preda's point. In Winance's view (2006), the patient and the artifact are both transformed in the encounter between "wetware" (the patient's body) and hardware (the mechanical structure of the wheelchair): "Both the device and the person are transformed; they form something new," Winance (2006: 58) says. In Winance's perspective, the very term materiality becomes an assemblage, a patchwork or composite structure constituting what Winance calls the "body-in-the-wheelchair-of-the-person":

> [The] transformation of Mrs. Atti and of her wheelchair is a transformation of their common materiality. Here materiality denotes the force of the ties that shape and hold the "body-in-the-wheelchair-of-the-person." Materiality refers neither to the body of the person nor to the wheelchair, which are set up through sound ties. Little by little, through the confrontation involved in testing and subsequently in use, the ties binding Mrs. Atti to her wheelchair are drawn. Through adjustment, a community is shaped. This community is material … but it is also emotional. (Winance, 2006: 58)

This heterogeneous material assemblage is thus a form of "community," a form of affinity across the included materialities including resources such as emotionality. Materiality is thus what is malleable and flexible, continually adjusting to the new entities encountered. In Preda's (1999) and Winance's (2006) views, materiality is almost enacted as a substance from which the appearances are constituted; materiality is not strictly defined on basis of its manifestations—artifact, tools, resources—but is what includes social and cultural resources. Conventional distinctions between materiality on the one hand and social resources on the other are thus collapsed into these "thing-centered forms of sociality."

This view of materiality applies to the studies of laboratory practices that have been reported by, for example, Barley and Bechky (1994). Galison (1997: 2) emphasizes that the laboratory machines used in technoscientific research "can command our attention if they are understood as dense with meaning," i.e. if machines are treated as if they have some intrinsic "symbolic connections to the outside cultures in which these machines have their roots." Galison (1997) thus says that in order to understand the functioning of advanced technoscientific apparatuses and equipment, they need to be examined as having operating relationships with what is outside the laboratory. This view is consonant with Latour's (1988) view that the laboratory is fundamentally open to the outside and that the laboratory practices are bringing in social and technical problems to fuel the research work while in turn sending out entities, theorems, facts, as they are produced. Laboratories are thus social inasmuch as close attention is paid to social problems and interests and they are material as they are ensembles of technologies and tools put to use.

Barley and Bechky's (1994) study of a life science laboratory and the work of laboratory technicians demonstrates the importance of minute attention given to the maintenance work and the work to care for the biological specimens (cell lines, laboratory animals, viruses, yeast cells, etc.) being used in the research work. Researchers do not merely produce data and theories out of thin air but are rather mobilizing a comprehensive series of resources to produce data which are translated into theories. The laboratory technicians are thus in the position to produce the preconditions potentially leading to legitimate scientific output. Barley and Bechky (1994: 115) testify to the importance of the work conducted by the lab technicians to uphold the laboratory procedures:

> [T]heir [lab technicians] role centered on managing irregularities, ambivalences, uncertainties, and other forms of trouble that plagued even the most well-practiced procedures. The management of trouble was critical because almost every problem that occurred, no matter how small, threatened either the staff's ability to create useable data or their ability to maintain equipment and materials in good working order. (Barley and Bechky, 1994: 115)

While the scientists were the "masters of formal representations" (expressed in findings, theories, research applications, etc.), i.e. the translation of "raw data" into written texts submitted to various stakeholders (e.g. research councils, financiers, journal editors), the lab technicians developed a unique contextual knowledge of empirical matters, i.e. how to run and maintain the machines and how to "keep the cells happy," i.e. to provide the optimal conditions for the cells serving as the model organism (Barley and Bechky, 1994: 119). Barley and Bechky (1994: 116) explain:

> [L]ab personnel constructed and employed a body of knowledge that most scientists lacked—a contextual understanding of materials, instruments, and techniques that was grounded in hands-on experience. The lab staff's contextual understanding of empirical procedures was an amalgam of formal and informal

knowledge whose mix was difficult to untangle. In addition to selected facts and propositions, contextual knowledge involved the ability to interpret subtle and situated signs, sensorimotor skills, heuristics cues to specific activities, personal and vicarious access to an unfolding history of events and fixes, and adherence to work styles marked by a concern for cleanliness, reflexiveness, and constant documentation. (Barley and Bechky, 1994: 116)

The scientists were thus serving the role of being the interface with the external world, the scientific community, the university administration, the research foundations, and the general public, while the lab technicians were managing the *infrastructure* of the research laboratory. As Star (1999: 382) emphasizes, infrastructures are by and large invisible for the ignorant user or the public as long as they function. The ignorance and cognitive limitations of humans in their everyday settings prevents them from appreciating electricity, public transportation and central heating, and so forth, as long as the technological system works smoothly, but are brutally reminded of the importance of such systems when they break down. "The normally invisible quality of working infrastructure becomes visible when it breaks," Star (1999: 382) notices.

The view of organization advocated by Orlikowski (2010), Leonardi (2011), Introna and Hayes (2011), and others stresses the relations between heterogeneous resources and that some of these resources are social and abstract (norms, institutions, professional standards, classification systems, and so forth) while others are material and tangible (e.g. machines, door-stops, desks, computer screens) and effective organizational practices are dependent on reconciling such resources. In studies of healthcare practices and technoscientific research work, for example, the material resources mobilized are in many cases conspicuous as in the case of the incubators wherein the embryos are grown in assisted fertilization laboratories while in some cases they are infrastructural (Star, 1999) and laid down into practices in the form of routines, standard operation procedures, classification schemes, and other standards that have been internalized and are at times almost unconsciously executed by skilled professionals (Dreyfus and Dreyfus, 2005). Material resources are thus operating on different levels and through various practices and they range from the unavoidable and immediately visible to what is buried deep beneath systems and structures (e.g. the code of computer languages regulating technological systems). Regardless of such methodological and analytical difficulties facing the practicing researcher, the analysis of technological systems on all levels demands an elaborated theory of how social and material resources are brought together and put to use in everyday work practices.

Summary and Conclusion

The social sciences and organization theory are torn between idealist and materialist theories. This volume enacts a materialist view of the subject matter, assisted fertilization as clinical practice derived from research in reproductive medicine, in itself a heterogeneous field within experimental medicine. The materialist perspective advocated in this chapter does not by no means exclude the importance of theories, symbolism, and other regimes of representation that are at play when intervening in and supporting human reproductive processes. Instead, such regimes of representation are always already bound up with the capacity to explore and examine the underlying material substratum of the human body, both directly in the form of visual inspection and diagnostic procedures and through the use of various technologies and tools being developed. Assisted fertilization work is therefore best understood as a form of sociomaterial practice including heterogeneous resources such as instruments, theories, scientific standards, biochemical resources such as hormones, and advanced machinery such as incubators and freezers. In the next chapter, the procedures developed on the basis of such heterogeneous resources will be examined in more detail as the practice of assisted fertilization work is examined.

2

Reproductive Medicine and Assisted Fertilization

Introduction

This chapter reviews the literature on reproductive medicine and assisted fertilization work in the clinics. Reproductive medicine has a complex and fascinating history and points at how various sub-disciplines such as endocrinology, cytology and veterinary medicine have brought certain issues and research findings to the table. Much reproductive medicine focusing on human reproduction has emphasized how to limit and control fertility and it was not until the late 1960s and 1970s that know-how of human reproduction was used to further enhance human fertility. This shift in focus, from prevention to promotion, overturned the predominant belief that overpopulation was a matter of human fertility rather than lack of supporting social and economic conditions helping families in overpopulated regions of the world to plan their families better. The pioneers of assisted fertilization realized that overpopulation is not a matter of the sheer number of children born but the number of *unwanted* children. As fertility is unevenly distributed in a population, some families had more children than they wanted or could provide for while other families (i.e. couples) had no children. In the late 1960s, an analysis of this problem separated reproductive medicine from a research agenda exclusively aiming at reducing the number of children born to pursue a more specific research agenda.

In many Western countries and welfare states, assisted fertilization is either organized by the public healthcare sector or funded by tax money. In these countries, including the Scandinavian countries, between 3 and 4 percent of the babies born are fertilized with assistance. In the United States, where assisted fertilization is covered by insurance, insurances that not all citizens can afford, the comparative figure is around 1 percent. This statistical difference is likely to be explained on the basis of economic conditions rather than family planning preferences or fertility. That is, when the state finances assisted fertilization, larger groups are capable of taking advantage of the services. However, in some countries, including Sweden, a "mixed economy" prevails wherein public and private clinics co-exist and complement one another. In addition, much research in reproductive medicine and the longitudinal research on the medical, psychological and social differences between naturally born babies and babies born through assisted fertilization is financed by public research funds. Reproductive medicine and assisted fertilization is in other words a field wherein both private and public interests are blended.

BIOPOLITICS, BIOECONOMY AND THE MANAGEMENT OF LIFE

In addition to the organization theory perspective, enacting the organization as a specific social arrangement open to both external influences and internal change initiatives and managerial activities, a societal perspective needs to be taken on the organization of assisted fertilization clinics. In the latter half of the 1970s, Michel Foucault became more interested in the concept of *biopolitics*, a term he coined to denote the totality of activities seeking to monitor and regulate the population in states from the end of the eighteenth century. Like most concepts in Foucault's work, the concept of biopolitics is a grand term, capable of accommodating a variety of discursive practices and institutional arrangements, and consequently the idea of biopolitics, and related terms such as biopower and bioeconomy, has gained a foothold in the social science literature.

At the very core of this literature is the concept of life, the Greek term *bios*, as what is separated from *zoe*, a lower form of life, the life of animals and less developed biological systems (Agamben, 1998). The concept of life has been a *philosophia perennis* in the Western tradition, being defined in numerous ways but mostly as what is in a state of becoming and change: "Life is open-ended: its impulse is not to reach a terminus but to keep on going," Ingold (2010: 98) says. While life may be conceived of as what is separated and freestanding from human interests, in contemporary life pervaded by technoscientific accomplishments and possibilities, life is becoming not only a philosophical or theological matter but is also what Thacker (2010) speaks of as a "technical concern": "The concept of life itself—the unmediated, essential core of biological life—is … as much a technical concern of the life sciences as a philosophical one" (Thacker, 2010: 121).

The line of demarcation between life and non-life is not strictly defined on the basis of natural processes but humans may intervene and technological possibilities by and large help defining the boundary between the two. For instance, Lock's (2002) study of organ transplantation medicine demonstrates that the shift from the traditional definition of death as being based on the collapse of the cardiovascular system to the relatively recent idea of brain-death as informed by the new transplant surgery expertise developed in the post-World War II period. The new definition of death as brain-death, the loss of functional brain activity, was first proposed in the 1960s and already in the early 1980s, "[v]irtually all medical professionals and academics writings about the subject in North America recognized the new death" (Lock, 2002: 110). For Lock (2002) this relatively swift redefinition of one of the key terms in medicine needs to be carefully reflected upon as the term "brain-death" is more complex than is commonly understood:

> Brain-dead patients will, we know for certain, "die" as soon as they are removed from the ventilator. We take comfort from this knowledge when proclaiming them dead even though they look alive. But patients in cerebral death are rarely on ventilators and can usually breathe without assistance. All they need is assistance with feeding—as do a great number of patients who are obviously fully alive. (Lock, 2002: 120)

Healy (2002) addresses this new definition of death as a shift from treating medicine as a practice of healing to an "engineering profession":

> Medicine had the power, it seemed, not only to decide who should live and who should die, but to redefine death … Medicine was changing from a healing ministry to an engineering profession. The desacralization of life proceeded to the extent that the imminent end of a tax year might influence decisions as to the best date on which to turn off a respirator. (Healy, 2002: 161)

For Lock (2002), the enactment of death as brain-death is partially but not wholly informed by the technological, scientific and medical possibilities enabled by such redefinition of life and death. Das (2000) is even more explicit regarding the definition of death as a being the effect of the advancement of transplant surgery:

> The classical definitions of death even in the clinical context were based upon permanent cessation of the flow of vital fluids. But as the perceived need for more

organs and tissues arose, the classical definition was sought to be redefined to meet this need. (Das, 2000: 269)

Sharp (2003: 87) asks, if brain-death is as unproblematic from a medical and existential point of view as it is portrayed in the literature, why are then brain-dead patients/cadavers being anaesthetized during the organ procurement? Hospital representatives respond that this procedure is done to assure the hospital staff that it is beyond doubt that the brain-dead cadaver may sense anything during the organ procurement. For Lock (2002), Das (2000) and Sharp (2003) the definition of brain-death is still a matter related to the technoscientific possibilities to make use of organs and tissues, and consequently the term biopolitics is expanding to not only life in the conventional sense of the term but also to organs and other biological resources that are in a liminal position between life and death. Therefore, in the contemporary period, life is no longer per se but *for us*, a condition, state of equilibrium—Xavier Bichat famously defined life in the beginning of the nineteenth century as an "ensemble of functions deployed to resist death" (cited in Rabinow, 1996: 80)—that can be renegotiated as soon as new discursive formations and non-discursive practices emerge.

Foucault's term biopolitics was primarily used to denote state-governed initiatives to regulate and monitor public health and sanitation, especially from the mid-nineteenth century when urbanization created major densely populated metropolitan areas in great need for political initiative to handle poor housing conditions and poverty. Today, after more than 200 years of advancement of the technosciences, the term biopolitics may be used differently as the elementary matters of biological systems are increasingly explored and manipulated. Lemke (2011) points at these changes in focus in the post-World War II period:

> [T]he image of a natural origin of all living organisms is gradually being replaced by the idea of an artificial plurality of life forms, which resemble technical artifacts more than they do natural entities. The redefinition of life as text by geneticists, advancements in biomedicine that range from brain scans to DNA analysis, transplant medicine, and reproductive technologies … represent a rupture with the perception of an integral body. The body is increasingly seen not as organic substratum but molecular software that can be read and rewritten. (Lemke, 2011: 93)

For Lemke this shift in focus from the analysis and control of "external nature" to "inner nature" is a major change in biopolitics, a shift from what Rose (2007) would call the administration of health to the "management of life": "Genetic engineering clearly distinguishes itself from traditional forms of bioscientific and medical intervention since it aims to 'reprogram' metabolic processes, not merely to modify them. Central to this political epistemology of life is no longer control of external nature but rather the transformation of inner nature" (Lemke, 2011: 94). While the biopolitics of the nineteenth and twentieth centuries was occupied with monitoring populations and health, the new regime of biopolitics of the late modern period has entirely new capacities for manipulating life even prior to health problems, making the question of life per se its responsibility. That is, biopolitics operates not only through *responding to* perceived health problems—the case of mass-vaccination in the face of pandemic outbreaks of influenza, for example—but primarily through the enactment of regulations and policies for how technoscientific practices including reproductive medicine and assisted fertilization should be organized, monitored and put to use.

Still, despite this shifting of the term biopolitics, Lemke (2011: 121) believes that "an analytics of biopolitics can bring together domains that are usually separated by administrative, disciplinary, and cognitive boundaries." As these new biopolitical and therapeutic possibilities emerge, scientists and policy makers can not only handle emerging problems but also anticipate them. For instance, in reproductive medicine, diagnostic methods are used to identify undesirable genetic variations in the fetus, proposing the abortion of fetuses failing to comply with certain standards (see, for example, Franklin and Roberts, 2006; Nishizaka, 2011; Shaw, 2012). For some commentators, such practices are immoral as they put humans in the position as the gardener of the human species, eliminating unwanted children, and passing judgment on what life that should be permitted and what should not. For others, this is a scientific possibility that needs to be exploited to avoid human suffering and, less articulated but undoubtedly part of the argument, the social costs for caring for disabled children, for example.

The Performative Nature of Technoscience

Today, students of laboratory practices such as reproductive medicine, in the science and technology studies tradition within sociology, commonly conceive of laboratory work as the re-creation of nature under controllable conditions.

"It would seem ... that nature is not to be found in the laboratory, unless it is defined from the beginning as being the product of scientific work," Knorr Cetina (1981: 4) says. In the laboratories, snippets of nature being under the full control and analytical gaze of the scientists are created. Using the vocabulary of the sociologist Andrew Pickering, the late modern technosciences are operating on basis of a "performative epistemology," "a vision of knowledge as part of performance rather than an external controller of it" (Pickering, 2010: 25). In a performative epistemology, the sciences then re-create rather than study nature "in the raw." In 1828, the German chemist Friedrich Wöhler managed to synthesize urea, thereby once and for all transgressing the boundary between nature and artifice (Bud, 1993: 10), paving the way for performative epistemologies in the technosciences.

In addition to this gradual decline and disappearance of the distinction between nature and artifice, many of the products produced on basis of technoscientific expertise and know-how operate under the same performative epistemology. For instance, as numerous commentators have emphasized, many drugs being registered and promoted are not primarily responding to specific health conditions but are on the contrary serving to define the illnesses which they are prescribed for. That is, rather than being the solution to a problem, they are a solution that seeks for a problem to gain legitimacy. For instance, Greene (2006) examines the case of Diuril, the world's first hypertension therapy developed by Merck Sharp & Dohme marketed in 1958, and shows that Diuril in fact serves to "stabilize" hypertension as a medical condition, making it a legitimate diagnosis as there were therapies that could be prescribed:

> Hypertension became a different disease after Diuril. It is equally true, however, that Diuril became a different drug after it encountered hypertension. If we look at a pharmaceutical as both a clinical entity and a branded consumer product, the relationship between drug and disease emerges not as a story of design or serendipity, control in production, but rather as a narrative of cumulative negotiation and reciprocal definition. The history of Diuril and hypertension ... illustrates the mutually constitutive processes of clinical research, clinical practice, and medical marketing in the postwar American pharmaceutical industry and traces the evolution of a set of hybrid structures that became central institutions of pharmaceutical promotion in the second half of the twentieth century. (Greene, 2006: 22)

The access to a safe and easily distributed therapy, Diuril served to "lower the threshold" for the prescription of the antihypertensive medication and thereby the population of "potential hypertensive patients" was enlarged, Greene (2006: 53–54) says. Greene is therefore concluding that rather than merely providing therapies for clinically defined health conditions, pharmaceutical companies are actively serving to define "disease categories": "[P]harmaceuticals have become central agents in the definition of disease categories ... briefly, drugs define diseases in seven ways: as agents of therapeutic safety and efficacy, as bearers of therapeutic pragmatics and convenience, as technologies of enhancement, as research tool, as functional diagnostic tests, as sites of regulation and political activism, and as marketing vehicles" (Greene, 2006: 225). Examining two additional drugs, the diabetes drug Orinase and the elevated cholesterol therapy Mervacor, Greene concludes that these three drugs served as "[a] technology of control, reshaping the formerly unruly contours of disease into forms of more acceptable to human lives and livelihood." In addition, and more importantly, "each of these drugs helped to make their associated conditions more manageable, and in the process the drugs themselves become defined in terms of the related disease ... As these terms become fused in the regulatory practice of the therapeutic indication, drug and disease become formally (and legally) understood in terms of each other" (Greene, 2006: 226).

Also in the field of psychopharmaceuticals, a similar pattern wherein the illness or disorder is defined on basis of "to what it responds" is observable. As a consequence, the access to so-called selective serotonin reuptake inhibitors (SSRIs) such as Prozac and Paxil has, Fishman (2004: 188–193) reports, led to "a rise in depression diagnoses, indicating that the SSRI market has contributed to an expansion (and commodification) of the disease." Especially in the field of psychiatry, suffering from a relatively low degree of evidence for an etiology for, for example, schizophrenia, vaguely defined illnesses are at risk to be defined on basis of what therapies they respond to. As the number of mental disorders are growing in number—the first edition of the *Diagnostic and Statistical Manual of Mental Disorders* published in 1952 included 106 total diagnoses and was 130 pages long while the last and fourth edition published in 1994 included 297 diagnoses and had grown to a total of 886 pages (Strand, 2011: 308, Table 3)—psychiatrists and other clinical practitioners are arguably in dire need of adequate therapies.

Taken together, much work conducted by pharmaceutical companies may be understood on basis of performative epistemologies; pharmaceutical companies not only develop drugs that respond to perceived health conditions but also actively medicalize certain conditions to market their therapies. Marshall (2009: 144) reports that in the case of sexuo-pharmaceuticals, drugs intended to either enhance sexual interests or sexual capacities (Fishman, 2004)—Pfizer's blockbuster drug Viagra being the most famous example— pharmaceutical companies "[h]ave invested heavily in the development of diagnostic instruments and symptoms inventories, often well in advance of an approved treatment for the disorders they purport to identify." Such "diagnostic instruments," e.g. questionnaires and other web-based tools for examining one's sexual preferences and activity, are thus preceding the production of the very drug, seeking to establish perceived loss of sexual interest or performance as medical problems that can be treated by consuming prescription drugs.

This kind of marketing activity under the banner of "scientific research" has been heavily criticized for medicalizing a variety of social and physical effects of natural ageing (see, for example, Conrad, 2007; Blech, 2006; Angell, 2004; Conrad and Potter, 2000; Brody, 2007; Åsberg and Johnson, 2009; Mamo and Fishman, 2001). Again, as in the three cases examined by Greene (2006), drug companies do not merely supply drugs to medical conditions with a high degree of what Lakoff (2008: 744) calls "disease specificity" but also shape the market wherein the drug-in-the-making may be launched. "The relationship established between the FDA guidelines, clinical trials researchers, and the pharmaceutical companies help to create a consumer market for a pharmaceutical product while also shaping ideas about normality, in this case, normal sexuality," Fishman (2004: 188–194) writes.

In addition, the regulatory control differs between countries and regions (Abraham and Sheppard, 1999) further loosening the coupling between disease and therapy. Much of the widespread use of pharmaceuticals in the Western world today (Petryna, 2009; DeGrandpre, 2006) is explained on basis of marketing activities and an emphasis on consumerist ideologies rather than actual scientific accomplishments: "Expansion in pharmaceuticalization cannot be explained by growth in techno-scientific discoveries of therapeutically significant innovations that meet health needs because no such growth has been forthcoming," Abraham (2010: 615) summarizes.

The field of reproductive medicine and assisted fertilization has not been surrounded by similar criticism and there are fewer possibilities for medicalizing infertility as there are no clinically tested and approved therapies that enhance fertility besides the hormone therapies being part of the assisted fertilization treatment. At the same time, clinical assisted fertilization has been subject to long-standing critique for being some kind of "luxury medicine" wherein substantial economic resources are used in domains of research and clinical practice benefitting only the economically endowed groups of society. For instance, Longino (1992: 333), speaking from a feminist perspective, says: "There is something terribly unbalanced about pouring millions of dollars in an effort to enable a small number of privileged women (or the men whose wives they are) to procreate, when there are thousands if not millions of children in need of adoptive or foster homes." Similar to the critique of pharmaceutical companies for fabricating diseases and medical conditions in order to create a demand by shifting the boundaries for what is normal and what is not, assisted fertilization is criticized for consuming resources that could be used elsewhere in the healthcare sector. In addition, the general belief that the world is overpopulated, a standing theme in the news and policy debates for at least half a century and thus firmly rooted in common-sense thinking, works against a general recognition of assisted fertilization as a legitimate and widespread clinical practice.

However, during the last few years and with Robert Edwards' winning of the Nobel Prize in medicine and physiology in 2010, such criticism has been less harsh and as clinical studies report that assisted fertilization is a safe therapy with good efficacy the clinical practice is more widely recognized as a contribution to modern medicine. Still, assisted fertilization is oscillating between the two end-points of being either a form of industrial production of babies in the Huxley tradition or a miracle business capable of helping despairing couples and single women fulfill their dreams of becoming parents. While poorly organized and cynical practices in clinics only limitedly monitored and controlled by authorities in parts of the world have been reported to exist, in most parts of the Western world, assisted fertilization is a well-functioning and closely regulated activity.

The other image, that of the assisted fertilization clinic as a site where the wonders of life are accomplished on an everyday basis, is a larger concern for the clinicians as increasingly older women, at times with various medical conditions or suffering from obesity, are entering the clinics, having expectations that clinical fertilization is capable of solving all their problems. Much counseling activities are thus spent on this group of women and couples to make them realize and accept that there may be only very limited chances that they will become parents, despite all the stories reported in the news about the merits of assisted fertilization.

A recurrent theme in the interviews with the clinicians was that schools should dedicate more resources to provide students with an elementary understanding of human reproduction. Especially today, when primarily women spend longer periods of time studying, making a career, and looking for a partner with whom they will create a family, such a basic know-how regarding the swift decline in fertility after the age of 35 and the quite limited chances of getting pregnant around 40 need to be taught. The "wonder-works" of reproductive medicine and assisted fertilization accounted for in the media tend to overshadow the roughly half of the cases wherein greatly disappointed couples and single women leave the clinics with their dreams of parenting shattered.

In summary, the performative epistemology proposed by Pickering (2010) helps students of technosciences including experimental and clinical medicine to see how heterogeneous resources are combined and used to accomplish certain objectives and operations. In the case of assisted fertilization, both advanced technologies and machinery (e.g. incubators and freezers) and relatively generic tools and devices (e.g. pipettes, dishes) are combined with medical and scientific know-how in a variety of disciplines including gynecology, endocrinology and embryology. In addition, being located in the late modern society pursuing various biopolitical programs, reproductive medicine and assisted fertilization as clinical practice are embedded in dense institutional arrangements. For instance, in the case of Sweden, there are both regulatory frameworks enacted by the European Union and national policies and monitoring bodies and the clinical practice part of the general public healthcare system financed by tax-money. In other words, there is no clear line of demarcation between the clinic and the outside world as social interests and various auditing and regulatory organizations and political decisions constantly penetrate the day-to-day work.

Assisted fertilization is in short part of the biopolitical practices of the late modern welfare state. This books aims at presenting how the assisted fertilization clinics are organized on the basis of, on the one hand, the technoscientific expertise developed over the last four centuries and on the other hand the "extra-scientific" influences (e.g. legal frameworks and policies) that shape and inform the clinical practices, at times expanding the domain of what is legally permitted, at other times shrinking the domain. The book is thus presenting how technosciences and wider institutional settings are co-aligned and brought into at least partial harmony in the day-to-day work in the clinics.

Studies of Reproductive Medicine and Assisted Fertilization

CONTROLLING HUMAN REPRODUCTION

In Clarke's (1990, 1998) account of the development of reproductive medicine as a branch of experimental medicine, the concern over how to regulate and control human reproduction has served as an underlying political and scientific objective in the modern period. In parallel to the study of reproductive medicine as being part the field of experimental medicine, there has been an interest among sociologists, social theorists, psychoanalysts, and so forth, to examine and understand human sexuality and sexual practices (Bullough, 1994). Bullough (1994) argues persuasively that the anxieties regarding sexuality in the Western tradition of thinking derive from Christian theology wherein the Church Father Augustinus declared that original sin is passed forward to the children through sexuality and birth; sexuality per se is already from the beginning bound up with the human fall from grace. As a consequence, the field of sexology emerged as a curious blend of scientific research and moralist thinking. The early steps toward a scientific field of sexology were not surprisingly taken in the mid-nineteenth century and scholars such as Karl Heinrich Ulrichs, Richard von Krafft-Ebing, Albert Moll and Magnus Hirschfelt in the German university system, and Sigmund Freud in Vienna, paved the way.

The period from the mid-nineteenth century was characterized by swift urbanization and major metropolitan areas in Europe and North America virtually exploded in size as rural populations flooded into the cities. In addition to the difficulties of controlling sanitation and lowering the mortality rate among newborn babies, leading to various social programs and projects, the turn of the twentieth century was also a period wherein women activist groups addressed reproduction as a feminist issue. "The modern birth control movement began in the United States shortly after the turn of the century as a progressive movement to enhance women's control over their reproductive capacities" (Clarke, 1990: 34). The last decades of the nineteenth century were also a period wherein the engineering sciences, championed by the new professional figure of the engineer, started to strongly influence society (Shenhav, 1999). The engineers' analytical methods and skills served as a general model for how to control and dominate nature. "Reproductive sciences were embedded within and dependent upon industrialization processes that enhanced control over nature and social life" (Clarke, 1990: 34). In the twentieth century, human reproduction was no longer simply conceived of as a "gift of

God" but increasingly became understood as a medical and social issue that could be subject to policy-making and political regulations.

The development of effective contraceptives was thus a standing research objective during the first half of the twentieth century, leading to the production of "the pill," the biochemical and hormonal prevention of ovulation launched in the early 1960s. The contraceptive pill carried substantial social significance and was persistently associated with the women's movement, the so-called "sexual revolution" of the 1960s, and with novel social orientations more generally. Unsurprisingly, feminist groups were part of the financiers of the research work preceding the commercial launch of the contraception pill.

The period from the early 1960s was characterized by great social, economic and cultural change and consequently the family structure in both Europe and North America started to change. Markens emphasizes these shifts in "sexual morals" and the accompanying shift in family structure:

> [B]etween 1960 and 1979, there was more than a twofold increase in divorce rate … Despite a slight increase in the late 1980s, the fertility rate for women had fallen from its peak in the mid-1950s. At the same time, the rate of childlessness for women had risen … In 1990, over 25 percent of births were to unmarried women, compared to only 5 percent in 1960 … Between 1960s and 1992, the proportion of children living in single-mother families almost tripled (from 8 percent to 23 percent). In the early 1990s, it was estimated that by the time they reach the age sixteen, half of all children would have lived in a single-parent family at some point. (Markens, 2007: 10)

As women were entering the labor markets and were no longer dependent on a partner supporting them economically, they could choose their partners and even life on their own as single parents. Out of wedlock births consequently grew in proportion during the period and there was also a growth in interest for providing commercial contraceptive drugs. "After 1965, both federal and industry (largely pharmaceutical) support rose dramatically … Funding jumped from under $38 million for 1960–1965 to $332 million in 1969–1974," Clarke (1990: 28) reports. The "sexual revolution" declared in the last years of the 1960s was thus no subversive underground phenomenon unaccompanied by commercial and political interests but was rather the immediate effect of investment in reproductive medicine research, economic growth and a more equal distribution of economic resources in the population in Western parts of the world. The pharmaceutical industry was not resting on its laurels but provided commercial products further reinforcing a shift in attitude toward sexuality, family life and parenting.

For feminist groups and activists, the sexual liberation was indicative of women's economic liberation but while the recognition of the female sexuality was perceived as a step forward in freeing equally men and women from unwanted traditional norms and values, in some cases dogmatically denouncing sexuality separated from reproduction, the new attitudes and norms were not only beneficial for women. For feminist commentators, sexuality and human reproduction are contested terrains and great controversies remain how to conceive of, for example, reproductive medicine. While most feminist commentators welcome reproductive medicine and assisted fertilization as one means for women to gain control over their reproductive capacities, some radical feminists conceive of assisted fertilization, for example, as a form of technoscientific and economic colonization of the female reproductive organs. Feminists, Briggs (2010: 361) argues, "saw in reprotech [reproductive technologies, including assisted fertilization] a male, technocratic effort to harness and control women's reproductive capacity for eugenic and oppressive ends." For instance, Waldby and Cooper (2007) speak of "post-fordist biotechnology" in the case of reproductive medicine, i.e. human reproduction is a form of industrial process governed by commercial interests.

While assisted fertilization has by and large been gradually recognized as a legitimate clinical practice, gestational surrogacy is subject to fierce criticism as is cuts through a series of social theory categories such as class, race, ethnicity and gender. Says Andrea Dworkin (1983, cited in Wilkinson, 2006: 136):

> Motherhood is becoming a new branch of female prostitution with the help of the scientists who want access to the womb for experimentation and power ... Women can sell reproductive capacities the same way old-timer prostitutes sold sexual ones but without the stigma of whoring because there is no penile intrusion. It is the womb, not the vagina, that is being bought.

For some feminist and critical commentators, gestational surrogacy represents little more than a neo-colonialist practice where rich Western couples are able to "rent a womb" to have their baby delivered. Says Twine (2001):

> Gestational surrogacy is embedded in a transnational capitalist market that is structured by racial, ethnic, and class inequalities and by competing nation-state regulatory regimes ... There is unequal access to assisted reproduction

technologies in most countries because the cost is prohibitive and if is not state
funded then only elites and the upper middle classes can afford to purchase
these services. (Twine, 2001: 3)

For instance in India, a country with a liberal legislation enabling commercial gestational surrogacy, Twine (2001: 17) reports, "surrogacy is estimated to be a $445 million business … The Confederation of Indian Industry predicts that medical tourism, including surrogacy, could generate $2,3 billion in annual revenue by 2012. Gestational surrogacy is an important gendered niche in the global medical market." Bailey (2011: 717) continues: "India is well-positioned to lead the world in making commercial gestational surrogacy a viable industry: labor is cheap, doctors are highly qualified, English is spoken, adoptions are closed, and the government has aggressively worked to establish an infrastructure for medical tourism." While there are arguably cases of blatant exploitation and a lack of international agreements regulating these activities, surrogacy may appear in many forms and is contingent on local and situated conditions and may thus be complicated to reject *en bloc*. Goslinga-Roy (2000), studying the American "market" for surrogacy, found little exploitative practices but also emphasized that it is primarily working-class women providing these services, and that their position in the American society is generally underappreciated:

Surrogates … are typically working-class women who, by receiving
remuneration for what are essentially devalued homemaking skills in American
culture, elevate their gender status by becoming professional homemakers. As
professional homemakers, they receive the attentions of wealthier middle-to-
upper class couples and are celebrated at their surrogate centers as commendable
altruists. (Goslinga-Roy, 2000: 133)

For feminist commentators, human reproduction is a complicated issue because it is located at the center of a variety of social relations and may be influenced and shaped by political decisions and scientific procedures. While pregnancy was once an obscure process deeply seated in the feminine body and outside of the human gaze, it is today explored in detail and many biological processes are mapped and displayed. For feminists and others, reproductive medicine and assisted fertilization has led to a general disenchantment, a devaluation of the mysticism of human reproduction, an accomplishment that on the one hand may be part of a liberating project while on the other could be used to exploit both women and men. Regardless of the view that is favored, assisted fertilization and other practices of the "baby business" such as adoption and gestational surrogacy must not be understood as isolated technoscientific or social practices but as practices determined by a variety of social, technological, juridical and cultural changes over the last century and especially the last four decades. Today, mankind is in the position to influence and control, at least partially, human reproduction and the outcomes and effects from such capacities are an empirical question that needs to be studied *in situ*.

STUDIES OF ASSISTED FERTILIZATION

Assisted fertilization is the clinical branch of reproductive medicine and the clinical practices can be separated into a number of distinct but interrelated activities. First, there are various activities pertaining to the donation of gametes—oocytes (unfertilized eggs) and sperm. Second, there is the work with the clients seeking assisted fertilization treatment after experiencing difficulties in becoming pregnant. The clinical work with the clients could also be separated into the "front-office" activities wherein the clients are encountering various healthcare workers such as gynecologists, nurses, midwives and psychologists, and the "back-office," the laboratory wherein the actual fertilization is conducted and where the embryos are grown for a number of days prior to their transfer to the uterus. This tripartite separation of the activities in space and time enables the safest and most effective therapy but also means that the clients or the patients are to some extent experiencing that they are separated from the very fertilization activities. In this section, studies of the first two activities will be examined.

Collecting the gametes: Gift economies, egg agencies and sperm donations

Some parts of the healthcare sector rest on what has been called a "gift economy" (Currah, 2007) and what Titmuss (1970) speaks of as a "gift exchange." Cheal (1988: 19, original emphasis omitted) defines a gift economy as "a system of redundant transactions within a moral economy, which makes possible the extended reproduction of social relations." While the contemporary competitive capitalist regime of accumulation is economizing and financializing a long series of assets and resources, rendering them tradable on a market (Çalişkan and Callon, 2009; Espeland and Stevens, 2008; Samuel et al., 2005; Power, 2004; Carruthers and Espeland, 1998), there are some domains wherein free gifts still dominate and where an economizing of resources is—perhaps seemingly paradoxical—preventing effective activities. As Zelizer (2005) has pointed out, some resources and services are poorly lending themselves to economic transactions because such an operation would violate instituted norms and beliefs: "[M]oney and intimacy represent contradictory principles whose intersection generates conflict, confusion, and corruption. Thus people debate passionately the propriety of compensated egg donations, sale of blood and human organs, purchases of child care or elder care, and wages for housewives" (Zelizer, 2005: 27). In such cases, gift relationships substitute market transactions.

In the contemporary period, gift economies and gift relationships are more widespread than may be recognized, Currah (2007) argues:

> *[G]ift economies continue to appear in many forms, serving myriad needs and interests in communities of different sizes and geographical reach — for example, Alcoholics Anonymous (and its progeny the Twelve-step programs), blood donation systems, charitable organizations, scientific research or community-led initiatives such as restoration projects. These activities are generally able to operate in a more and efficient and desirable fashion without the alienating and calculating power of the market.* (Currah, 2007: 475)

Richard Titmuss' (1970) study of different national blood donation systems indicated that the safest and cheapest systems for supplying blood did not rely on market-based activities wherein donors were paid for their blood but rather on a gift relationship between individuals donating their blood for relatively low economic compensation. If blood is commodified, it will lead to a market for blood and consequently economically deprived people having little to offer other than blood donations would supply the system. Consequently there would be increased costs for controlling the quality of the blood. If the economic compensation is low but supported by a sense of community and shared obligations, more healthy individuals would be the principal donors. Titmuss (1970) therefore advocates a *Gemeinschaft*-based model for blood donation used in the UK, for example, rather than the market-based model used in the United States. In the healthcare sector, gift economies are quite widespread. For instance, in the domain of transplant surgery, there are monitoring bodies controlling that the supply and demand of donated organs are not becoming economized, i.e. that policies and agreement regarding the distribution of organs are followed and that there is no trade of organs. However, as there is an endemic shortage of organs, overseeing the circulation of organs is easier said than done:

*In the US alone, 76,000 people were waiting for transplants in 2000 (up from
18,000 in 1989), but there were only 6,000 donated organs (including from
cadavers). The figures indicate that 5 per cent of Americans need a transplant
at some point in their lives and half of these die while on the waiting list.
(Wilkinson, 2006: 116)*

While the field of transplant surgery is anxious to avoid any critique regarding
the handling of available organs (Healy, 2004), there are some researchers
pointing at the difficulties to keep the commercial interests at bay and to
maintain the gift economy agreement: "Although veiled in a complex array of
euphemistic constructions, organ transfer and in turn, the donor body are sites
of a lucrative medical practices," Sharp (2003: 26) writes. For instance, China
has been criticized for selling organs from executed prisoners (Dickenson,
2008) and there are rumors of organ theft in poorer parts of the world that have
not been verified. Such rumors are nevertheless indicative of the low trust in
the international regulation of organ trade.

While transplant surgery may be an extreme case in terms of the shortage
of organs leading to difficulties in upholding a bureaucracy-mediated gift
economy, the access to gametes and especially unfertilized eggs is limited.
Mitchell and Waldby (2001: 339) use the term "clinical labor" to denote the
"processes in which subjects give clinics and commercial biomedical institutions
access to their in vivo and in vitro biology, the biological productivity of living
tissues within and outside of their bodies." That is, the donors of eggs and
sperm participate in clinical labor to supply the assisted fertilization market
(market being here in the widest sense of the term including gift economies).
While sperm donation is relatively uncomplicated, albeit surrounded by mildly
intimidating procedures as the donor has to masturbate in the clinic to be able to
ejaculate, egg donations involve complicated endocrinal processes wherein the
donor needs to undergo hormone therapy to enhance ovulation. In addition,
the retrieval of the eggs demands some clinical work. As a consequence, eggs
are in short supply and there is a growing market for egg donations.

To some extent, there are donors willing to donate eggs regardless of the
economic compensation to help siblings become parents, for example, but
there are also students donating eggs for money to support themselves (Beck,
2008). More problematic is the trade of unfertilized eggs in poorer regions of
the world such as Eastern Europe where some women have been encouraged
to donate more eggs than is clinically recommended in the Western part of the
world, Dickenson (2008: 5) reports. As Dickenson (2008) and Twine (2001) point

out, referring to these women as donors is a misnomer as they are definitely selling biological resources to support themselves. Dickenson (2008: 6) also stresses that these eggs are retrieved relatively cheaply as patients in private assisted fertilization clinics in Cyprus, for example, are paying five times as much for the unfertilized eggs.

Regardless of the pricing of oocytes, the use of the term "donor" is in many ways a euphemism used to maintain the idea that the donor is making a heroic contribution to the recipient rather than participating in an economic transaction. Almeling's (2007) study of egg agencies and sperm banks shows how staff are instructing the egg donors to think of themselves as donors operating on basis of altruism rather than thinking of the clinical labor as a form of "paid work" to veil the economic interests involved. As around 10 percent of the American population has been estimated to suffer from infertility problems, egg agencies may be expected to be here for good. While the US assisted fertilization clinics are based on market activities and obeying general demands for profitability and turnover and other relevant economic performance measures, the egg agencies are still stressing the gift relationship ethos in their work: "[E]gg agencies structure the exchange not only as a legalistic economic transaction, but also the beginning of a caring gift cycle, which the staff fosters by expressing appreciation to the donors, both on behalf of the agency and the agency's clients," Almeling (2007: 333) says. That is, agency staff "[s]imultaneously tell potential donors to think of donation 'like a job,' while also embedding the women's responsibility in the 'amazing' task of helping others" (Almeling, 2007: 334). This is the paradoxical message sent to the donor: on the one hand, egg donation is a "job" but at the same time it is a job that is not to be conceived of as a "career opportunity" with economic compensation but rather as a form of "gift giving."

To pursue the former view, the egg agency encourages dedicated and committed donors taking their assignment seriously; when stressing the "gift of life" they can downplay the economic interests involved and avoid criticism for exploiting both the donors and "life per se." If the donors fail to get this message and start to think of themselves as "professional donors," they were corrected by the staff: "[W]omen who attempted to make a career of selling eggs provoke disgust among staff, in part because they violate the altruistic framing of donation," Almeling (2007: 334) writes.

While there was a clearly demarcated institutional boundary between donations and other economic transactions, in fact the relationship between donor and recipient was characterized by the hybrid nature of the trade, i.e.

the "gift of life" was compensated by "counter-gifts" (as prescribed by the gift economy cycle, see e.g., Cheal, 1988) and in many cases the donors were given "flowers, jewelry, or an additional financial gift." This gift exchange was encouraged by the agency staff because it effectively contributed to the construction of egg donation as reciprocal gift-giving "[i]n which egg donors help recipients and recipients help donors" (Almeling, 2007: 334). However, regardless of all the cultural and institutional conditions regulating the relationship between the egg donor, the egg recipient, and the intermediary, the egg agency, there is little doubt that the entire relationship is embedded in economic interest and calculative reason. Egg donation is an economic activity disguised as a gift relationship to not violate any cultural norms regarding the economizing and pricing of the "priceless," life in the form of a living baby.

In addition to the economic transactions and gift relationships, Almeling (2007) also reports that the egg donors had to conform to two complementary gendered stereotypes to qualify as donors. Either they had to be "highly educated and physically attractive," i.e. holding a socially prestigious position, or "caring and motherly with children of their own," i.e. have a "track record" in reproduction. Sperm donors were generally expected to be tall (serving as some kind of general biological marker for physical attractiveness and vitality) and college educated (indicating social aspirations) but what primarily mattered was "sperm count"—the concentration of sperm and sperm motility (Almeling, 2007: 327). As an effect of the clinical labor invested, men were, unlike the female egg donors and their eggs, not expected to have any close connection to their reproductive materials.

Almeling's study demonstrates that the retrieval and handling of gametes are by no means separated from wider social and cultural beliefs and institutions. Socially prestigious qualities—e.g. tall men and physically attractive women—are projected onto the eggs and sperm as if these elementary biological specimens, cells, would be able to carry within such qualities to be actualized in the yet-to-be-born baby, representing some kind of Aristotelian entelechism wherein the potentiality of the thing-in-the-making is already in place in elementary entity—the acorn always already contains the full-grown oak; the egg and sperm contain the qualities of the grown human being (see, for example, Tober, 2001). Almeling (2007) thus shows that social beliefs play a key role in regulating the field of assisted fertilization, at least in markets dominated by commercial actors that can never fully recognize such economic interests. The donation of eggs and sperm operates under its own economic conditions and institutional norms.

An ethnography of the clinical work

The collecting of and markets for human tissues in the form of reproductive cells is one area of studies of reproductive medicine and assisted fertilization. Studies of organizing and practices at the clinics is another, though less common. Cussins' (1996, 1998) ethnography of clinical assisted fertilization work is one of the few studies available. Her work primarily emphasizes the view of the client or patient as being located in a healthcare process wherein her body and reproductive organs are treated as if they were disjointed organs barely maintained within one single biological structure:

> The organs become a focus of repair and therapy, with all the qualities of the classic specimen of study. The uterus and ovaries and tubes are represented sui generis, as if were, on the monitor, floating apart from the context of the rest of the body, and of the whole person. (Cussins, 1996: 586)

Rather than being a process where the patient is at the center of the relations, Cussins (1996) suggests that a series of organizational and bureaucratic procedures constitute the work process and render the activities separated and isolated from one another. First, Cussins (1996: 596) speaks of the "objectification" of the female body and its reproductive organs inasmuch as "the woman is rendered into multiple body parts many times during a treatment cycle." Second, the process of "naturalization" means that as the woman is translated into a female patient, most of her social roles are temporarily bracketed and instead it is her body as a biological system to be explored and modified that is constituting the center of interest (Cussins, 1996: 596). Third, the entire procedure is tempospatially structured in accordance with a bureaucratic organizing scheme and consequently it is of key importance that she "arrives on time," participates in the activities and follows instructions. In short, the female patient is subject to various disciplinary and organizational activities that reduce unnecessary time and efforts in the clinic. Fourth and finally, the female patient is subject to what Cussins (1996: 597–598) calls "epistemic disciplining," a complex term that denotes a "characteristic form of objectification" within the scientific discipline of reproductive medicine including "epistemic standards" that "normalizes diagnoses" (see also Beynon-Jones, 2012).

Cussins (1996: 599) summarizes: "[O]perationalization renders us as mechanistic discrete body parts, naturalization turns us into objects of experimentation and manipulation, bureaucratization turns us into institutional cogs, and we are hoodwinked by our epistemic disciplining." These activities are not exclusively orchestrated in assisted fertilization clinics but appear to be generic procedures for all sorts of healthcare processes. Still, Cussins speaks of assisted fertilization as a form of "ontological choreography" wherein the body and its reproductive organs are enacted to be operable within the pre-existing regime of technoscientific procedures and techniques and to be subject to interventions:

> *The objectified body must not lose its metonymic relation to the whole person, and neither must the instruments lose their acquired properties of personhood in virtue of which they fix, by-pass or stand in for stages in the woman becoming pregnant. I called this process of forging a functional zone of compatibility that maintains referential power between things of different kinds ontological choreography. (Cussins, 1996: 600)*

The ontological choreography of assisted fertilization is thus a matter of relating the patient's biological body and its reproductive organs to the scientific know-how and expertise and the totality of technologies, tools and resources at hand; in order to accomplish anything at all, the body needs to be enacted as a certain biological surface subject to various practices that are at the same time generic and situated.

In addition to the ontological choreography constituting the patient's body as a biological specimen subject to examination and manipulation, Cussins (1996) emphasizes the wider institutional frameworks supporting and determining the clinical work: "Extensive legislative and bureaucratic standards penetrate the lab, inscribing every embryo, and prescribing reproducible success rates" (Cussins, 1996: 587). As being part of experimental medicine, assisted fertilization work is propelled by the collection of data that are examined to identify "normal cases" serving as reference points in the work. The preoccupation to define metrics for the normal and its counterpoint, the abnormal or "pathological" (see Canguilhem, 1991; Jeacle, 2003), is of key importance in the day-to-day work:

> *What skills and expertise are routinized depends … on what is normal and natural; values for diagnostic tests, possible explanations for responses to drugs, and so on, are routinely recognized and recorded from the range of possible (normal and natural) values. (Cussins, 1998: 68)*

Consequently, all kinds of statistics and clinical data are collected at various stages of the process. Cussins (1998) argues that the entire "epistemic culture" of reproductive medicine and assisted fertilization work is very much concerned about the "production of statistics," both supporting future practices but also serving to market and promote the clinic:

> By this I mean that what it is for a procedure to work and be an indicated therapy is expressed statistically, rather than say, as a matter of experiments, or a matter of fact. Fertility clinics, particularly private ones, are increasingly in competition for patients. Reputation draw patients, and these are built primarily on successfully initiating pregnancies. A patient calling an infertility unit has a right to, and often will, ask what the center's success rates are. (Cussins, 1998: 85)

In the commercial clinics, the success rates of the competing clinics are monitored and reviewed: "Much energy, then, goes into compiling the statistics and generating success rates. Competitors' rates are viewed with interest and sometimes with suspicion, and ways in which reported rates from center to center might not be comparable are much discussed" (Cussins, 1998: 85).

The assisted fertilization clinic must first establish routines and procedures for transforming the patient into a biological system that can be effectively controlled and manipulated on the basis of technoscientific know-how and expertise, and secondly, it needs to compile data and information both further enhancing the clinical work (see, for example, Frandsen, 2009) and serving to portray the clinic in favorable terms. This dual nature of the statistics as what is both an input variable for the clinical work and publicly displayed information reveals the complexity of the data collected and how it can be staged and interpreted differently on the basis of local interests and objectives. One of the features of the field of assisted fertilization, Franklin (1998) remarks, is that it tends to portray its own role as being of marginal importance, enacting involuntary infertility as a "minor obstacle" that needs to be passed, needing only a "little correction" or a "little push" to be handled:

> The tantalizing feature of IVF is the idea that there is just a minor adjustment to be made, just a small gap to be bridged, just a little push in the right direction, just the need for a "helping hand," as the technique is often described. More often than not, several adjustments are needed, and consequently there is a significant component of trial and error in identifying them. (Franklin, 1998: 109)

In the same manner, proponents of cosmetic or aesthetic surgery, being more widely criticized than assisted fertilization procedures, are eager to portray their own role as not modifying the face of the patient to accomplish a "new look" but rather to "restore" or "further enhance" what is "already there." That is, Brooks (2004: 231) says, "cosmetic surgery promotes the assumption of an inner self apart from, or superior to, the body." In Brooks' view, such a narrative of "minor corrections" is based on a "fantasy," a "symptom of Western, Protestant, liberal, humanistic, capitalist, patriarchal dominance" that invokes an "egoistic, individual subject, a subject 'without ties, dependent on no-one' who objectifies and denies the agency of nature (the body)" (Brooks, 2004: 232). Cosmetic surgery is here granting much agency to the subject, suggesting that anyone can "become what they *truly are*" and that cosmetic surgery is one of the means for surfacing such inner selves. Also Pitts-Taylor (2007) emphasizes this new strategy when promoting cosmetic surgery:

> [T]he dominant logics of contemporary cosmetic surgery now reach significantly beyond beauty ideals. Such logics depend upon essentialist notions of authentic inner selves. They require an understanding of the body and its surface as a signifier of authentic inner meaning. They recruit psychiatric strategies—or alternatively, political or consumerist ones—to decode the meanings they find. (Pitts-Taylor, 2007: 35)

Needless to say, there are substantial differences between cosmetic surgery and assisted fertilization therapies, but the underlying shared narrative is that nature can be "corrected" through relatively simple technoscientific interventions. While cosmetic surgery is shaped, as Brooks (2004) put it, by paternalist and gendered ideologies portraying women as a surface that needs to be sculptured to erase facial features deviating from prescribed beauty norms and natural signs of ageing, the ideology of assisted fertilization is that reproductive medicine and experimental medicine and the technosciences more broadly are potentially capable of "helping nature on its way." While this is actually (statistically speaking, that is) the case in roughly half of the couples and single women seeking assisted fertilization treatment, there is a lot that remains to be known regarding human reproduction.

In addition, the uses of adjectives such as "minor," "small" and "little" are indicating that the patient is making only a marginal, almost negligible, effort when lending her body to the assisted fertilization therapy. However, the hormone therapy and the egg retrieval are by no means trivial biochemical and mechanical interventions into the human body and the reproductive organs.

The male gametes, the sperm, are relatively effortlessly retrieved but the female patient's efforts are substantially more demanding. Consequently, the narrative of assisted fertilization as being a "minor adjustment" of what is already in place is veiling both the accomplishments made in reproductive medicine and assisted fertilization practice and the clinical labor of the female patient. If nothing else, such persistent use of the narrative of "minor adjustments" is indicative of the marketing of assisted fertilization therapies as the safest and "most convenient" path to parenthood.

In summary, the work in the assisted fertilization clinics is no different than other healthcare processes in being structured around a series of activities and processes rendering the human body as what Mol (2002) speaks of as "the body multiple," a material substratum that is enacted on the basis of various professional domains of expertise and consequently unfolds as a series of medical gazes; a gynecologist, a psychologist and an embryologist are in their own ways conceiving of the patient's body and reproductive organs on the basis of individual professional knowledge interests and practical concerns. While the ontological choreographies derived from such multiple visions on the material substratum, the patient's body, may be stressful or intimidating, it is a *sine qua non* of democratized, modern healthcare, seeking to optimize every single step in the healthcare procedure. In addition to these clinical practices, the assisted fertilization work is accompanied by the ceaseless collection of data and information that is both fed back into the analysis of the clinical work and used to promote the clinic in the market. Finally, regardless of the difficulties to help more than 50 percent of the couples and single women to become parents, assisted fertilization is surrounded by an air of positive thinking wherein infertility is narrated as a "nature going astray" and being in need of some clinical support to get back on track.

Such a positive—critics may say "trivializing"—view of medical therapies and technoscientific interventions into biological systems seems to be present in market-based healthcare services where clients needs to be assured that what they are participating in is not violating any biological order but merely serving to influence what is already in place a little. As, for instance, Pitts-Taylor (2007) remarks, having her own rhinoplasty operation—a "nose-job," for short—as part of her ethnography of the field of cosmetic surgery, the almost unbearable pain that she endured during one full week after the operation was never mentioned or addressed in the promotional material or other studies of cosmetic surgery. If nothing else, the patient hoping to bring forth the inner self has to pay the price of a few days of intense suffering, partially handled by potent painkillers. To correct and push nature in any direction is potentially not as easily accomplished as we are informed by the professional communities offering the services resting on such promises.

Summary and Conclusion

The technosciences are commonly portrayed as the triumph of human reason over nature, the heroic accomplishments gradually advanced over centuries of systematic inquiry into the elementary matter of our existence. This narrative of triumphalism and dominance, assuming that man stands apart from nature, now being its master rather than its serf, is gradually exchanged for a more "environmentalist" view wherein man not only explores nature but essentially *is* nature, a biological species or developmental system based on what Oyama (1997, 2000) calls *ontogeny*, the reciprocal relationship and development of organism and its habitat. "A developmental system is emphatically not bounded by the organism's skin, but includes nested systems on a variety of scales from the molecular to the ecological," Oyama (1997: 122) argues. Being articulated as a critique of a reductionist view of the human organism as being exclusively determined by its genome, its hereditary material (see, for example, Lewontin, 2000), Oyama and other evolutionary biologists want to conceive of the human organisms and other biological systems as being the outcome of dynamic interactions between the biological organism and its environment. In reproductive medicine and assisted fertilization, such views would imply that human reproduction is not simply matter of selecting eggs and sperm from individuals whose phenotypes—the physical constitution—comply with predominant aesthetic and cultural preferences and beliefs, but that researchers need to extend the medical gaze to the interaction between the embryo and the endometrium and the uterus more generally, i.e. the post-transfer life of the embryo.[1]

While this stage of human reproduction has been subjected to few studies because of the methodological and ethical difficulties involved—during regular intercourse, it is complicated to determine the exact point of fertilization and, in the case of clinical assisted fertilization, there are few patients agreeing to participate in such studies of the early stages of long awaited pregnancies—it

---

1   For instance, Kelly (2012) reports that research demonstrates that the so-called maternal-fetal interface is quite fluid and permeable and cells from the fetus circulate in the mother's blood system in what is referred to as gestational cell transfer during the pregnancy. Such observations are suggesting that the interaction between the mother and the fetus is complex and not yet fully explored.

may be that this relationship between the embryo and uterus is a key to a more elaborate understanding of human interaction. Before assisted fertilization was developed as a clinical practice, conception, the "process of genetic combination" (Franklin, 1998: 104) and fertilization, "as the fusion of gametes," were not analytically separated. Today, in the new medical gaze, fertilization occurs prior to the conception that occurs over the succeeding 36 hours. Fertilization and conception are therefore today conceived of as separate biological events. Such a more refined analytical vocabulary—one a matter of biomechanics, one of genomics—is indicative of the advancement of reproductive medicine and assisted fertilization.

In the future, after more research efforts and additional clinical experience and the advancement in adjacent medical domains of expertise, an even more detailed understanding of human reproduction may be accomplished; after some 40 years of assisted fertilization as clinical practice, significant mechanisms have been mapped and understood while many remain concealed. Among the many merits of the technosciences, it is instituting *hope* as a human virtue, the cultural belief that strenuous effort may eventually be rewarded, if not in life, then as a forerunner in the history books—as in the case of Mendel and other countless scientists whose work was only credited after their death (Kohler, 1994: 25–26; Canguilhem, 1988: 112). In the domain of medicine, dealing with issues of life and death, hope is an indispensable element motivating both scientists and patients to carry on their work and therapies. If assisted fertilization will be able to move beyond the 50 percent success rate in the therapies is then a question to be answered in the future.

PART II
Assisted Fertilization as Practice

PART II

3

Developing Assisted Fertilization

Introduction

Since the early beginnings, Swedish scientists and clinicians have taken active part in the development of assisted fertilization. In this, the first of the four empirical chapters, the development of the field as a clinical practice is addressed. Relying on interview material with some of the key figures in Scandinavian reproductive medicine and pioneers in assisted fertilization, the chapter demonstrates how reproductive medicine was enacted as a professional field, characterized by the ambition to delimit and control human reproduction rather than to further enhance it. Assisted fertilization represents a major shift in this ambition. In addition, some of the scientific, technological and institutional arrangements and advancements being of key importance for the field are addressed.

The history of human assisted fertilization is comparatively short, a definite starting point being set at 1978 with the birth of the first successfully in vitro fertilized baby. However, this event was a result and a continuation of earlier developments in reproductive medicine such as surgical repair of reproductive organs for the treatment of infertility as well as developments in other fields of experimental and applied sciences. The initial development and spread of the practice of assisted fertilization was rapid and then stabilized, resulting in the four million children in the world today that are estimated to have been born following this treatment. Several important steps were taken along the way to becoming an established and accepted branch of research and clinical medicine. Quite a few of these steps were accomplished through the development of new technology, such as transvaginal ultrasound, freezing techniques and the so-called ICSI procedure. Some developments were also related to new hormone treatment programs as well as the growth and selection of the embryos. However, the simultaneous changes of the societal norms and regulatory legislation that accepted the treatment have also been crucial. When the treatment was first introduced, infertility was experienced as shameful and there was an initial and lingering political and normative skepticism toward medical and scientific intervention in this intimate process of life.

The Beginnings of Assisted Fertilization

The original demand and thus also a basic rationale for the development of assisted fertilization as a branch of reproductive medicine is due to the prevalence of unwanted infertility. Sometimes attributed to the sexual revolution of the late 1960s, untreated sexually transmitted diseases were one common cause of infertility in the 1970s and 1980s. However, the root causes are often difficult to diagnose. Diseases and birth defects are combined with the fact that human reproduction seems to be naturally limited, and thus approximately 15 percent of the population suffer from infertility or low fertility. This demand for treatment of infertility was highlighted by several interviewees, not being a fact that the general public is commonly aware of. One interviewee illustrated humans' low fertility rate with a comparison with other animals:

> We human beings are not very fertile animals, we're not. The biggest chances of conception when animals mate is about 90 per cent success rate, but for humans it is like 30 per cent. That is the difference between us and the animals; the animals mate once or twice ... We are not really fertile. (Gynecologist, Clinic #1)

In the beginning of the development of assisted fertilization, around 1950, reproductive medicine was intensely preoccupied with the opposite of infertility: developing methods to prevent unwanted pregnancies and children. Thus, at the advent of assisted fertilization the concern for the low fertility rate of humans or those couples or persons who experienced a complete lack of fertility was a problem rarely considered in mainstream research or clinical practice. Despite this, the English biologist and medical scientist Robert Edwards, eventually together with gynecologist surgeon Patrick C. Steptoe, and later a large team, worked to find a solution to infertility. In Sweden, one of the pioneers of assisted fertilization describes the reactions within the field to the early developments:

> We thought the world's problem was not that there were too few kids but too many, and if there was something to be worked in, it was to work on pregnancy prevention. I happen to know Robert Edwards as a physiologist and I was listening to his lectures during international conferences and everyone thought

he was a little bit crazy because he advocated the wrong concept, you may say.
(Gynecologist and entrepreneur, Clinic #4)

The first time a human egg was reported fertilized outside of the body was in 1944. However, this research was not continued until 1965 when Robert Edwards discovered, after much experimenting, the necessary factors to prepare egg cells for fertilization. Using findings from fertilization of hamsters, he then determined the necessary conditions for the sperm cells to survive in vitro. The introduction of laparoscopic surgical techniques in 1970 made it possible for Edwards, now joined by Steptoe, to harvest mature egg cells from a woman's ovaries. After learning to grow the embryos into 16 cell organisms and attempting more than 100 transfers to the uterus, the accompanying hormone treatment was changed and as a result in 1978 the first IVF baby, Louise Brown, was born. It took two years before the treatments were successful in other teams and countries, a team in Australia being the first to follow Edwards and Steptoe's accomplishment (see, for example, Fauser and Edwards, 2005).

In Sweden in 1981 a team of Swedish gynecologists and experimental medical scientists attended the first IVF conference where 28 participants from around the world met, all working to copy Edwards and Steptoe's feat. The development was too fast for the results to be written up and taken through the scientific publishing process of medical journals. Instead, the knowledge of the brand new techniques and the development was shared generously through personal relationships and visits, said one of the Swedish pioneers:

> In the late [19]70s, early [19]80s, we were trading know-how not through published journal papers but verbally. We were travelling around between clinics, looking at their work and tried to change things for the better ... This [private] clinic was at an early stage connected to the [public] University Med School clinic and they were communicating closely, that is: what they did, we also did. (Gynecologist and entrepreneur, Clinic #4)

Soon after the first IVF conference, in 1981, a US team had their first baby born by assisted fertilization, soon followed by France, and the year after by the Swedish team. Sweden was thus the fourth country in the world to succeed with the assisted fertilization innovation. In Sweden 25–30 attempts were carried out before the first two successful pregnancies were achieved (Cohen et al., 2005). Since the techniques were so new, no one could know for certain the effects of the treatment on the children. In an article following the Nobel Prize to Edwards, the leaders of the Swedish team commented: "[I]magine if the first child had been born with birth defects, then heck knows if this technique would have existed at all today" (Leman, 2010: 14).

One of the interviewees in the study remembered the early days of assisted fertilization as being a time of many concerns regarding the safety of the methods. The first 100 pregnancies and children were monitored particularly closely:

> *The first concern was naturally this theoretical issue if things would come out as a real disaster, if monsters were to be born, quite simply. That concern was not very strong but it was still present in some way. There was all this talk about "artificial babies" and so forth … Eventually it was realized that there were no monsters being born. So the safety issue was abandoned because it was observed that the first 100 children born were very well. (Gynecologist, founder of Clinic #7)*

In the beginning the techniques used could be characterized as experimental and particularly due to the laparoscopic surgeries they were too expensive and time-consuming to be used in large scale. In 1984 the Swedish team developed an ultrasound led transvaginal method of retrieving the egg cells from the ovaries (Cohen et al., 2005). When experimenting with the method, a pediatric heart probe was first used. Finding a company that was willing to produce the new ultrasound technology proved difficult, the idea seemed crazy or even vulgar to the representatives of the major medical technology corporations. In the end, a small Danish company started the production. Again the spread of the know-how was rapid and mostly carried out through personal encounters and demonstrations:

> *We developed among other things this technique as the first clinic in the world. I travelled around the globe demonstrating how we were using it during a few years … It is a method for egg procurement. We were the first clinic to use it in the world and we were happy to demonstrate how we used it. (Gynecologist and entrepreneur, Clinic #4)*

This ultrasound technique is now used in assisted fertilization clinics all over the world and also widely used in general for diagnostic gynecology. In hindsight, one of the pioneers expressed regret over not patenting the invention. Yet no one could predict with certainty the future of assisted fertilization. More developments of the treatment were to come, but first assisted fertilization needed to be fully accepted and grow from only a few experimental teams into a widespread and common clinical practice.

Becoming a Clinical Routine Practice

Bringing the brand new innovation of assisted fertilization to the patients who needed it required the start-up of geographically dispersed clinics. The treatment needs to be offered relatively close to the patient, since it involves several steps and visits in order to first investigate the couple's reproductive capacities, then prescribe medication to stimulate the natural egg cell production, harvest the reproductive cells and then perform one, or more often than not, several repeated transfers of embryos to the womb. However, starting new clinics for medical practice demanded investments, something hospitals and the authorities in Sweden were unwilling to provide. The need and rationale for assisted fertilization was questioned. One of the interviewed pioneers remembered how the management at his hospital perceived of assisted fertilization only as an experimental research project:

> The then current management would not allow us to start IVF in the beginning, they thought so much research had already been done, in essence, and other things … [should be done instead]. (Gynecologist, head and founder of Clinic #3)

Another argument against investing in starting new assisted fertilization clinics in Sweden was related to the decision whether or not the treatment should be covered as part of the general public healthcare. The social and cultural norms of primarily reducing pregnancies influenced the question of how to view the problem of unwanted infertility. Infertility was not considered a real problem, and thus helping people become pregnant was outside the scope of what was considered healthcare, explained one interviewee:

> They were not willing to invest in this, thinking it was "some luxury health care" and unnecessary. And the National Board of Health and Welfare were also quite negative and asked whether this was really part of their [responsibilities] … Whether it could be classified as an illness to not get pregnant, that was a central concern for them. (Professor and entrepreneur, Clinic #4)

Due to the lack of interest and support among the public healthcare actors, the solution that remained was to start privately run clinics. Thus, in the major metropolitan areas of Sweden the first private clinics were started around the middle of the 1980s. The pioneers privately invested their own capital and found risk capital to start the clinics to meet the demand among patients. However, in order to avoid a situation where only patients of means could access this kind of care, the public healthcare actors soon followed suit. In this way the Swedish social democrat norm of healthcare being an equal right for all was used to the advantage in creating publicly financed assisted fertilization clinics. One of the interviewees describes this relationship between the starting of privately and publicly run clinics as a trick that was played in several regions of the country:

> [The Stockholm regional healthcare politician] rejected [our proposal] on the basis of political concerns. Then someone said to me, "open a private clinic. They will never be able to tolerate that" ... Back in Gothenburg, there were not too many children made at the time. And they [politicians] didn't want to provide any money. So, we did the same trick one more time, starting [a private clinic] in 1986 and then we received money immediately [for a public clinic]. That is so sensitive, that there should be a public access and not only being something for the rich to be able to afford getting children. So, we didn't start [the private clinics] at all to make money but to provoke the public sector health care system. (Professor and entrepreneur, Clinic #4)

The methods of financing the private clinics were sometimes unexpected. One clinic received risk capital from an insurance company and a vermin prevention company. The latter company found the idea of assisted fertilization interesting and wanted to support further research, the founder explained:

> They did not care about making any money but reinvested the profits in further research, telling us that "you have better use of the money than we do so take the money and plow it down into new research". This clinic was almost more research-intensive than the university hospital clinic. (Professor and entrepreneur, Clinic #4)

The motivation for the private clinics is thus described by the founding figures as mainly altruistic and as a way to further the development within the area. The interviewees described an open climate of sharing knowledge between the clinics:

> During the years there has been a remarkably open climate between the IVF clinics. There never been a situation of real competition. Partially, of course, because there has been an excess supply of patients. (Lab researcher, Clinic #2)

Most of the early founders of the private clinics, if not all, were working at or simultaneously running the public clinics. This was accepted in the beginning until competition for competent clinicians was experienced by the management of the public hospital clinics:

We were four back then, with the permission of the hospital management. So, we started this with our own capital and debts and everything. We had a leave of absence from the hospital about a month at a time, taking turns so as not to be away from the hospital too much. At that time the activities were still rather limited here and also at the hospital. Then when the level of activity increased, at the hospital and in other places none the least, then it became a certain situation of competition and then we were not allowed to continue moonlighting, so to speak. There were new rules about this at the end of the 1980s or beginning of 1990. (Gynecologist, founder of Clinic #7)

When looking back at the development of the clinics, the beginnings seem daring and also almost haphazard. The development is often described as driven by a handful of committed scientists and clinicians motivated by the need they saw among the patients and the excitement of the continual and rapid developments of the research and techniques. All of the clinics had to create themselves from nothing, with few models to follow. In the beginning, in the small teams that worked together, the gynecologists were involved in and handling all the different elements of the treatment. However, only a few years later, the internal organization of the clinics and the techniques used were stabilized, with accompanying stable results, says one gynecologist:

When you think about the first period, when I came in contact with all this, it was ridiculous; we were doctors trying to handle everything but we did not have the equipment or know-how or anything, basically. We started from scratch and every clinic should learn on its own so there was an enormous development. All these organizations setting up meetings and knowledge sharing activities — things moved quite fast when you think about it. '84-'85 was like the middle ages: we knew nothing and had nothing but in '86-'87 things started to move. From the early 1990s we were doing quite well regarding the results. Around '90 was a milestone where we started to establish a certain order and where the hormone stimulation model worked. (Gynecologist, Clinic #1)

In a matter of only a few years from the starting of the first private clinics, assisted fertilization was accepted as a part of the regular healthcare sector, according to the interviewees. However, according to societal norms and in the eyes of the general public, the treatment was still not fully trusted and infertility still bore an air of stigma for several more years. One of the interviewed nurses remembers how most patients kept their treatment secret, to avoid negative reactions from others:

> *In 1990 when I started here, IVF had been around for some time but it was still quite new and a bit special, even a bit suspicious in some quarters. You did not exactly publicly announce you were coming here and they [patients] had to sneak in here from work, inventing all sorts of stories and return too late, and so forth. (Nurse, Clinic #3)*

The patients who received assisted fertilization treatments were made out as selfish and suspicious because adoption was considered the philanthropic solution to the problem of overpopulation and thus also a natural choice for people with infertility problems. The lack of understanding for the choice or need for IVF was sometimes harsh, as one gynecologist remembers: "That was the argument when the thing was discussed in Sweden: you just need to adopt [a child]. Stop whining and adopt a child!" (gynecologist, founder of Clinic #7). Another interviewee explained the initial reluctance of acceptance for assisted fertilization as connected to a general fear of the unknown. The choice of words to describe and name the new treatment was thus of utmost importance in order to avoid further fueling what were deemed as "emotional reactions" instead of appealing to reason. Hence the preference for "assisted" versus "artificial." Also, presenting the technique as routine and the standardization of the clinics helped decrease the suspicious and negative attitudes within and without the medical community.

As the clinics grew, the techniques were developed and the level of activities increased, the competencies necessary to perform the treatments became more specialized. A division of labor became necessary to increase efficiency and so that gynecologists were not performing every element of the treatment. Laboratory technicians, biomedical scientists and biologists specialized in the handling of the human tissues once they were retrieved, while the gynecologists increasingly specialized in diagnosis, prescription, managing the treatment, retrieving the egg cells and then restoring the embryos to the patient. Also, as experience of treating infertile patients increased, the need for related advice, education and support were acknowledged. These were time-consuming work activities that a knowledgeable midwife or nurse could provide. In some cases specialized psychological care was required in order for the patients to be able to go through with the treatment or handle the fact that treatment was unsuccessful. Thus, the variation of professional categories working at or affiliated with the clinics increased as part of the sophistication of the organization of the treatments:

The physicians did most of the work themselves ... quite soon we learned that there was a need for two additional professional categories. Professionals working in the lab, embryologists, and then we realized we needed counselors, mid-wives or nurses that could take care of the patients, advise them, sort out those suffering psychological conditions, normally around 20 percent, and send them to the psychologist that we also hired. (Gynecologist, founder of Clinic #7)

The motivation to work with assisted fertilization for the employees was often, as mentioned previously, the attraction of working with cutting-edge research and technology. Traditionally clinical research in Sweden is conducted at the publicly funded and organized university hospitals. This has posed a challenge for the private IVF clinics who describe their profits as mainly being invested into research for the employees, as a way to be an attractive employer.

This kind of activity is dependent on recruiting qualified competence since it is a knowledge-intensive field. This field has developed clinically during the period, the last 30 years. It is a young science and a clinical science and in order to excel there is a need for qualified co-workers and we believe that you may only get that as long as you can offer interesting work assignments. If you become a pure business enterprise it wouldn't attract interesting persons because they will lose some of their incentives and return to the university because what they do is closely associated to our activities, the scientific part, that is. (Gynecologist and entrepreneur, Clinic #4)

The challenge for the private clinics to keep the research work going was thus solved through making use of a steady profit. One representative describes how their clinic started making a profit already in the first year of business and could eventually even invest in major reconstruction. The competition for patients among the clinics is described as minimal, even between the private enterprises. The development of the 16 clinics in total became mostly evenly spread in the country, with the exception of the capital region where the years 2000 and 2006 marked the start of two new private clinics. The Stockholm area is thus the home of one public and three private clinics, and within commuting distance Uppsala has one additional public and one private clinic. Around 2005 a consolidation of the majority of the private clinics in the country into one company occurred, making transfers of capital and employees between the clinics easier. However, some interviewees described the newest private clinics as struggling more to become profitable.

Setting Standards

The stabilization of the basic treatment techniques at all the clinics happened in a matter of approximately five years. However, besides the development of the ultrasound guided transvaginal collection of egg cells described earlier, a few other important steps were taken that changed the treatments later on during the development. The hormone stimulation programs and the single embryo transfer technique developed so that the initial clinical practices shifted in an important way, here described by one of the founding gynecologists:

> *During a fairly long period, we were [hormone] stimulating quite extensively, we retrieved like 20 eggs from every woman and produced many embryos and transferred three, four. Today, we transfer one embryo. You may then ask yourself what's the use of retrieving 20 eggs to produce one embryo? The rest are put in the freezer but there is evidence of epigenetic changes in the eggs after the strong hormone stimulation. If you retrieve many eggs you wouldn't get the same quality in the last eggs as in the first ones. So, there is a qualitative disadvantage to retrieve many eggs and besides that it is dangerous to over-stimulate. You can induce this overstimulation syndrome and patients may even die. (Gynecologist, founder of Clinic #7)*

In 1991, the practice of transferring several embryos to the womb meant the birth of twins in about a third of all pregnancies. This was due to the drive to increase the chances of pregnancy. However, pregnancies with multiple babies involve substantial risks to the health of both the mother and babies, both in the short and long term. As the awareness of these risks increased and the treatment itself developed, the frequency of single embryo transfers in Sweden diminished gradually. One interviewee commented on this development:

> *The goal is to reduce the twin frequency and we are practically down on the natural level … Some percent or so, but initially it was like twenty or twenty-five. (Biomedical scientist and head of clinic, Clinic #2)*

One recent development recognized was the significant shortening of often expensive and uncomfortable hormonal treatments of the female patients. One interviewee called this development a revolution: "What we are accomplishing today demands a minimal medication of the patient, minimal time actually, and that is revolutionary, I'd say" (biomedical scientist and head of clinic, Clinic #1). Besides the development of the hormone treatments, the technological and scientific development has included a range of new media which enabled longer growth of embryos and freezing techniques that make it possible to store fertilized embryos and recently also egg cells and ovarian tissue. Longer growth of embryos outside the body was found to in some cases increase the effectiveness of the treatment, though increasing the complexity of both the control and selection of the embryos. However, the technology that made it possible to achieve assisted fertilization through the micro-injection of a sperm directly into an egg cell was highlighted most of all by the interviewees, as an important developmental step. This technology and technique is called ICSI, which is short for intra-cytoplasmatic sperm injection. Again, a Swedish team was early in this development, being the second in the world to succeed with a baby born as a result of the treatment. The ICSI treatment is estimated to be the solution to 90 percent of male infertility. A summary of the milestones in assisted fertilization are accounted for in Table 3.1.

Table 3.1   Milestones in assisted fertilization

Year	Milestones in assisted fertilization
1981	The use of gonadotrophins to increase the number of growing follicles
1983	Transvaginal ultrasonography for oocyte retrieval
1984	Gamete intra-fallopian transfer (GIFT)
1984	Pregnancy following cryopreservation
1986	Pregnancy after human oocyte cryopreservation
1988	Pregnancy after subzonal sperm insertion (SUZI)
1989	Partial zona inspection (PZD)
1992	Intra-cytoplasmic sperm injection (ICSI)
1997	Re-introduction of single embryo transfer
1998	Pregnancy after in vitro maturation of oocytes prior to IVF
1999	Clinical application of pre-implantation genetic screening (PGS)

Source: Adapted from Hamberger and Wikland, 2010: 1502.

The stabilization of the techniques and practices used has thus continually been related or intertwined with the development of the technology and knowledge of the methods. The development is described by the interviewees as fast and rather dramatic in the beginning. After that it has been characterized by a couple of significant leaps during the 1990s before reaching a plateau of minor changes during the last decade, say two interviewees:

> *I think I would say it is a linear [development] even though there were a few*
> *leaves … Now, it starts to decline. We have reached some kind of plateau, I'd say.*
> *(Gynecologist and entrepreneur, Clinic #4)*

> *In the case of Sweden, there have been little changes during the new millennium.*
> *(Gynecologist, Clinic #1)*

In Sweden, ICSI is currently used in about a third of all successful assisted fertilization treatments. In many countries this is the technique of choice, irrespective of the origin of the infertility. One reason for this could be that it is associated with higher prices for the treatment. Regarding the general development of pricing, this has varied in different countries. In Sweden, for patients who pay for their own assisted fertilization treatment, the prices have been quite stable and similar, when comparing clinics. However, comparisons are not always straightforward, since different "package deals" and models are used, as one interviewee explained:

> *The average costs for an IVF, and ICSI treatment—they are a little bit more*
> *expensive—is around 23,000 and 27,000 crowns [approx. 2,800 euro]. But*
> *there are different models. There are the private clinics where they set a package*
> *price so you get a package of three to a lower price. I don't know what this costs*
> *but something like 60,000 crowns [approx. 6,700 euro]. (Biomedical scientist*
> *and head of clinic, Clinic #1)*

The prices in Sweden are seen as rather low, just about covering costs and leaving only what is considered a small profit. The developments of new technology and techniques have included much specially designed and thus relatively expensive equipment. Medical supply and technology companies have come to appreciate this niche and the costs are high to the clinics, says one interviewee:

> *I don't think [the price] is unreasonable because our costs are quite substantial*
> *… the stuff we use. I ordered catheters we are using to store the eggs recently:*
> *200 cost 60,000 crowns [approx. 6,700 euro]. (Biomedical scientist, Clinic #6)*

In Swedish society, the price level makes it possible for most couples to afford the treatment, if the private alternative is favored or necessary. However, when asked, one interviewee at a private clinic described situations where an unemployed couple or patients with a low income went to great lengths in order to raise the money necessary:

In the low-income groups struggling with unemployment or those having the least well-paid jobs are having a hard time saving 25,000 crowns [approx. 2,800 euro] for the treatment. They sell the car or take a loan from their parent or relatives or wherever. You can have loans without safety but you need to have an income, so things are a little bit better ... But there are still couples telling us that "now we need to take a break [in the treatment] so we can save some money." (Biomedical scientist, Clinic #6)

The Swedish banks offer loans to those who are employed and in 2005 the possibility for employers to pay for the private treatment as part of a tax-exempt benefit was approved by the Tax Agency. For those who are granted this benefit, approximately 30–55 percent of the price is reduced.

Through the development of the public as well as private alternatives for treatment, assisted fertilization has become comparatively accessible to the population in Sweden. In countries with only private options, the number of treatments and the proportion of babies being born are fewer per capita. These statistics and facts were mentioned by the interviewees who often compared the current Swedish practices of assisted fertilization to the situation in the United States:

Three percent of all children born in Sweden on the basis of assisted fertilization. In the US, the comparative figure is merely one percent. So, you can claim "the technique is underutilized in the United States," as they say themselves. This is because the technique is so expensive that the one half of the population would never think of ever getting close to an IVF-clinic since they couldn't afford it, quite simple. (Gynecologist, founder of Clinic #7)

Comparisons of the development of the treatments in different countries is related thus partly to differences in the general organization of healthcare into public and/or private sectors, but also differences in the national legal frameworks. The development of the legal aspects and the current status of assisted fertilization when it comes to social acceptance are discussed in the next section of this chapter.

Legal Aspects and Current Status

Throughout the development of the field of assisted fertilization, an issue has been the legal recognition of the treatment and regulation of the handling of the human tissues involved. At the start the public support and inclusion as part of general healthcare was the main concern. In 1997, Sweden decided to follow the WHO recommendation to categorize unwanted childlessness as a disease. According to public health prioritization lists it was placed in "group 3," e.g. less prioritized diseases which might be chronic but are not considered to be a cause of invalidity. This is the second to lowest priority group of the Swedish healthcare system which covers most non-acute diseases.

The first Swedish law related to assisted fertilization was instituted in 1984 and dealt with "insemination." It was followed by a law concerning "fertilization outside the body" which was instituted in 1988. A major investigation into the research, results and laws in 2000 led to a revision of both these laws in 2003 as well as those regarding parenthood and secrecy. The revisions were instituted so that donation of egg cells became legal and it was also made clear for all donors of gametes that at the age of 18 the child has the right to know the identity of the donor. In 2005 another revision was instituted mainly changing the requirements for the investigation into the health of the presumptive parents and allowing lesbian couples to use assisted fertilization. The revisions of the laws represented a major victory and liberalization in making it possible for women without functioning egg cells and for lesbian couples to receive the treatment. The only restriction was that the handling of donation of eggs and sperm cells as well as the assisted fertilization with donated egg cells is only allowed at public university hospitals, unless a special license is obtained.

However, despite the liberalization, the laws still do not accept assisted fertilization for single women, embryo donation or surrogacy. Since the legal framework has varied and still varies in different countries, sometimes in the quite near vicinity such as the Nordic countries, this has opened a market for people who travel to receive treatments elsewhere. The common and derogatory term for this phenomenon was explained by one interviewee who discussed the gradual loosening of the legal restrictions in Sweden:

> Sperm donation was first, in the middle of the 1980s, and then egg donation not until 2003. Embryo donation is not legal in Sweden in any way or surrogacy for that matter. This has led to what is referred to as reproductive tourism … where people are travelling to other countries to legally undergo the treatment that is illegal in Sweden. (Professor and entrepreneur, Clinic #4)

The reluctance to fully deregulate all forms of assisted fertilization in Sweden can be seen as related to the lingering skepticism, societal norms of parenthood and the arguments used are often related to the primacy of the concern for the children. In the case of surrogate pregnancies the risks to the women's physical and emotional health are also considered too great. Despite many forms of assisted fertilization now being legally accepted and legitimate, one interviewee claims that the whole field of assisted fertilization is still treated as a lesser form of medicine of low priority:

> *"This is luxury health care, it is nothing we should prioritize ... The state shouldn't sponsor this, they [patients] have to use their own money" and so forth. This is what we've heard over the years. (Gynecologist and head of clinic, Clinic #1)*

Also, still the norm of adoption being the solution to infertility is sustained. One interviewee described how the costs of assisted fertilization are questioned, with adoption being promoted as the better solution. The problems surrounding adoption are seldom recognized:

> *We hear that comment, "there are so many orphans that may be adopted. Why spend all this money to give birth to a few children in Sweden when all these orphans are around?" Well, they do exist but these countries are not so keen on adopting them away no more. So, there are limitations in that respect. (Physician, Member of Parliament of Sweden)*

Similar negative attitudes were described when it came to affording grants for research projects in the field. Some researchers had thus learned to rephrase the research problem to regard treatment specifically for infertility in cancer patients, a popular research area, instead of research regarding infertility in general. At the same time, a few uncertainties regarding the long-term effects of in particular the ICSI method were also voiced from representatives within the field. Here the need for longitudinal population studies, one strong research area in Sweden, was highlighted:

> *What is done in Sweden which is good and not done in too many places, that is the longitudinal studies. It is not enough to just monitor the first generation, as I see it, but when the first test tube babies become grand-mothers we can close the case. And the entire ICSI procedure, that is a major question mark since they have not yet become parents. (Professor and entrepreneur, Clinic #4)*

Despite these normative challenges, sometimes affecting the resources available within the field, the current clinics in Sweden can be described as embodying and making accessible state-of-the-art assisted fertilization. By current standards, this means that an average couple without any particular complicating factors has a 50/50 chance of becoming pregnant within the limits of the publicly financed treatment regime. This is a dramatic improvement, compared to the low percentage of treatments that were successful at the advent of the method. Still, many couples who attempt the treatment are unsuccessful, often without the causes of continued infertility being clear. The interviewees in our study did not fail to mention the large proportion of unsuccessful treatments:

> *About 30 percent may be pregnant after one treatment, and then you make an additional one, you may add perhaps 10 percent and then another 10 percent—something like that. But 50 percent won't get a child. It is easy to remember the successful half, but there are still many couples failing. (Gynecologist, Clinic #1)*

One interviewee even joked about the comparison of the precision of assisted fertilization compared to other medical treatments. If compared to the surgical removal of a (life threatening) infected appendix, assisted fertilization can be seen as a feeble treatment:

> *We need to know that we are working in an industry where the success rate per case is not very high. If we had a similar success rate in caecum/appendix operations at two-thirds, after trying like five times to remove the damn caecum/appendix, then you wouldn't be too impressed, right? (Gynecologist, Clinic #5)*

The continued high proportion of unsuccessful treatments was explained largely by the increasing age of the patients who attempt to get pregnant. Also, despite general principals and average percentages that describe the statistical effects of ageing on fertility, the exact ageing process is individual to each person: "After all, we do age at different speed, having little to do with the year we are born. The ovary capacity matters too, and the sperm quality naturally" (gynecologist, Clinic #1). Also, the natural low fertility of humans and the lack of knowledge about the causes of infertility in many patients present a natural barrier to succeeding in many cases. What the highest level of assisted fertilization could be remains to be known, and the interviewees expressed both a constant need to improve results and a respect for the probability that only small future improvements might be possible. Unless some completely unexpected development occurred, one interviewee expected only improvements by a few percent:

I have a hard time seeing how we could improve things. A few percent
perhaps and we always want to perform better but we won't be able to reach
100 percent. That is impossible! Not all patients can become pregnant.
(Gynecologist, Clinic #5)

Working with the human material of reproduction means that many embryos
are non-viable by nature, something that current understanding, technology
and medicine is unable to bridge. Another interviewee agreed that the
development to this day probably has reached a natural steady-state and only
if the selection of viable embryos could improve, an increase in results might
follow:

If we look at the material substratum, perhaps about half of all human embryos
are not genetically normal. We cannot move much further. But what could be
improved is knowing what embryo to select, which one to return [to the womb].
That is something we have been working on quite extensively, morphological
analysis, examining the embryos and selecting them. We use a computer
program with a unique prognosis model now being used elsewhere. (Biomedical
scientist and head of clinic, Clinic #2)

Recent developments of transnational standards for the selection criteria of
embryos will be discussed in Chapter 5. However, one scientist interviewed in
this study observed a gendered focus on the embryo, compared to the study of
the womb, during the history and development of assisted fertilization:

At times you can see the gender perspective in all this … [Leonardo] Da Vinci
drew what is called a humanoid and there he painted a small sperm with a little
man inside, a little baby travelling into [the womb] … Basically, the woman
is seen as an incubator producing a fetus. A few centuries later the egg is
discovered but still the woman is regarded as an incubator. A lot of the research
has been conducted on the embryo … If you check on the Internet, you notice
that there is ten times as many articles about the embryo as the endometrium.
(Lab researcher, Clinic #2)

Thus, taking into account factors that might originate from the environment
in the womb is another area of possible future development. This chapter,
describing the main elements of the development of assisted fertilization until
2011, ends with the mentioning these hopes and possibilities of the future.

Summary and Conclusion

In 1978, the birth of the first baby conceived through assisted, in vitro fertilization, also marked the birth of a completely new technique to treat infertility. However, both this event and the following children being born first in the United States, followed by France and Sweden, were part of an ongoing development which combined new and old techniques in the fields of, for example, veterinary medicine, experimental biology and surgical gynecology. Many experiments and years of attempts preceded the first successful pregnancies. In the beginning the technique could be characterized as experimental, as it was time-consuming, expensive, invasive and only a few percent of the attempts gave the desired results. However, as the development continued, the community of scientists and clinicians working with the techniques and methods increased and the method became more common. Enabling this process was a generous and open knowledge sharing, accomplished initially mainly through personal contacts, visits, meetings and demonstrations of each new development.

Many essential development steps were taken in just a few years following the start-up of teams working with the technique in several Western countries. In the period of 1985–1990 a Swedish team developed the less invasive and cheaper ultrasound guided transvaginal collection of egg cells. The medical treatments with hormones used to stimulate egg cell production were also developed (Roberts, 2007; Fujimura, 2006), in order to harvest more eggs at a time and thus increase the chance of successful fertilization. Several embryos were then transferred back to the womb resulting in a high proportion of twins and multiple pregnancies, with risks to the health of mother and child. Single embryo transfers have since then become more common, in Sweden becoming standard practice, without affecting results. In 1992 another developmental leap occurred in the field, as the ICSI method became successful in treating male infertility. Later developments have primarily focused on the storage and growth of the gametes and embryos through new media and freezing techniques, the selection of embryo through genetic testing, for example, and the morphological qualities of visual inspection of the embryos. Also, the variation of professional categories working at or affiliated with the clinics increased as part of the sophistication of the organization of the treatments, including gynecologists, embryologists, midwives or nurses and counselors.

The most significant developments have thus often depended heavily on the use of laboratory or medical technology such as micro-injection needles, microscopes, ultrasound transducers and freezers but also medical treatments such as hormones. All of this has naturally been related to the physical practices of retrieving, handling and restoring the human tissue to the body. However, as the possibilities of what can be done have increased, choices have also been made in tandem with societal norms and the existing healthcare systems that the clinics became part of.

This development has been characterized by individuals and small groups of mainly physicians stretching and using the existing institutional arrangements and regulation of healthcare. As an example of this in Sweden, despite public healthcare being a "right" of all citizens, defining assisted fertilization as part of this system was at first contrary to the wishes of politicians and hospital management. Instead, the first clinics were created through private initiatives, funded by the involved individuals' own capital, private loans and risk capital from outside the field of medicine. This development then quickly provoked the public hospitals to start their own clinics in order to avoid a situation where only patients of means could have access to this type of healthcare. However, continued national and regional differences in regulatory and financing frameworks have resulted in what has been labeled as "reproductive tourism," where patients travel to gain access to techniques that are restricted or expensive in their own country. Thus, the demand is not always fully met locally, in the "market" for assisted fertilization.

In sum, reproductive medicine has a history and tradition of focusing on controlling reproduction seen as otherwise mostly unwanted and problematic. Developing methods of contraception has been a *raison d'être* for the field that still lingers. Thus, the current stabilization and standardization of the techniques used for assisted fertilization has happened both *in spite of* and as *an extension of* societal norms and institutional arrangements of healthcare. Still today, assisted fertilization is sometimes accused of responding to a luxury problem that is not a disease and should instead be solved through adoption of orphans, from anywhere in this overpopulated world. Yet, in Sweden and in many other countries, assisted fertilization has become an accepted and common clinical practice as well as area of research within reproductive medicine.

4

In the Clinic

Introduction

In this chapter, the work conducted in the clinics to receive, inform and counsel patients is examined. Being based on the separation between front-office work including all engagements with the clients and the back-office activities in the laboratories, essentially separated from the clients, the chapter is pointing at the need for providing a range of professional expertise to be able to handle the clients and their concerns. Being populated by a number of professional groups including gynecologists, midwives, nurses and psychologists, the clinics are sites wherein heterogeneous professional categories are complementing one another to serve the clients and patients during their treatment. Communication between the front- and back-office areas of the clinics is necessary and the findings show that the clear demarcations of responsibilities, standardization and high levels of control support this division and integration of labor.

The demand for the treatments offered is seen as an individual problem for the couples who come to the clinics but also a result of current lifestyles, the educational system, job market arrangements and governmental support to families; and thus a socioeconomic problem for society at large. In the clinics, social and cultural norms of gender status and nuclear families intersect with the medical-technical possibilities as part of the everyday focus on the embryo, the screening of potential donors and the logic of a successful pregnancy being a lucky "gift," both in assisted fertilization with a couple's own gametes or in the case of donor-material being used. The jobs in the clinics are described as attractive, even if assisted fertilization is still treated as being of lower priority in the healthcare in general.

The Demand for the Treatment

Working in the assisted fertilization clinics, the different professions involved become experts on the patients' problems. Unwanted childlessness, as the many different conditions causing infertility are often termed, involves physical, emotional and social issues that the clinics respond to. Regarding the physical problems that cause infertility, one complicating factor in the care of the patients is that a clear-cut diagnosis is often missing. Many patients, while going through the treatments, live with the uncertainty or hope that a natural pregnancy might still be a remote possibility for them.

Often the clinicians work simultaneously with diagnosing infertility problems as well as with the treatments. In the case of the private clinics, sometimes the diagnosing has first been done within the public health system, since the free public option most often is the first choice for treatment. However, since the treatment of assisted fertilization is often the same, no matter the cause of the infertility problem, one interviewee was of the opinion that a search for a diagnosis was seldom given priority:

> This group of unexplained infertile women is a special group. They do not have a diagnosis. If you do not find anything immediately then you do not bother to understand the underlying causes [of infertility]. (Lab researcher, Clinic #2)

Even if a diagnosis or root cause is identified, the patient's physical conditions are often complex. For instance, the diagnoses of the chronic inflammatory disease endometriosis or polycystic ovarian syndrome (PCOS) are common causes of female infertility. However, both of these diagnoses have unclear causes and present in many different forms and levels of severity. The system of diagnosis used in healthcare in general is simple and multiple causes are seldom made explicit, even if they are evident when looking at the patient couple's history/anamnesis and general condition. There is often a combination of factors that can be related to a couple's difficulties in becoming pregnant, one interviewee explained:

> The patients are often classified in accordance with relatively simple diagnosis systems. "Why doesn't this couple get a child?" is the question being asked. "Because she suffers from endometriosis," period. But in fact, she's 41, smokes too much, is slightly overweight, the ovulation does not work very well all the time, and the sperm sample is so-so, and then "she's got endometriosis". This

is what everyday life looks like and classifications of endometriosis are often
deceiving. (Gynecologist, founder of Clinic #7)

The man's reproductive health issues can of course also be the underlying
cause of the couple's infertility. The most evident cause of infertility in a
couple is a low sperm count and/or sperm cells whose ability to move, the
so-called "motility," is reduced. This can be relatively easily observed under
a microscope. Similarly, the fertilization and growth of the embryos can be
observed in vitro, without disturbing the process. However, what happens
when a specific embryo is transferred to the womb of a female patient is beyond
the reach of the gaze of the clinicians, and thus shrouded in a veil of obscurity.
One interviewee highlighted this lack of observation methods as a reason for
the continued lack of diagnosis and knowledge of the causes of infertility:

> *The woman's womb cannot be studied because there are no methods ... or there*
> *are no good methods, and of course when the day comes when it will be ethically*
> *possible to study [it would be of great interest]. It has been very complicated to*
> *intervene and study a woman's womb during pregnancy. (Gynecologist and*
> *entrepreneur, Clinic #4)*

The lack of diagnosis and specific causes of the infertility also makes prediction
of the outcomes of the treatment difficult or impossible. The clinicians must
inform the patients of their chances, without knowing for certain how each
couple fits the statistical categories. Despite the uncertainties involved, the
interviewees described the importance of offering support by informing the
patients of the hopefulness of the situation. Since reliable predictions are
impossible, everyone has at least a similar statistical chance. However, in the
case of private treatments, as one interviewee pointed out, financial abilities
might limit the number of attempts possible for a couple, and thus also their
statistical chances:

> *You need to support them and tell them that "things are not totally hopeless for*
> *you." But then it depends on their financial situation and other things we do*
> *not have a clue about. (Nurse, Clinic #3)*

The physical diseases and general health conditions aside, the main reason
described for many couples coming to the clinics was their age. The increasing
demand for assisted fertilization in Sweden is often explained by the increasing
age of primarily the mothers of first-born children. In many metropolitan
areas in Sweden the average age of mothers having their first or only child is

approaching 35 years, which is also considered the age when fertility generally starts declining rapidly. Most interviewees mentioned the age factor as significant for many of the patients:

> *The reason for the number of patients is of course that we have older parents and especially older women, because the woman plays the largest role. The man's age matters too but that is later in life. The family life is postponed; around 31 years of age is the average [for the first baby] and that makes a difference for these activities, because they get started too late, quite simply. (Gynecologist, Clinic #1)*

Thus, a preventive measure in order to avoid many of the patients of assisted fertilization would be for the populace to have children earlier in life. This was something one of the interviewed gynecologists working at an IVF clinic wished for: "If I could wish for something, it would be that people would consider getting children as early as possible in life" (gynecologist, Clinic #1). However, the interviewees were also quick to point out the undesirability of going back to a social order where women are excluded from education and the job market because of becoming mothers early in life. One interviewee related the issue to her own daughters and reflected on the support that young couples get in society, instead wishing that it would be easier to have both a family and a career, at the same time:

> *I have a couple of daughters and of course I want them to get their education and do what they want to do, no doubt, but there should be a society enabling students to get children so you could get children between the age of twenty and thirty. (Gynecologist and head of clinic, Clinic #1)*

Another gynecologist emphasized that labeling many of the patients in the clinics as infertile in the sense of being a disease is hardly correct, since it is a natural process to become less fertile with age. He preferred the term "sub-fertile" for this growing category of patients. Low nativity might be considered a social problem for society at large and the interviewee pointed to the role of politics and institutional arrangements for parents as an important factor. The level of benefits provided by the state to families has been shown to have an effect on nativity in some countries, she said:

> *We can see that clearly, for those coming here, it is not always the case that they are infertile or suffer from some kind of disease but they have quite simply been waiting for too long until they have reached the age wherein they are*

facing problems to get a child. So, many of our patients are not to be considered as infertile but rather sub-fertile. If they tried to get their child earlier they wouldn't have so many problems. It has been demonstrated that politics matter, like in Germany where they changed the rules regarding child support benefits and how [parents] were reimbursed. Political decisions have substantial consequences. (Gynecologist, Clinic #5)

However, with the organization of the job market and the increasing time invested in higher education among many young adults in Sweden, it was not seen as surprising that family-building has been postponed. Also, the education of young people about the statistics of fertility and reproduction was highlighted by many as important. A general lack of awareness of the significant decline in fertility after 35 in women and the extremely slim chances of becoming pregnant after 40 was described. One explanation offered was the lack of information given to teenagers:

We have this society where women want a career and a job and both men and women work. There are no women willing to be housewives and getting their first child at 22 and having no education and then ... it may take some time to meet a man they would like to live with and the years pass. That's what society looks like today ... And there is relatively little information in the schools and in the high school that after 40 it is very hard to get pregnant. (Biomedical scientist, Clinic #6)

The tradition of reproductive knowledge and sexual education focusing on preventing unwanted pregnancies, especially among young people, might contribute to young couples postponing family-building too long. The increasing demand for the IVF clinic's treatments was seen as a signal that could be used to heighten the awareness in society:

Sexual education is much more about how to protect oneself against pregnancies and infections than to think of to start on time. But as more people come to IVF clinics, it will become an issue. (Physician, Member of Parliament of Sweden)

Thus, an increasing demand for the treatment was described as an individual as well as societal problem. Also, IVF is portrayed as a last resort, natural fertilization being the norm. This is not surprising, due to the socioeconomic costs of the treatment, for individuals and society through public reimbursements, as well as the uncertainties regarding the results for a little over half of the patients.

Organizing Inside the Clinics

The work in the clinics is clearly divided in a front-office and back-office distribution of labor. These different areas are related to two types of physical spaces at the clinics, as well as the content of the work practices and areas of responsibility. Also, the different professions involved in the treatments are usually focused on one of the two areas, communicating when necessary to manage the integration of the parts into a whole. One interviewee who managed a clinic described these two separate parts and their connections. It is clear from his description that the work is standardized and follows a routine procedure:

> One part is the laboratory and the other part is assisted fertilization. We take care of the eggs and fertilize them and make a selection to bring it back to the woman after the so-called in vitro period lasting for two to five days. The eggs are procured, it is fertilized and selected. That is a very brief version of what happens on the way. The embryo is transferred [to the woman] and patients return after twelve days to make their pregnancy test … That is the whole cycle. (Biomedical scientist and head of clinic, Clinic #1)

The gynecologists working in the clinics are responsible for the medical treatments that most assisted fertilizations involve. The gynecologists' role as responsible for the medical treatments of patients is of course supported by law and through the legitimacy of their training, even if they at the advent of the treatments, as described in the previous chapter, also were in charge of the laboratorial procedures. Since the comprehensible division of labor between the laboratory and the front-office area of the clinic became the norm, the responsibility for the transformation of the separate gametes into viable embryos belongs to the embryologists, i.e. biomedical scientists or biologists. One interviewee working in the front-office described how the selecting of the fertilized egg cells and deciding the timing of the transfer back to the womb is conducted by the back-office laboratory employees while the decisions about the procurement of the gametes is in the hands of the front-office who receives or retrieves them from the patients:

> We're in charge of the hormone stimulation and we decide when the eggs are procured … it is then brought into the laboratory where the egg is fertilized, when egg and sperm is transformed into the fertilized egg we call an embryo. It is the laboratory who is deciding when the egg is brought back to the women. (Gynecologist, Clinic #1)

After the embryos have been prepared in the labs, the clinicians in the front-office then perform the transfer to the womb of the patient. The handing over of the human tissues was thus the point where the work within the two areas and professional groups intersected. This means that the employees working in the front-office areas of the clinic alone have almost all of the direct contact with the patients. These connection points and the integration between the two parts of the clinic were described as rather trouble-free, the clear lines of demarcation being respected. Communication is however of course necessary, in order for the treatments and routine work to run smoothly: "[There is] an interface between lab and clinic that needs to be attended to through a tight dialogue. Otherwise, it runs on rails, basically" (gynecologist, Clinic #1). The IVF process usually involves a hormone treatment for the woman whose egg cells are going to be used, which stimulates and also regulates the ovulation cycle synthetically. The medical control of the patients' bodies ensures that enough egg cells can be "harvested" in order to increase the chances of having a selection of embryos to choose from and some embryos left after the first attempt, for additional attempts, if necessary. Also, the hormone treatment has practical advantages for the organization of the work in the clinics. The controlled regulation of ovulation makes it possible to plan the date and time of the retrievals and transfers, one interviewee explained:

> It [regulated ovulation] is a bit safer. Practically speaking, we are able to plan a bit better. So the patient can get a certain date, perhaps a week prior to the transfer [of the embryo]. She can get a more clear decision rather than just waiting. So there's been a development. That has been a good thing. (Biomedical scientist and head of clinic, Clinic #2)

However, despite the increased control, the treatment steps still demand much precision in order to be in step with the short window of opportunity for fertilization. Thus, some procedures cannot be planned to normal office hours. Also, the even distribution of patient case loads might be hard to plan, since it is impossible to know how long it will take for a patient to get pregnant or before the decision is made to stop the treatment. One interviewee remembered times when working hours had been quite irregular and long, in order to meet the specific demands involved in the treatments:

> [In the early days], there were egg procurements between six and seven in the morning and we were working late nights to make all ends meet. (Biomedical scientist, Clinic #6)

The work at the clinics is in general aiming at maximum level of control, particularly when it comes to traceability of the human tissues. The many patients' tissues and cells must be kept separated and their development traced. Without documentation and labels, the cells are impossible to connect with the patient that they belong to. Mix-ups, e.g. not knowing which patient a gamete or embryo belongs to, could have enormous consequences for people's lives. Also, if for some reason embryos or gametes would not survive in vitro, technical faults need to be excluded as the cause, such as broken thermostats in incubators or faulty media-chemicals or gaseous environments for the storage of the cells. Thus, much work is done to prevent any loss of control. This is mainly accomplished through standardizing all procedures into many clear steps and through documenting what is done with each sample of cells and each embryo in order to create "full traceability."

The standardization and control was a common theme that connected the front-office clinics with the back-office labs. Traceability and documentation started in the clinics with the collection of the gametes, continued in the labs and was then dependent on the front-office again as the embryos was transferred to the patients. Also, constant checking of the technology used is necessary. One interviewee compared the work at an IVF lab with that of a blood-bank, where the wrong blood-type being distributed to a patient can have fatal consequences. The whole organization is built to prevent any mistakes from being made:

> There are many similarities between an IVF lab and a blood bank really, when it comes to organization and structure. Much of what we are doing in the IVF lab is to keep order among all the tests and test tubes and dishes from all the patients. In most cases there are quite a few patients and couples being handled in tandem. So it is critical for an IVF lab to have documented routines. That you are planning for the activities and that you have a good structure in what you're doing. There are certain work elements where you need to really be sure about the identification of the test, all the time. You want total traceability and so forth. The very organization and structure is very important. (Gynecologist, Clinic #5)

The work conducted in the clinics thus largely consists of highly routinized and strictly controlled work. The assisted fertilization clinics were also operating under quite tight regulatory control and detailed monitoring by the authorities. The interviewees regarded this as being of great value at the same time as it consumed some of the resources at hand. "Today, there is a regulation prescribing that all clinics and laboratories dealing with [human] tissues need to implement this quality control system and as a part of that there is this deviancy analysis system," the founder of Clinic #4 argued. Another interviewee stressed that this regulatory control was highly efficient and served its purpose—to provide full transparency and safety:

> *[The activities] are most efficient ... There are few other health care activities that are as monitored. Since it is a young discipline, there is much regulatory control; anything we do can be checked by someone to control how well we perform, and that is an advantage when you want things to work well. (Gynecologist, Clinic #1)*

The routines for quality control are also checked and accredited through certifications, something that was appreciated by another interviewee working in the front-office area:

> *There are demands on the quality systems which has led to a situation where all IVF clinics in the country are certified by ISO, i.e., an international standard. That means an increase in quality too. That has generated very positive effects. I think everyone would agree on that. There's been much work, it cost a bit, but it also came out well. (Nurse, Clinic #3)*

In general, assisted fertilization as a practice was described as heavily influenced by the trust in systematization and in numbers. The statistics and figures representing the results of each clinic are constantly registered and discussed. However, one interviewee was critical of the selection of some of these numbers. Counting the number of treatments and pregnancies should be related to the number of babies actually born, she pointed out:

> *IVF is characterized by all these figures in a way that isn't optimal. They count embryo transfers, implants, number of pregnancies. But they do not count the number of babies born. That would be a natural end-point and what they declared at the first conference 20 years ago, yet still they do not count the babies born. You do your study and submit it and you don't care to see how many babies are born. They just check the pregnancies.[1] (Lab researcher, Clinic #2)*

---

1   One of the reasons for accounting for pregnancies rather than babies born may be that many clinicians are also active researchers publishing their studies in double-blind review journals. Waiting nine more months would then delay the publications.

When reporting the "results" of the treatments, time is saved by focusing on only the number of pregnancies instead of waiting to count the number of children being born. Since longitudinal studies have previously shown that pregnancies following assisted fertilization are the same as others if using the single embryo transfer method, the pregnancy with all its normal risks is considered the end-point of assisted fertilization.

An important part of assisted fertilization treatments is the possibility to use donated gametes, as described earlier in the book. In Sweden, the work of recruiting and taking care of the persons acting as donors belongs to the front-office area of the clinics. "Assisted fertilization is not just IVF but also egg donation, sperm donation," a gynecologist reminded us (Clinic #1). This part of the work was described as less obvious by the interviewees, perhaps since the common image of assisted fertilization easily becomes aligned with societal norms of the heterosexual nuclear family, i.e. that of helping heterosexual couples to become parents and helping their *own* reproductive capacities along, when they run into trouble. One interviewee made the observation that the donation and storage of sperm cells has remained unregulated by legislation in Sweden. In theory, sperm-banks might be started easily by anyone who is willing:

> Sperm donations are unregulated, curiously enough. Anyone can freeze sperm and so, you can do that. There is no law regarding for how long they can be stored and so forth, which is quite strange considering how long you are allowed to freeze embryos. (Gynecologist and entrepreneur, Clinic #4)

The future organization of the donations of gametes thus might be different. So far in Sweden, it has been an integrated part of the clinics performing assisted fertilization, in particular the public sector financed clinics, adding to the complexity of the work and organization of the clinics.

Professions and Tasks

However, besides the work of conducting the assisted fertilization, most clinics and many of the clinicians are involved in research work to further improve the knowledge in reproductive medicine and the treatment of assisted fertilization. This was described as a motivation for the gynecologists who worked in the clinics. In the publicly financed university hospitals, teaching and research is a necessary part of the work. However, research was also described as related to the credibility of the clinics, mostly aimed at the scientific community. One clinic had employed a communications expert, particularly working to inform the public and the new patients about assisted fertilization. She thought that the credibility gained by the clinics from the research in the eyes of the patients was rather small:

> We are communicating that there is a tight integration between research [and the clinic] and we invest a lot in research. It is in the brochures and home pages to promote that part. I think that is creating a credible image when promoting that part. But then I do not know if the patients care. They are more of an additional target group really. They are fully focused on their things, their treatment. (Public relations manager, Clinic #1)

Among the interviewees there was some disagreement whether the private clinics were able to provide the same support and natural environment for the research of the employees. However, the argument that research is important as part of the image of the clinics was used to support the private clinics' investments in research:

> [About research in a private clinic] Of course it isn't only costs, there are other values as well, I mean. If you look at it crassly, it is a little bit of goodwill, you are marking your territory in this world. And hopefully patients will think that if you have serious research it might be a good place to come to, even if this is nothing you calculate with in a budget negotiation. (Gynecologist, head and founder of Clinic #3)

A reason that research was seen as important to attract competent clinicians was the shortage of personnel. Especially IVF-trained gynecologists came in short supply in Sweden at the time of the study. However, this was a lack that was described as chronic. Other professional categories working in the clinics were also popular on the job market, said one interviewee:

> There is always a shortage of physicians. Always! I think the same goes for the entire health care sector. So, that's a common problem. Embryologists are just in balance. If you have been working in IVF and know this industry, you wouldn't have a problem getting a job, I'd say. (Gynecologist, Clinic #5)

The lack of gynecologists with relevant training for working in assisted fertilization had led to some discussions about the division of labor in the clinics. For some of the tasks, midwives were qualified and also a cheaper source of labor. In 2003, a Swedish randomized study reported that embryo transfers conducted by midwives had similar clinical results compared to gynecologists (Bjuresten et al., 2003). The patients themselves preferred being treated by the midwives, with whom they often have more contact and thus a stronger relationship:

> When you have this shortage of physicians and they are by far the most expensive labor, other groups can do the job they do not need to do ... I guess this is what is happening in most of the public clinics. It has been proven that it works just as fine with a midwife doing this job. Otherwise they wouldn't be allowed to do it. (Gynecologist, Clinic #5)

The decisions about which professional category should do the different elements of the treatment are thus still to be completely settled in the field of assisted fertilization. In Sweden, the line of demarcation between gynecologists and midwives is a contested area in general, something that some of the interviews in our study also noted:

> There is a certain competition between midwives and gynecologists. The midwives have been keen on taking care of the gynecologists' traditional domain of jurisdiction ... The physicians [i.e. gynecologists] are a bit anxious to just let it go. But at a few places the midwives are trained to transfer embryos or making ultrasound diagnoses and so forth. (Gynecologist, founder of Clinic #7)

Thus, despite the lack of qualified gynecologists, there was reluctance in allowing midwives or others to take over some elements of the treatments. One midwife expressed disappointment in not being allowed to do routine ultrasound check-ups, which is something she was trained to do for normal pregnancies:

> When I was hired I was promised to take care of the ultrasound we do on all patients during week seven or eight when they are pregnant. I have still not been able to do this because then we are in the physician's domain [of jurisdiction]. That does not work, that is a gated territory. Especially when it is a midwife, the territories are quite well protected. (Midwife, department director, Clinic #1)

Instead, midwives, nurses and nurses' assistants did less qualified tasks such as assisting the gynecologists and handled the most extensive contacts with the patients, giving them advice and instructions regarding the treatment plans. The most labor-intensive part of the work in the clinics was described as the giving advice and counseling, often answering questions to help patients handle the emotional stress of the treatments. This was described as particularly important for the patients who had to leave the clinics without a pregnancy:

> *Of course there is a lot of telephoning, for example, lots. It isn't always the technical side but it is the emotional: questions and worry. One is really sad, it hasn't worked or they have to get information about how the treatment is done … The goal is kind of that even those who do not become pregnant should feel that they got the best and leave here satisfied. Those are the ones you work for. Those who get a child are happy no matter what you have done. (Gynecologist, head and founder of Clinic #3)*

Contributing to human life and reproduction can be seen as part of the motivation for many to take a job in an assisted fertilization clinic. Several interviewees found the job highly attractive and once they had started, found it hard to leave. One interviewee described her appreciation of working with the emergence of life, where existential and ethical issues are common:

> *I think this sense of being close to life is what makes it special. We had a few chaplains coming here, lecturing about ethical issues and grief and such things. We had this one chaplain saying that [we were] working in almost the same field … They work with death and we work with the emergence of life … so there are all these grand ethical issues and a discussion and that makes the whole thing very inspiring to work with. (Biomedical scientist, Clinic #6)*

Often comparisons to other areas of work were made, such as in the previous quote, comparing it with the important work of a chaplain. One researcher in the field instead compared it to a job she would not have enjoyed, explaining:

> *I would have a hard time studying some enzyme someplace that you do not really understand what it does. After ten years or so you might be able to point at some possible function. (Lab researcher, Clinic #2)*

However, even if the job seemed highly appreciated by the interviewees working in the clinics, they described their relationship to other medical fields as somewhat frosty. One interviewee felt that assisted fertilization clinics were isolated: "IVF clinics are quite independent and somewhat isolated from the rest of the health care system. That's how things are, for some reason" (gynecologist, Clinic #5). Perhaps the isolation of the clinics was mostly due to their independence, performing most if not all of the necessary procedures and treatments within their own units, without the assistance of external parties. It could also be, at least in part, due to the recurring questioning and the comparatively low priority given to offering the treatment, compared to treating life-threatening diseases, as described in the previous chapter. In this relatively new area of medicine, the political and social dimensions are more explicit, even though it revolves around an area of life that is usually considered very intimate and private to the individual:

> Other political health care issues are not pursued at the patient level; it is more about waiting times in general. There is no one at least that dares to say that for example "should we really have gastric by-pass operations?" but rather, "they are so obese they are suffering", and then the question is only how much we should help them and so forth. In this issue however, this is part of it. Such a deeply human, political, social and legally anchored issue around an imagined third party—which the child is—combined with the medical developments and possibilities of health care and then it is something that is very, very individual. It is a situation that most others never need to share, that people are not prepared to share in this way. (Psychologist, Clinic #8)

An example of the political dimension of the treatment and the social status of the clinics is also the gender issues involved. One interviewee explained that high priority is systematically given to areas of medicine requiring more expensive technology and which treat mainly adult men:

> I believe this is a gendered issue, a political decision … You get resources for technical development. And that is what politicians want to invest in, in technical devices like MRI [Magnetic Resonance Imaging].
>
> Q: But isn't IVF quite technical?
>
> A: There's some technology in IVF. But the reason for not investing more in obstetrics, even though it is to some extent technical, is because it is not adult men delivering babies. (Biomedical scientist and head of clinic, Clinic #2)

Thus, the tasks in the assisted fertilization clinics were experienced as being given less priority, compared to the areas of medicine being awarded higher status in the healthcare system based on cultural and societal norms. One explanation is that this situation reflects the gender relationships in society at large and because of reproductive labor resting on women, being the ones to carry the pregnancy.

Encountering the Patients

Patients coming to the clinics have tried for some time to become parents and are in most cases worried and concerned whether they will be able to become parents at all, and are consequently under significant stress. The patients are thus in need of information, counseling and discussions throughout the treatment. Many of the interviewees emphasized that the work in the clinic was more labor-intensive than was commonly understood, both in terms of dedicating time to listening to the patients' stories and in informing the patients how to handle their hormone therapies. For example, the information to the patients regarding the preparations before the egg procurement was quite detailed and it was of great importance that it was followed as prescribed, the managing director of one lab emphasized:

> It is quite important that things are done properly. For instance, they [female patients] need to take their shots at a certain time and they mustn't forget it. And they shouldn't change the dosage during the therapy. There could be devastating effects if you take too much or too little or forget about it for a week or so. Forgetting about one or two shots ... and then you may ruin all of the treatment. (Clinic #2)

A psychologist working in one of the public clinics described how couples were affected emotionally and their image of what it is like to become a parent was threatened. When she met the patients, many doubted if they could go through with further treatment attempts:

> Maybe they have done one treatment and kind of realized that it isn't certain that this is going to work. And it has started to feel difficult in such a way that it feels challenging to the image of how it would be when I wanted to be a parent. That is part of the heavy load in this life situation, I believe, that we are not prepared that it will be a load to carry. This willingness to get pregnant when you actively want it, it is incredibly romantically packaged in some way: you wait until it is right, you meet the right person, then you have the coolest sex you have ever had then "woo", that is it ... But living under this load that some couples experience year in and year out, and trying to keep that feeling [is difficult]. (Psychologist, Clinic #8)

Also, during the treatments, the patients' work situations were often affected. This was in part due to the treatment itself and the need to visit the clinic regularly, but also due to the uncertainty about the near future:

There are very few of us that have a work situation at this age where you can kind of come and go as you wish and only know two days in advance that you need to be somewhere at nine in the morning. So, it is hard to be committed when one doesn't know if one will be able to participate the way one wants to … How should I dedicate myself to this when all I am really hoping for is to be on maternity leave at that time. One realizes, I think, that nine months is too short of a time perspective to feel well … And conversely too, I think I can see, that if you succeed in keeping your work situation reasonably intact, it is a very good protective factor or support. (Psychologist, Clinic #8)

A biomedical scientist (Clinic #6) addressed the need for not only informing the patients but also to listen to their stories and concerns: "I don't think [the lab work] is the tricky part; the big part is actually to pay attention to and speak to the patients. There is so much worry and sadness they bring with them when they come here. So, it is more about listening to and talking to patients that is important." She continued:

These patients are of the same age as my kids. I believe the patients think that is comforting that you are a bit older and are experienced. We are a few here with different experiences and I myself have twins. I have one [colleague who has] been through IVF having "IVF children," one [colleague] has adopted a child, and one has donated sperm so we have … quite a bit of life experience. (Biomedical scientist, Clinic #6)

At times, there were expectations on part of the clients that the medical practice could not live up to. In the public Clinic #6, the biomedical scientist argued that, over the last few years, there has been a significant increase of women in the age span of 40–43 coming to the clinic and that they were devastated to learn that they were too old to be eligible for the treatment. One of the nurses exemplified how she had to address delicate issues in her conversations with patients:

It could be quite demanding to inform a 45 year old woman that there is nothing we can do to help her, especially when she's got no idea at all that such could be the case … [some women say] "I have just met my husband … we would like to have a child so we're choosing IVF," and then they believe that is the solution to everything. But we are dealing with what they are producing [egg and sperm] and we cannot produce anything new. So, there is both sadness and anger, of course … Those are not uncommon conversations. (Nurse, Clinic #3)

In the private clinics the age limit was slightly higher, even though the chances of pregnancy were only very small for these couples, it was seen as reasonable to try: "We do have a slightly higher age limit at 42. If there is a reasonable chance and reasonable means around 10 percent's chance" (biomedical scientist and head of clinic, Clinic #2). The interviewed psychologist argued that popular media reporting cases of ageing celebrities becoming parents served to establish assisted fertilization clinics as magic workshops, as the full story was never told:

> [There is a] quite unreflected media image where handsome celebrities at the age of 45 are giving birth to children and are on display, but there is no one mentioning the egg donation … Today, we are misled by the fact that we stay young on the outside, while on the inside we're ageing just as fast; biologically speaking. (Psychologist, counselor, Clinic #8)

Reproductive medicine was in this case "contaminated" by celebrity culture prescribing that you can always accomplish what you want through the help of money and science and that youth is unconditional. "There is a new and open attitude, but on the other hand this attitude makes people think, falsely, that 'this is no problem, we can always get help,'" the psychologist remarked. The interviewees working the clinics had no illusions about their abilities to conduct miracles and conquer the physical limitations of human fertility. When to draw the lines for treating patients and charging them money for a hopeless endeavor was seen as a professional judgment that should be based on statistics and science, not on the wish of the patient. Here, comparisons to other countries can be made. In the free market of the US assisted fertilization clinics, the patient's own wishes are given higher priority, said one interviewee:

> We have this entirely different view in Europe. In the US, patient autonomy is prioritized. What the patient wants, they get quite simple. In Europe or at least the Nordic countries we don't accept that … We believe it is a matter of professional judgment what is possible to do and what is not … That is for instance why a treatment cycle in a private clinic is four times as expensive in the US as it is here. (Gynecologist, founder of Clinic #7)

Becoming a parent was not seen as something that can be guaranteed for every adult. One interviewee described pregnancy as a lucky gift:

> It is no human right to get a child. Absolutely no right, but something you get, if you're lucky. But it is no human right … That's my view even though I help

> *them getting a child. [But] I definitely think one should help those having a*
> *problem getting a child. (Lab researcher, Clinic #2)*

In Sweden, the clinics experienced a shortage of donors, affecting the encounters with the patients in need of donated egg or sperm cells. These patients were forced to wait, sometimes for years, making the treatments different compared to treatments using only the patients' own gametes:

> *We have barely no waiting times for our couples. When it comes to fertilization*
> *by donation, there is a waiting time because there is a shortage of donors*
> *limiting how fast we can proceed. (Gynecologist, Clinic #1)*

The waiting times and shortage of donors was an issue that concerned the interviewees working at the clinics. Ideas about how to change the situation were offered by several. A person working as the head of one of the clinics wished for an international collaboration to pool resources in the form of the donated cells, something which was however considered impossible with the current legislation:

> *In some areas such as corneas or heart valves there are Scandinavian bio-banks*
> *and one can conceive of something similar [in assisted fertilization] … but that*
> *would demand an entirely new legislation in Sweden and in Scandinavia. But*
> *it is a good idea. (Biomedical scientist and head of clinic, Clinic #1)*

The current legislation prevents donors from earning money, allowing only compensation for the loss of income caused by the time spent visiting the clinic. Most interviewees pointed to the low economic compensation, particularly for women who donate egg cells, as a factor in the shortage of donors. Donating egg cells means going through a large portion of the whole IVF treatment, in order to procure the cells, including hormone treatments and the ultrasound guided vaginal egg retrieval with local anesthesia and some moderate discomfort or pain:

> *Donating sperm is a quick job but donating an egg, that is an ordeal. She has*
> *to go through 75, 90 percent of the IVF process including many visits at the*
> *clinic, stimulations, monitoring of the stimulation, egg procurement being not*
> *exactly a pleasant experience, just in order to donate. For that you receive two*
> *and a half or three thousands crowns [approx. 250 euro]. So, who's interested?*
> *(Biomedical scientist and head of clinic, Clinic #1)*

However, the most important reason for the shortage of donors was the legislation that prevents donors from remaining anonymous, regulation that is less common in other countries, said several interviewees:

> In Sweden, the donor is not anonymous for the child and that has been the case since '85 and egg donation has been permitted since 2003 … It could be that there are persons that do not want to be donors for that reason. Abroad you may find anonymous donors accessible for the patients. (Gynecologist, Clinic #1)

Since 2003, when egg cell donation became legal in Sweden, this treatment has remained quite infrequent and is only a small share of the total number of assisted fertilization treatments. One interviewee estimated it to be only 150–200 egg cell donations per year out of 12,000 IVF treatments in total. If a woman who is waiting for an egg donor has a friend or relative willing to donate, a "cross donation" can be arranged so that someone else who is also waiting gets her cells and the first woman is given priority and moved ahead in the waiting list. The people who do choose to be donors in Sweden have often experienced infertility among their family or friends. Becoming a donor is often seen as a "good deed," a sentiment that fits well with a gift economy instead of a "free market" of demand and supply.

> Mostly it is persons who in one way or another have experienced infertility. And there are for sure other groups. At times, we are contacted by persons who want to do good, to make a contribution. (Gynecologist, Clinic #1)

One of the clinics explained that they regularly ran ads in the local newspaper to recruit donors. When the Nobel Prize was awarded to Robert Edwards they hoped that new donors would be easier to recruit, as the awareness of the needs of these patients might increase among the general public:

> It's been a real challenge to recruit [donors] … This is a major decision, so you have to make up your mind on your own, so to speak. We're trying to use subtle [promotion] while at the same time I have this feeling that we need to attract the attention because people may not be fully aware that they can donate. (Public relations manager, Clinic #1)

On a webpage and in the waiting room of one of the public clinics a picture of gift-wrapped presents in the shape of an egg and a sperm are accompanied by the question "Do you want to give away something really, really valuable?" in big red letters. This is one example of the promotion to potential donors.

However, promotion of donorship is also balanced in the clinic by control of potential donors. As part of the process, all potential donors are screened and their reasons for wanting to become a donor are scrutinized. One interviewee explained that he had denied many potential donors because he believed they were too immature and unaware of the future consequences:

> Over the years I have been speaking to many donors and it is a very subjective [decision]. Of course, they have to be socially in order, they cannot be intoxicated by drugs and they need to be able to understand what they are embarking on and so forth. Given these conditions, I have refused many donors over the years. A young girl with a somewhat rosy image of how to improve the world, well, they do not always understand that in twenty years time, then they are married and have children of their own, there may be someone knocking on the door telling them "You're my mom!" You need to demonstrate a certain maturity to know what you are doing here. (Gynecologist and head of clinic, Clinic #1)

Taking care of the patients offering this "gift" was described as rather costly since it involved several steps. One interviewee explained and compared the care for this additional category of clients to the organizing in the neighboring country of Denmark:

> You need to check infection tests to make sure the donors do not have HIV and so forth. Viral diseases and so forth. It is a quite substantial and costly apparatus. Private sperm banks have proved to be a better alternative and for instance we have the Danish Cryobank starting ... They are incredibly skilled but they are doing nothing else. (Gynecologist and head of clinic, Clinic #1)

The interviewee thus suggested that privately owned and specialized banks for the collection and storage of the reproductive materials would be more efficient, something yet unheard of in Sweden. In sum, the patients in the main focus of the clinics were naturally the couples receiving IVF treatments. Donors are seen as a means to this end and the complications involved are thus an impediment to the treatments.

Summary and Conclusion

The work in the assisted fertilization clinics does not deal with inert, mute matter but with patients failing to become parents and them therefore expressing their concerns and emotions, for example with anger or sadness. The front-office staff including nurses, midwives and gynecologists therefore needs to dedicate time and efforts to inform and communicate with the patients. Assisted fertilization is thus not strictly an intervention into the human reproductive apparatus but is also the procedure of creating a situation where patients can make sense of the situation to emotionally and practically cope with the treatment they are undergoing.

Often a clear-cut answer to the reasons for a lack in fertility is missing, though the generally increased age of parents was a common explanation for the increasing demand for the treatment. "Natural" or unassisted fertilization is the norm that the treatments are measured against. The increasing demand was thus seen as a signal to society to inform individuals and reform institutional arrangements, in order to maintain or improve nativity in the population and to prevent further increase in assisted fertilization treatments. The demand for the treatments is seen as both an individual problem for the couples who come to the clinics and also a result of current lifestyles, the educational system, job market arrangements and governmental support to families; and thus a socioeconomic problem for society at large.

Inside the front-office areas of the clinics, some competition for tasks was perceived in the relationship between the midwives and gynecologists. Counseling and advising patients, often in a sensitive emotional state, was time-consuming but seen as important. Offering possibilities to do research as part of the job was described as important in order to recruit and keep gynecologists and other highly qualified employees. The job was experienced as meaningful and attractive, even though assisted fertilization is treated as a lower prioritized part of the healthcare system at large. Besides the regular assisted fertilization treatments, many clinics also organized the donation of gametes, based on the logic of a gift economy.

There is thus a series of activities and encounters intersecting with the material and biological manipulation of reproductive materials such as eggs, sperms and embryos. While the front-office work included all patient contacts, the work was embedded in the technoscientific possibilities of reproductive medicine and clinical assisted fertilization work, determining the interactions between staff and patients. The timing of the treatments being controlled through hormone regimes; the need for high level of traceability and cleanliness, in particular in the handover to and from the laboratorial (back-office) areas of the clinics; the legal arrangements and regulations, particularly of the donation of reproductive materials, are some of determining factors which have been described in this chapter.

5

In the Laboratory

Introduction

While much of the work of handling the patients occurs in the clinic, the interface between the patient and the assisted fertilization practices, the laboratory is the site where most of the scientific work is organized and taking place. Patients are in many cases worried and concerned whether they will be able to become parents and consequently much effort is invested in the capacity to inform and counsel the patients. In many ways, the patients are integrated into therapy, for instance during the hormone therapy phase preceding the egg retrieval, and consequently very detailed information must be provided on how and when to take all the medications at home. This chapter addresses the activities taking place in the laboratory—the back-office of the assisted fertilization clinic. It is in the laboratory that the gametes, the unfertilized egg and the sperm, are brought together to fertilize the egg and where the embryo is grown for a period of two to six days in various media. Finally, it is in the laboratory where embryologists are visually inspecting and selecting the most suitable embryo for the embryo transfer to the woman's womb. Most embryo transfers in Sweden today are single embryo transfers; single births have significantly lower risks than multiple births and patient safety and the safety of the unborn child are at the center of the therapy.[1] Since only one embryo is transferred, the selection procedure is of key importance. Assisted fertilization clinical work is an activity monitored in detail and preoccupied with statistics and metrics, and there are much empirical data collected and stored pertaining to the embryo selection process.

The work in the laboratory is also structured around specific regimes of division of labor, professional categories and technological development.

---

1 "After legislation declaring that only a single embryo could be implanted via IVF, Sweden saw its NICU [Neonatal Intensive Care Unit] usage rates plummet, as did Belgium, and now much of the European Union has followed suit," Rapp (2011: 211, note 7) reports.

Sharing these generic analytical categories with any other domain of science-based work, assisted fertilization laboratory work is one of many examples of how biological specimens, scientific and technical know-how, and technologies and tools are constructing an experimental system capable of producing embryos that hopefully are received favorably in the uterus, eventually leading to the birth of a baby. While the entire discourse on assisted fertilization is surrounded by the concerns for "life" and "babies," there is a tendency that the technical and technological aspects of the work conducted are downplayed, very much in order to conceal the "engineering-oriented" aspects of assisted fertilization. While this laboratory work is by no means concealed for the patients, they tend to be separated from the laboratory activities in order to reduce costs and to avoid misunderstandings. For instance, in the domain of embryo selection, there are certain risks involved in letting common-sense thinking intervene in what is a professional domain of expertise. Goslinga-Roy (2000) offers an illustrative example of how patients may easily project their beliefs regarding "life" on biological specimens. One female patient was invited to take part in the embryo selection process:

> Her doctor had let her see, right before their transfer into Julie's uterus, through the microscope, the five choice embryos he had picked. One of these five embryos wiggled as she peered through the lens: "Gee, I wonder if this one in the left corner will get us pregnant!" she remembers exclaiming. The vitality of this embryo seemed to exhibit a will-to-live commensurate with her and her husband's desire for a child. (Ironically, the wiggle was an optical illusion according to the reproductive laboratory director whom I later interviewed). (Goslinga-Roy, 2000: 129)

A perceived evidence of vitality and a life force was apparently merely an optical illusion and consequently much professional expertise and visual skills need to be acquired before qualified assessment of, for example, embryos may be articulated. Consequently, and also for reasons of strict cleanliness, the work in the laboratory needs to be a secluded area, and thus becomes a domain wherein the patient's role is marginal.

Uses of Technology

Needless to say, the work in the laboratory is heavily determined by the technologies being developed and implemented in the practices. The laboratory work includes a variety of technologies and tools, both "hardware" such as microscopes, incubators, dishes and pipettes, and cabinets and freezers for the storage of gametes, and "software" such as computer programs and administrative routines to monitor and control the work. One of the interviewees pointed at the capacity for storing and handling the embryos and oocytes, the unfertilized eggs, as one key to the increased success rate in the therapies:

> *What has been of great importance is that we have learnt to understand how to handle these fertilized eggs. We did not know that from the beginning and we will still be able to make a little progress but we have not reached all the way. I think that is a key factor. (Gynecologist and entrepreneur, Clinic #4)*

Speaking in more detail, another interviewee pointed out that one part of the work involves manipulating the gametes, i.e. to actively insert the sperm into the egg in the so-called ICSI (Intra-Cytoplasmatic Sperm Injection) procedure, and called for more advanced technologies further enhancing the work: "Above all, there is a need for better microscopes and desks for the microscope and manipulators [sic] to be able to operate the pipettes and to insert into the eggs. So there is quite a bit of mechanics involved" (professor and entrepreneur, Clinic #4). Most of the interviewees emphasized that major scientific and technological leaps were accomplished in the late 1970s and the 1980s but that after the early 1990s, there has been a slowing down of the technological development. One of the most significant technological changes in this 15-year period was the development of the ICSI method for mechanically injecting a sperm into the egg. "From a male infertility perspective, the possibility for microinjection, that was a huge leap ... Prior to that, not very much could be offered men with infertility problems. IVF wouldn't help if there were no [functional] sperm," the head of Clinic #1 said. One of the interviewees pointed at the influence of the method:

> *About 20 percent of all IVF cases were caused by a male factor [i.e. poor sperm quality] and we did a few studies comparing ICSI and other methods. Since ICSI was a little bit more effective, the technique just took over. In the US, they could get a bit more pay and that was of great importance when promoting the technique ... In Turkey for instance, 98 percent of all IVF is using ICSI. In Sweden, 60 percent. And that is not in parity with the male infertility factor ... it will be interesting to learn if the boys have inherited this male factor because that has not been studied ... We do not know what is happening to all these children. (Professor and entrepreneur, Clinic #4)*

The ICSI method was developed to handle the cases of male infertility but because the method proved to be highly effective, it is today widespread, even in cases when male infertility has not been clinically proven. Some of the interviewees recalled that when the method was first developed and put to use in the early 1990s, there were some laboratory researchers that felt a little bit uncomfortable when using it, primarily because of its limited clinical evidence regarding safety and efficacy: "In every new development phase, there are ethical discussions … When microinjections were developed, there were many who thought that intervening into the egg felt a little bit uncomfortable" (biomedical scientist, Clinic #6). In general, as being part of experimental medicine and reproductive medicine, issues pertaining to safety and efficacy are given much weight. The entire laboratory work and assisted fertilization in general is surrounded by a ceaseless collection of clinical data in various ways contributing to the understanding of how assisted fertilization works. Regarding ICSI, there were reasons for being concerned regarding safety and efficacy because the fertilization of the egg is different than in natural fertilization:

> *To really take it as far as you can, they [children born of ICSI] are of a different*
> *kind, another race than us. When an egg is fertilized, it is fertilized by the head*
> *of the sperm and then the middle section of the sperm, the mitochondria, is*
> *never internalized by the egg but it is left outside. So humans just inherit the*
> *female DNA mitochondria [the part of the cell that produces energy]. But the*
> *ICSI children … there you place the entire sperm in the very heart of the egg*
> *and it is likely that the paternal mitochondria will be part of the development.*
> *That does not mean that it is dangerous but it is on the other hand not what*
> *happens during natural fertilization. So there is this little question mark and it*
> *is interesting to see what happens when these children are starting to reproduce.*
> *(Professor and entrepreneur, Clinic #4)*

The argument here is that especially the boys being born on basis of the ICSI method may inherit a poor sperm quality from their fathers. Since the first babies were born in the early 1990s, these boys may not have started to reproduce, have kids of their own, and it is therefore still an unanswered empirical question whether male infertility in terms of sperm motility and concentration is caused by genetic factors or it if is a matter of environmental conditions and influence. There is in general a concern that male fertility seems to be in decline, both in terms of sperm motility and concentration and some researchers have pointed at environmental conditions such as the presence of estrogen in drinking water. In some cases, there are evidence of fish becoming infertile as the waters become contaminated by too high levels of sex hormones. Under all conditions, the issue of male infertility has historically been relatively marginal in the domain of reproductive medicine, one of the interviewees argued:

There has not been very much thinking about what the sperm is and what genetic material it delivers. That is something I have studied and written my dissertation about, how the sperm chromatin is structured ... In the beginning, the sperm is a circular cell having no motility and no tail but that is developed during the last eight weeks ... The chromatin is then loosely structured as in a large cell but eventually when the sperm become a small cell the chromatin is much more tightly structured. The hypothesis is that the chromatin is being protected during the transportation to accomplish a natural inception. It has been observed that infertile men ... have a different chromatin structure than fertile men ... So the interest for the sperm has been reawakened during the last years. (Biomedical scientist and head of clinic, Clinic #1)

"There should be more focus on male infertility," another laboratory researcher (Clinic #2) added.

The development of new technologies and tools is continuous and relatively linear during the last two decades. Being able to deliver a 50–60 percent "hit rate," the key to further enhance this figure lies not primarily in the development of new technologies such as microscopes or freezers but in a more elaborated understanding of the human reproductive organs and processes. Instead, one of the interviewees argued, in the future there should be more emphasis on developing cheaper yet reliable technologies and tools helping to lower the costs and to "democratize" assisted fertilization—to take it to parts of society and the world having little economic resources to invest in clinical assistance: "The IVF technology is all too sophisticated, too technical and focused on being at the frontline. The equipment in the laboratories, like the heating cabinets; you can almost fly to the moon with them, damn it! What we need is simpler stuff" (gynecologist, founder of Clinic #7). In Sweden, Denmark and other countries where assisted fertilization is part of the public healthcare system offering, between 3 and 4 percent of all babies born are fertilized in the laboratory. In the United States, where there are no such public health sector offerings, the comparative figure is around 1 percent, i.e. one-third of the Scandinavian level: "If you examine the US, they are below one percent and that is what you may expect when people are paying themselves. You cannot assume that [they] do not want children as much as we do, because they do, but they simply cannot afford it" (professor and entrepreneur, Clinic #4). This indicated, everything else equal, that the presence of a public healthcare system offering assisted fertilization under determinate conditions strongly increases the number of babies born.

In other words, cost and access to adequate financial resources play a key role in assisted fertilization. Therefore, rather than merely promoting assisted fertilization for people in economically endowed welfare states in the North or for the richer strata of any society, there are ample possibilities for developing what may be called "low-cost assisted fertilization," yet with good clinical safety and efficacy. In order to be able to provide such offerings, less sophisticated and costly technologies need to be developed. The professor in reproductive medicine expressed his hopes for the future: "Today, there are these Chinese companies that try to develop much cheaper ultrasound machines at the fraction of the cost we're using but still serve their purpose. There are companies in the US developing much more elementary incubators than the ones we are using" (professor and entrepreneur, Clinic #4).

Taken together, the laboratory work is heavily structured on basis of the technologies used while at the same time it is not reducible to the technologies; technologies constitute the backbone of the laboratory but the know-how and expertise in handling the gametes and embryos are what play the key role. The development of new technologies such as for instance incubators with cameras built into the cabinet, enabling a series of photos to be taken during the first five to six days of embryo growth, eliminates the need for taking the embryo out of the cabinet to visually inspect it and therefore the disturbances during the first phases of embryo growth may be reduced to a minimum: "Another thing being developed is a new type of incubators, something called EmbryoScope where they have built a microscope where you can take photos [of the embryo] … These photos helps you monitoring and controlling in much greater detail" (biomedical scientist and head of clinic, Clinic #1). Such new technologies may be of great importance or may play a relatively marginal role, but it is complicated to determine such outcomes prior to the clinical work.

Like all experimental sciences, assisted fertilization is advanced on the basis of clinical trials and the assessment of outcomes. Such a view is summarized by one of the interviewees: "There are new things coming up all the time, like 'this is the future!' But then it needs to be validated and it should be studied and randomized and so forth before you can see [the application]. For 25 years, I've heared that 'this is the breakthrough!' but in 99 out of 100 cases, it's nothing" (gynecologist and head of clinic, Clinic #1). What may appear as a solution to a perceived problem may after being clinically tested have little effect or relevance; on the other hand, what may appear to be of marginal interest may be of great importance. The experimental sciences are filled with such narratives of disruptive or non-linear innovations and improvements.

Scientific Practices

The more than 30 years of clinical experience from working with human reproductive material and embryos has led to a very well monitored and controlled process for handling the biological specimens. The retrieval of eggs, their storage, fertilization, selection, and the transfer of embryos are a series of events in the assisted fertilization practice that are mapped and understood in detail. At the same time, assisted fertilization work is riddled by certain areas wherein human reproduction is not yet mapped, for instance how the embryo is connected to the endometrium inside the uterus and how the embryo and the uterus and the placenta are interacting and mutually responding to one another in the early stages of pregnancy. In addition, prior to the embryo transfer, there are more things that need to be known regarding, for example, embryo selection. Several of the interviewees pointed at the field of embryo growth as being one field where there had been some progress during the last few years. New media for growing the embryos and new storage media were two recent changes that had favored healthy embryo growth. In addition, new scientific methods such as metabolomics, the analysis of the metabolic processes of the embryo, were identified as promising methods in the field of embryo selection. "What substances these embryos are emitting could mirror their genetics and that is important," the founder of Clinic #4 argued. "It is called metabolomics: to review what substances in the medium they [embryos] have consumed and what they have 'spitted out,'" a gynecologist in Clinic #1 added. The underlying scientific program to metabolomics is genetics and genomics, the study of the hereditary material of the biological system.

The period from around 1990 to the early years of the new millennium has been characterized by a strong belief in the human genome as being the "book of life" capable of revealing the underlying mechanisms of the human organisms. However, as the human genome was mapped in the so-called HUGO project, researchers were disappointed when they learned that the human genome was somewhat limited and that the transcription of genetic sequences into proteins was far more complicated to understand than to merely map the genome. Today, there is widespread skepticism regarding what Griesemer (2006) calls "gene-centric biology," and instead there is an emphasis on what has been called "post-genomic research" emphasizing, for example, the production of protein (in proteomics) and metabolites (in metabolomics) in relationship to the genome and more specifically sequences (so-called SNPs or ESTs) of the genome.

The field of assisted fertilization also received its share of the "genomics craze," i.e. studies where the genome of the female patients has been examined. According to one of the professors in reproductive medicine, such studies have been able to explain very little of the fertility variation in the population. In addition, one of the embryologists pointed at one study demonstrating that the hormone therapy plays only a marginal role in preparing the endometrium in the uterus for receiving the embryo and therefore milder hormone therapies can be prescribed, primarily supporting ovulation but having few other objectives:

> There are a few studies published recently that show that the hormone treatment done in IVF actually fails to improve the endometrium — quite the contrary [to what we previously believed]! There are these new "ray technologies" where you can examine 30,000 genes and then you notice that 500–600 in the endometrium are different because of the hormone stimulation in IVF in comparison to a regular cycle. It is widely recognized that the endometrium does matter, and therefore the [hormone] treatment is milder. There are lower levels of hormones. (Embryologist, Clinic #2)

In general, genomics research seems to have a marginal influence in the field of assisted fertilization. Instead, interviewees emphasized the need for mapping and understanding quite practical procedures such as embryo selection:

> What I believe is in the pipeline to advance the field, or what should be in the pipeline, that is better methods for choosing what embryo to return to the uterus. That would be the most important issue. And a lot of research is done in order for us to understand what happens on the molecular plane, in the hormone stimulation phase in the laboratory; why are some eggs failing while others are developing? (Gynecologist and head of clinic, Clinic #1)

While metabolomics analyses, for example have been advanced as a field of research that may support the embryo selection, today the embryos are selected primarily on the basis of visual inspection, a so-called morphology analysis:

> A: Today we choose embryos on the basis of how they look in the microscope, right.
>
> Q: So you inspect them visually?
>
> A: Exactly! (Gynecologist and head of clinic, Clinic #1)

The practice of embryo selection is thus indicative of the visual practices in medicine and the need for developing professional vision in experimental medicine and reproductive medicine and the clinical work of assisted fertilization more specifically. The capacity for looking at and assessing biological specimens lies at the very heart of medicine and the laboratory work in assisted fertilization is no exception. For instance, one of the gynecologists pointed at the scale wherein the work is conducted:

> *The eggs are relatively large cells but an egg is one tenth of a millimeter in diameter. And transparent too! … Pipetting the eggs between dishes, and handling several eggs from one patient, is really one practical element; moving them without losing them. You freeze them and inject sperms into them in volumes of a few nanoliters. To accomplish the work is technically demanding and requires manual skills and long training. At the same time as it is a technically demanding procedure it is also routine work, you could say. (Gynecologist, Clinic #5)*

Working on the micro scale puts certain demands on the analyst:

> *It is technically demanding and you work a lot with microscopes … All work with the eggs, the movement between dishes and when assessing them … [you need to] magnify them 80 to 100 times … these morphological assessments, there are routines and rules and documents prescribing how to do it; what parameters that are of importance and what are less important and how to choose, and so forth. (Gynecologist, Clinic #5)*

Not only does the embryologist need to have adequate theoretical understandings of the biological specimens, he or she also needs to be able to visually inspect and to mechanically manipulate the gametes being worked in. The work is thus mediated in every sense of the term by the microscopes and other technical resources being involved in the work. Later in the process, in the case of embryo selection, the embryologist is facing an even more difficult challenge, that of selecting the most suitable (i.e. vital) embryo.

SELECTING EMBRYOS

The embryologists are handling all laboratory procedures involving the gametes, including the fertilization of the egg through in vitro fertilization in the test tube or the injection of the sperm into the egg (the ICSI procedure), the growing of the embryos in incubators, the selection of embryos, and the freezing of surplus embryos that are not selected for the transfer for later use. While there has been much emphasis on methodological development, e.g. genomics (the screening of the DNA sequence of the embryo) or metabolomics (the measurement of metabolites emitted in the media), the principal method for selecting the embryo for transfer is morphology analysis (from Greek, *morphe*, "form"), that is, the visual inspection of the embryo after around either two or five days of growth in the incubators. One of the embryologists accounted for the procedure:

> We primarily check the number of cells. We select on day two ... By that time, the embryos should have ... between four or six cells, and then they mustn't be too fragmented, not have a too ugly cytoplasm, not too uneven size of the cells which we have a limit for. (Embryologist #3, Clinic #8)

She continued:

> We look at the cytoplasm in the cells, we look or vacuoles [enclosed cavities in cells] and if there is more than one nucleus per cell, and we are looking for something we call a fragment, a form of cellular garbage that can irritate [the embryo]. We select on basis of a predefined criteria list what to transfer and freeze. When there are fine embryos it is not the least complicated. But these boundary embryos, can we really justify to put these back? We look in the computer files what has been done previously [with the patient] ... We have become more liberal in terms of what we transfer because it is still counted as one attempt [even if no embryo is transferred]. And if we return something, then there is at least a chance. If we transfer nothing, there is no chance at all. (Embryologist #3, Clinic #8)

The morphological analysis is based on a predefined list of qualities (see Table 5.1) including the evenness of cells, the speed of the cell division, and the absence of vacuoles and fragments in the cytoplasm. Embryos that divide too quickly, before the 25–27 hours range of time, are also excluded because too quick cell growth may indicate genetic deviation: "If it moves too fast and cleaves to a three cell by the 25th hour, or a four cell, then it's also an indication of chromosome abnormalities" (embryologist #1, Clinic #8). In addition, the embryos should preferably divide evenly (into even number of cells) to comply with the predefined standards: "We exclude some embryos from the very beginning ... unless they are fertilized normally, they are excluded. If they have an irregular first divide, if they move directly to three or four cells [instead of two cells], then we remove them as well, we don't select them in the first place. We choose those which have divided into two cells within a certain time after the fertilization" (embryologist #2, Clinic #8). By and large, the principal aesthetic criterion of the embryologist was *symmetry*—the evenness of the cells and the absence of fragments and other aesthetically disapproved features of the embryos. One of the embryologists stressed the "appearance" over measurable qualities in the work:

> We're looking at different morphological characteristics or, you know, appearance. Characteristics of appearance … Everyone else is trying to look for … Other ways that you can quantify what a good quality embryo is … You can quantify chromosomes, you can quantify RNA production, you can quantify … You know, protein levels. Or you can either, indirectly get an idea of the viability of the embryo, by looking at, when it grows in a culture drop. (Embryologist #1, Clinic #4)

As a consequence from the reliance on aesthetic features, the embryologists debated the vitality of embryos that did not comply with the predefined parameters: "Some people get pregnant, even with a non-optimal embryo … We don't know everything. Some embryos that we don't think are optimal actually can produce a baby," one embryologist (#1) said. Regardless of such insights, the knowledge that even "sub-standard embryos" at times led to pregnancies, the embryologists were concerned that the patients would ask about their opinions about their view of the embryo transferred. One of the embryologists said that she tried to avoid such questions altogether if possible:

> There is no problem when there are beautiful embryos to transfer but to demonstrate a crappy one, that is not great fun. At the same time, when we do a transfer of a non-top class embryo, we don't tell them anything unless they ask. Then we say, "well, we have chosen an embryo for the transfer" and have little else to say about the quality. But if they ask us, of course we answer them. Unless they ask, though, we try to avoid the topic. If I tell you that this [embryo] wasn't too good but we'll give it back to you anyway, then you might think you're not getting pregnant. We really don't know how the brain affects the body. You mustn't say that, but that is how I think. If you eliminate their hope, I think that makes a difference. And unless they ask they won't get an answer. (Embryologist #3, Clinic #8)

Knowing that we do not fully understand the somatic role of expectations during pregnancies, the embryologist thought it was important not to disappoint the patient. Still, the absence of qualified embryos led at times to crucial discussions:

We have some patients that get no nice ones, and which one to choose in that situation to be able to give her something back. That is the worst part ... At times, we are asking a physician whether we should terminate the therapy or if she should get something back. That has changed over the years because it used to be the policy that they get three transfers ... for economic reasons, we have changed the policy to be three egg retrievals so if you get no transfer it is still counted as one trial. In that respect, there is no benefit in not transferring [the embryo]. On the other hand, we have decided not to transfer anything we do not believe in. Statistically speaking, though, these grade-three embryos have been proven to lead to pregnancies but at a lower frequency. So the chances are not zero. (Embryologist #4, Clinic #8)

The embryologists had clinical data supporting their choice of embryos complying with predefined standards yet it also testified to the limited understanding of the biological processes of the post-transfer pregnancy.

Organizing Professional Vision

The embryologists' work to visually inspect, assess and select the most suitable embryo was both based in individual skills and competencies and collective practices of visual inspection. While the visual inspection was trained individually, it was always from the very beginning informed by professional vision derived from previous experience and clinical data. That is, while the visual inspection is of necessity conducted by individual embryologists their professional vision is constantly subject to comparisons and corrections. One of the embryologists explained what qualities were required to perform the work: "You need to be both quick and very careful, well, a combination of that. You need to maintain an oversight of the whole, sort of, have a sense of responsibility for what you are doing and do your best no matter what" (embryologist #2, Clinic #8). Since the embryos were grown in incubators designed to recreate the uterus, the embryos were kept outside of heated and protected environments for a minimal amount of time. The assessment thus called for a combination of great carefulness—dropping the dishes on the floor, spoiling weeks of pains and efforts by both patients and professionals, is every embryologist's absolute nightmare—precision and speed. One of the embryologists explained:

Someone that's good is also someone that's quick at making a decision. Knows what a good embryo is. Has a "gut feeling" is terrible way to say ... I think, a good embryologist should have an open mind as well; of what can be a pregnancy

and what not. But it should be very, sort of strict in how they're determining,
when they're grading. So they're always grading the same embryos the same
way. (Embryologist #1, Clinic #4)

Being able to combine carefulness, precision and speed made experience a key
quality in an embryologist: "This is where experience matters," embryologist
#2 said. "One may have seen 100 embryos and the other 100,000, so there are
these small differences [in perception]. But it is not only a matter of experience;
the more you've seen, the more you believe you know."

At the same time as experience was highly valued, the inspection of embryos
was always a collective procedure. First, in the laboratory where the day-to-
day work was organized in teams of two or more embryologists working
together and secondly in the joint inspection of embryos in collaboration with
other clinics, so-called validation. The capacity to collaborate with others and
to have your assessments scrutinized by others were thus important qualities
in an embryologist: "You need to be able to appreciate collaboration because
you are always dependent on other persons doing their share … When you
are hiring another person [it is important] you feel 'this person would fit with
the others.' So we're not hiring odd personalities because that might risk our
collaboration," embryologist #2 argued.

Despite resting on an international system of criteria, recently further
developed on basis of the Istanbul consensus, the visual inspections were after
all, one embryologist argued, "subjective" and not an "exact science" since
nothing was "measured" (embryologist #4, Clinic #8). Like in many other
scientific communities (see, for example, Sommerlund, 2006: 918), "subjectivity"
was the demon of the scientific procedure that needed to be handled properly:
"In our clinic, we have this routine that we are several participating in the
assessment of the embryos, to be able to discuss and share a view, so we're
not sliding into completely different opinions," embryologist #2 said. To
accomplish disciplinary objectivity in the embryo selection, the embryologists
were using a system based on an international scoring system (see Table 5.1)
where the embryos were graded. Embryologist #1 explained:

This blastocyst [pointing at a picture] is the type of blastocyst which I would
call a 4-0-0, or a 4AA, that's 4 grade of expansion, top grade of inner cell mass
and a top grade of trafectoderm, we call a 4AA.

A: Where does this "4" come from?

B: The four is a type of grade of expansion. This fluid-filled cavity has now stretched so much that the embryo is not its original size, it's past its original size, of the egg. (Embryologist #1, Clinic #4)

Table 5.1   Consensus scoring system for cleavage-stage embryos, in addition to cell number

Grade	Rating	Quality assessment at ~48 hours
1	Good	< 10% fragmentation Stage-specific cell size No multinucleation
2	Fair	10–25% fragmentation Stage-specific cell size for majority of cells No evidence of multinucleation
3	Poor	Severe fragmentation (>25%) Cell size not stage specific Evidence of multinucleation

Source: Istanbul consensus.

"It's a numbers game, I choose the best. She gets 10, I choose the best, I freeze the rest," embryologist #1 eloquently summarized. Embryologist #2 continued, emphasizing the effects of the most recent international standards for embryo inspection:

If we write grade A it is fragmented, and B means the cells are uneven in size, C means that the cytoplasm is sort of gritty, a little bit dark and there can be vacuoles in the cytoplasm. Now we're starting to assess vacuoles per se according to the consensus document, because it appears as if they are negative for the embryo and the granulates don't make any difference. So that is a new thing to do on basis of the article. (Embryologist #2, Clinic #8)

The embryologist lists their assessment in a protocol and eventually the selection of the embryo can be verified empirically in terms of pregnancy or miscarriage. In order to calibrate individual and laboratory-based differences in assessment, the different laboratories were collaborating to make joint assessments of embryos:

We do the validation jointly with a few other clinics in Sweden where they have filmed the embryos in different stages … You sit on your own looking at these films

and make your assessment … well, looking for differences. [Afterwards] we jointly
examine the embryos to see if there were cases where we made different assessments
and then we examine them one more time. (Embryologist #2, Clinic #8)

The uses of computer-based media rather than the microscope posed a few challenges for the embryologists, normally manipulating the microscope to inspect the embryo from different magnitudes and angles. After making their individual assessments the embryologists discussed differences in assessments and specific features of the embryo that were problematic to reach an agreement on. Again, it is the embryos deviating from the norm that cause the most discussions: "I can imagine there are a few differences [in how individuals evaluate]. You notice when we are like five persons looking at the same embryo. And if you have a patient with—how should I put this—somewhat lower quality [of the reproductive materials] you notice that we make different assessments than what we would do if we have a top quality patient" (embryologist #3, Clinic #8). She continued to once again emphasize that quick assessments are important:

In the cases which are crystal clear, then there are no problems doing it on your
own, but in these questionable cases it is a good thing to discuss them with
someone. "Is this about 20 percent fragments or is it more like 30 percent?"
"What can we agree on in this case?" "Are there two nucleus in this cell or is
it just one?" The more eyes that see, the better it is. And then there is the time
factor; it is supposed to be done quite fast. The one sitting by the microscope is
the person having a final say regarding what is written in the document. At the
same time, anyone can say what they think and of course we're trying to reach
an agreement. (Embryologist #3, Clinic #8)

In other cases, there were more discussions and different embryologists had at times alternative views: "In this grey zone, they may have more fragmentation; uneven in size. A few embryos have all these characteristics, you know. They are complicated to assess. Some of us say 'that's good quality!' while other thinks 'I wouldn't go for that one!'" (embryologist #5, Clinic #8).

CLINICAL EVIDENCE AND PROFESSIONAL VISION

Regardless of all the difficulties involved in assessing and selecting both eggs prior to fertilization and embryos after between two and five days of growth in the incubator, the embryologists were convinced their expertise made a difference in the end:

Q: What's your sense, how much of your assessment makes a difference, do you think? How does it feel when you are working on it?

A: I think it makes a substantial difference … If you would choose embryos that don't look great at all, then there wouldn't be any good results. So it really matters. (Embryologist #2, Clinic #8)

One of the embryologists addressed her role in the industry as being the one to select what embryo to transfer:

At times there is this weird feeling that "here I am, making all these selections: this one I accept, that one I don't." At the same time, we have our reasons for doing this, but still "who am I to decide"—those thoughts may come. But we are educated and trained, and who else could make the decision? … It is us working in the lab that take care of them [the embryos] all the time, handling them, and know how they are, based on the knowledge we have today. There are plenty of things we don't know, for instance, now we're starting to measure the metabolism of the little creatures. So there is plenty of things to develop that we know little of today. (Embryologist #3, Clinic #8)

The selected embryos could eventually be verified against clinical data—the patient's reported pregnancies. When collecting the clinical data, low-quality embryos had a lower pregnancy frequency:

We had this issue six months ago or so, what are the success rates for these grade three transfers? It is not that complicated to get statistics out of the data base, so we retrieved the data and we learned that the pregnancy frequency was between ten and fifteen percent rather than 35 and 40 percent. So it is definitely not zero so if you have nothing else it is worth trying. (Embryologist #4, Clinic #8)

For the embryologists, the clinical data served both to verify their professional expertise but also to motivate them to continue their work as they learned after a few days whether their work had led to any pregnancies:

We always have statistical reports so, we're looking at data, our data is always captured into an Excel sheet, and there we have all of the grades, and you can basically sort them and say, what top qualities gave us pregnancy, what poor quality embryos gave us pregnancy? What is the implantation, that is the pregnancy rate, for this embryo type compared to this embryo type? So you can always look back into the data and everything. We also have a very fun report every morning that we talk about, where we show a list of the pregnancies that have been reported to the nurses. Patients calls us up on a certain day and say, "We're pregnant!" And what we do is we can say "Ah, this pregnancy, lets pull the file." And then we go in and we look in her record and we look: what did the embryo look like? Because we always take a photo of the embryos that we transferred. "What did he look like?" (Embryologist, #1, Clinic #4)

Since the clinical practice in Europe and the Nordic countries stresses the importance of single embryo transfer to reduce the risks involved in the pregnancy and delivery of the baby, there are good clinical data supporting the visual inspection:

In the Nordic countries, we have very good results … Above all in the Nordic countries, but also in Europe in general … We have much experience from single-embryo transfers so we know which embryos that are transferred. If they transfer more embryos, as they do in the US, then you cannot tell which embryo [that became the fetus] … so we get a good quality control on what we're doing. (Embryologist #2, Clinic #8)

Regardless of such statistics, the post-transfer life of the embryo remains relatively obscure for the embryologists as there is a lack of clinical studies of how the embryo, the endometrium and the uterus are co-aligned and integrated post-transfer. One of the gynecologists pointed at the methodological difficulties in moving beyond the morphology analysis of embryos:

One of the reasons for all this emphasis on the embryo is that you can hold it in your hand and study it … (Gynecologist and entrepreneur, Clinic #4)

Despite much research efforts to develop omics methods (e.g. genomics and metabolomics) that could further strengthen the embryologists' assessment of what embryo to transfer, this work is still playing a relatively marginal role in the clinical practice. Instead, the individual and collective professional vision of embryologists embedded in an internationally enacted grading scheme taking into account clinically relevant parameters is the principal means for selecting embryos. Potentially, future advancement of omics analytical technologies may shift the focus from visual inspection and professional vision but for the time being the morphology analysis are dominating in the field.

In summary, the embryologist's professional vision is on the one hand embedded in individual skills in discerning the morphological features of the embryos, e.g. the evenness of the cells, the qualities of cytoplasm and its degree of fragmentation and vacuoles, and the collective capacity to align and balance individual accounts and professional objectivity, the joint routines for assessing the embryos. The coding schemes and the international standards being enacted here served a key role in determining standardized professional vision ultimately being determined by clinical data. Even in cases where there is an agreement regarding the low quality of the embryo, 10–15 percent of the transfers lead to pregnancies, testifying to the limited understanding of the post-transfer life of the embryo in reproductive medicine. As a consequence, regardless of the advancement of the field and the clinical performance of assisted fertilization, the professional vision of embryologists, their examination of life-in-the-making, is thus limited and partial, still not anchored in a comprehensive understanding of human reproduction. The examination of life is still a matter of diligently combining morphology analysis and clinical data rather than operating on basis of a more solid theoretical framework.

Professional ideologies and aesthetic norms

After the embryo is transferred to the womb, the embryologist can only await the results but once they know if the transfer is successful, i.e. the pregnancy is developing as anticipated, new data is fed into the system, providing further guidance on what embryo to select. In her study of assisted fertilization clinics, Cussins (1998) suggests that the selection process is embedded in a typical Western aesthetics wherein the symmetry of the embryos and how "round" they are—already Plato portrayed the circle as the perfect shape, a belief that has been maintained throughout the Western canon (Hallyn, 1990: 159; Stengers, 1997: 21)—and therefore the embryo selection is partially based on what Plato speaks of as "justified true beliefs":

> The evenness of the cells, the similarity of cell size, and the presence of "blebs" [asymmetries] are also recorded. The embryos are given a "grade" to reflect how "pretty" they are. Round evenly developing embryos are good, and uneven, "misshapen" embryos with blebs are not good. The "not good" embryos are routinely referred to collectively as "crud." (Cussins, 1998: 93)

Embryologists apparently need to base their joint decision on some shared belief and to draw on the aesthetic ideal of symmetry and circularity is as good a basis for decisions as any as long as there are no clinical evidence suggesting otherwise. Cussins' (1998) critique of the embryologists is thus of relevance for understanding how technoscience and medical practice are embedded in shared social beliefs, at times of marginal relevance for scientific pursuits. However, the critique ignores the relatively limited information on which the embryologists may make their judgment. Students of decision-making have emphasized that there is a tendency to collect excess information (Feldman and March, 1981), information that influences the decision per se only marginally but that helps portraying the decision-makers as acting in accordance with instituted beliefs and norms, i.e. that any decision should rest on available and relevant information.

In the case of embryo selection, there is some information to be collected prior to the embryo transfer and this is the reason why, for example, metabolomics may be of interest for embryologists, but post-transfer there is a shortage of information. Either if the pregnancy continues as anticipated or leads to a miscarriage, there are few women interested in any further clinical studies beyond the point of the embryo transfer, leaving the embryologists with decisions to be made on the basis of limited information. Hence they recourse to the shared aesthetic norm of symmetry. Seemingly ironic given that the clinical practice includes highly sophisticated know-how and advanced technologies, the embryo selection process is centered on visual inspections, albeit supported by the use of standard technologies such as microscopes. At the end of the day, professional vision is what determines which embryo is selected for the embryo transfer.

Professional and Regulatory Control

In addition to the technologies and scientific practices mobilized in the laboratory work, different domains of expertise are represented in the laboratory. Historically, as indicated in Chapter 3, gynecologists in the field of reproductive medicine have been the principal professional category developing assisted fertilization as a clinical branch of reproductive medicine. However, relatively early in the process, the pioneers of assisted fertilization identified the need for professional groups being qualified to handle the social and emotional needs of the patients. In the early private clinics, midwives, nurses and counselors were recruited to support the day-to-day work in the clinics. At the same time, the gynecologists were in charge of the laboratory activities but eventually they saw the need for hiring more specialized workers to handle the laboratory work. Today, the laboratories are populated by embryologists, cytologists, microbiologists, biomedical scientists and biochemists having little or no background in reproductive medicine but in various domains of professional expertise in the life sciences. While the gynecologists still play a key role in monitoring and overseeing the operations, taking the medical responsibility for the patients, the actual work in the laboratory is conducted by embryologists and the like. One of the interviewees, an embryologist, emphasized how they complemented the gynecologists in having more detailed expertise in certain areas of the life sciences:

> They [physicians] do not have the basic training in cell biology and biochemistry. It is part of their training but it is like it is forgotten and once they finish their training and have done their internship they start their resident training as gynecologists or further specialize and then this basic cell biology is lost since long. The most advanced research is thus conducted by embryologists. (Embryologist, Clinic #2)

"In an IVF lab you find molecular biologists but primarily biomedical scientists … There are a few gynecologists too, but they are exceptions," a gynecologist in Clinic #5 remarked. This shift from gynecologists ensuring medical safety and efficacy to the increased role played by new professional groups has also been accompanied by new professional standards. The gynecologist pointed at an emerging European standard for practicing embryologists leading to the issuing of certificates:

> There is a European organization issuing certificates in embryology. If you have been working under supervision for a long period in an IVF lab and have been examined there, then you may get this certificate. More and more people are taking that certificate and that may [be a standard] sooner or later, I think. In the long run, you need this certificate to work in an IVF lab. (Gynecologist, Clinic #5)

Such certificates are based on both formal credentials—university degrees and similar—and practical experience: "Within a year, they become junior embryologists. After conducting a number of practical elements and passing a theoretical test. After six years of experience, they become seniors," a biomedical scientist and head of Clinic #2 said. For instance, in order to perform ICSI sperm injections, there is a need for a year of training, the biomedical scientist said. In general, in Europe, assisted fertilization is a heavily monitored and regulated activity, governed by the European Tissue Directive specifying in detail how human tissues should be handled and traded. One of the consequences of the regulatory control is that the entire field is emphasizing the collection and analysis of clinical data revealing how well the various clinics are performing. Cussins (1998) remarks that the entire "epistemic culture" of assisted fertilization is embedded in the use of statistics.

While there is ample evidence of professional communities and groups evading bureaucratic and regulatory control, in the field of assisted fertilization, the interviewees expressed their firm belief in the need for a close regulatory control of the activities. In addition to the compilation of statistics of National Board of Health and Welfare [*Socialstyrelsen*], the monitoring body in Sweden, individual clinics were collecting their own data to know how they were performing and if they were able to present stable performance ratios over time. In some cases, the clinics were using such data to calculate an estimate for the chances of individual couples to become parents. The head of Clinic #2 pointed at the benefits of this estimate:

> *There may be marginal differences if you examine the annual statistics between clinics, basically depending on what kind of patients you have so making a comparison is a bit tricky. That is why we do not publish these statistics. Instead, we have this model ... When a new couple arrives at the clinic, we're trying to estimate their individual chances. But people still ask about the performance without really knowing what they are asking for. (Biomedical scientist and head of clinic, Clinic #2)*

Rather than being a "general" estimate, the method took into account individual conditions:

> *What are the conditions? Most of them derived from the woman: what ovaries do you have? How many eggs are there to procure? There are different models estimating the chances, based on age, menstruation data, ultrasound analysis of ovaries, etc. All this is brought into the model we use, giving an individual prognosis for each couple being correct to plus/minus five percent. (Biomedical scientist and head of clinic, Clinic #2)*

The "hit rate," ratio of successful pregnancies to failed pregnancies, is thus the golden standard for different clinics and interviewees argued that the clients were in many cases well informed regarding what clinics could present the most solid performances. Of course, there are biological conditions that differ across patient groups. After all, assisted fertilization is no miracle work but the clinical branch of reproductive medicine; the clinicians are only capable of manipulating the gametes being brought by the patients and they have few possibilities for adding any vital components to the existing biological specimens. For some patients, as indicated in the previous chapter, too high expectations of what reproductive medicine is capable of accomplishing are leading to disappointment and despair. As many of the interviewees pointed out, assisted fertilization is a technoscientific practice operating under determinate conditions and becoming a parent is by no means a human right. For those learning this lesson the hard way after numerous trials and embryo transfers, little chances beyond gestational surrogacy and adoption remain to become parents.

Summary and Conclusion

The laboratory work of assisted fertilization is here defined as being the totality of activities that is conducted in separation from the patients, the work in the clinics accounted for in the previous chapters. In the laboratory work, an experimental system composed of professional know-how and expertise, technologies and tools, and regulatory practices are interrelated and designed to handle the biological specimens, the productive materials (gametes, embryos). Regardless of the technological and scientific know-how developed over the last decades, there are difficulties in reaching beyond the 50–60 percent success rate in assisted fertilization, indicating that there is a need for developing new theories and methodologies for understanding how the embryo is developed and especially how it is interacting with the endometrium and placenta after its transfer to the womb. While there are some hopes for the future regarding new methods in embryo selection, e.g. metabolomics analyses of the metabolites in the media wherein the embryos are grown, there is still relatively elementary visual practice determining what embryo to transfer. While the entire handling of the reproductive material has been successfully mapped and clinically developed—eggs, sperm and embryos can today be stored for years in the freezers—the relationship between the embryo and the uterus is perhaps the most promising path forward for reproductive medicine and assisted fertilization. Unfortunately, there are few ethically sound and practically useful methodologies for studying how the embryo is interacting with the endometrium and the placenta and consequently the way forward may be more cumbersome than the advancement of assisted fertilization during the last few decades.

As will be discussed in the next chapter, the possibilities for studying human reproduction are determined by political and scientific decision-making bodies and are ultimately embedded in a "benefit to risk" ratio wherein the individual and collective risks are evaluated in relationship to the potential benefits. By and large, it may be complicated to study the embryo's first hours or days in the uterus because few women, especially with a history of involuntary childlessness, would be interested in lending themselves to such research work. Still, reproductive medicine and assisted fertilization is a relatively new discipline and what the future may look like is as always notoriously difficult to speculate about.

In addition to the advancement of the study of human reproduction, assisted fertilization remains primarily an option for the well-off or for citizens in countries where the state is investing resources in reproductive medicine. The global demand for assisted fertilization treatment may be substantial but today more pressing concerns including virus-based diseases and malnutrition are naturally higher prioritized than help for couples suffering from infertility. Consequently, "low cost" assisted fertilization programs would demand cheaper but reliable technologies. To date, the tendency is on the contrary to develop even more sophisticated technologies and tools to further advance the safety and efficacy of the field.

6

Regulations and Controversies

Introduction

Assisted fertilization has consistently been associated with either artifice and "unnatural ways of making babies" — Huxley's test-tube babies — or with some kind of "luxury medicine" for the economically endowed classes and strata. Such common-sense thinking is complicated to handle for social actors because these beliefs reside in emotional responses to perceived problems or emerging challenges. One of the great paradoxes of contemporary society is that despite the remarkable success of the sciences and more recently the life sciences, enabling various ways to intervene into the human biological system, there is a growing skepticism regarding the influence and the status of the sciences (Gauchat, 2012). While science has been a heroic pursuit to master nature on all levels, in the last few decades the attitude has potentially changed; genetically modified animals, cloned sheep, and the manipulation of the human genome have been some recent scientific accomplishments heavily debated in both the media and in scholarly circles.

For some people, the sciences and especially the life sciences capable of producing teratological creatures such as Dolly the sheep, an ordinary looking sheep, but nevertheless an engineered organism based on advances in cloning techniques, represent a shift from a sound and relevant research agenda to what is less sanctioned by wider social interests. "Seldom has the future of human nature been the subject of such concerns and in-depth discussions by our wise public intellectuals as in our globalized age … This technophobic reaction to our bio-technological progress has led to a return to Kantian moral universalism," Rosi Braidotti (2008: 10) writes. Similarly, Sarah Franklin (2001: 342) says: "[I]t is clear that both governments and industries increasingly fear the costs of miscalculating public distrust in science, and these fears are, if anything, especially predominant in the fields of biomedicine and biotechnology."

When the sciences are manipulating inert matter as in the case of physics and chemistry, being more emotionally neutral than the life sciences, there is little moral concern involved. When it comes to the life sciences, and especially the life sciences handling human tissue and human organs, worried commentators are more prone to discuss issues such as the "dignity of life." Life science expertise can be legitimately used to cure illness and restore injuries but when it comes to engineering life on the elementary level or the use of transgenic organs from animals in transplant surgery, the status of the human species is put under erasure, critics contend.

In the case of assisted fertilization as clinical practice, these two critiques have led to two parallel activities. The first is to collect and analyze clinical data to be able to provide evidence that assisted fertilization is a safe and effective therapy and that the babies born are not suffering from any deviations from natural born babies. Second, the issue of being addressed as a form of luxury medicine, an unnecessary expenditure of resources in a world filled with babies losing their parents or with no parents capable of caring for them, is handled by a combination of information and policy-making. The first activity can be done by the scientific and scholarly community itself by organizing longitudinal research projects demonstrating the safety and efficacy of the therapy; the latter activity needs to be a collaborative effort with various social actors. In both these two activities, protagonists of assisted fertilization have done a good job in the Western part of the world but in parts of the world where fewer resources are invested in the healthcare sector, assisted fertilization is still branded as a prerogative of the well-to-do of society.

This final empirical chapter addresses the policy issues, regulatory control and controversies that surround assisted fertilization. It is emphasized that rather than being what works against the interest of the protagonists of assisted fertilization, clearly articulated and well-functioning policies and regulatory frameworks support and legitimize the work in the clinics. In fact, there are tight and ongoing connections between on the one hand the practitioners and the politicians and the regulatory bodies in order to continuously modify the policies and regulatory framework to adjust to social needs and technoscientific possibilities. That is, rather than the one determining the other, there is a recursive relationship between practice and policy, and policy makers are closely collaborating with the practitioners to avoid any "grey zones" (Anteby, 2008) wherein there are ambiguities regarding what can be legitimately accomplished.

This does not mean that the relationship between practitioners and policy makers is devoid of controversies and conflicts; on the contrary, the political system in Sweden has been very skeptical in its reception of assisted fertilization, and not until a few entrepreneurial researchers started their own private clinics, the public healthcare system followed suit to provide assisted fertilization therapy for all categories of patients. These close contacts and a moderate degree of controversy has served to produce a regulatory framework that serves its purpose very well in terms of balancing patient safety, alternative choices of clinics for the patient, and entrepreneurial possibilities for enterprising researchers and clinicians. Still, the issue of what has been called "medical tourism" and the possibilities for undergoing therapies abroad in countries being less regulated and closely monitored is a concern for practitioners and policy-makers equally; assisted fertilization is taking place in an open world and couples and single women being denied the therapy in one place are likely to seek help elsewhere. This mobility of patients easily leads to opportunistic behavior and as will be discussed in this chapter, there are concerns regarding, for example, multiple embryo transfer being done on regular basis in the United States and elsewhere. Assisted fertilization may have reached maturity but it is still riddled by debates regarding patient safety vis-à-vis economic interests.

Regulations and Control

Organizationally, the Swedish healthcare sector is separated into regional administrative units referred to as *landsting*. Each such healthcare region is an independent and politically determined unit, capable of enacting its individual healthcare policies. As a consequence, there are some, but commonly relatively small, differences between the healthcare regions. For instance, while one region may accept women up to the age of 38, another region may accept them up to the age of 39. Such decisions are based on medical expertise but are also shaped by demand and healthcare budgets and priorities. "There is a regulatory framework being politically determined and then the health care authority has a framework for the entire southern health care region. There are similar frameworks elsewhere. They are not exactly the same but they are very similar, very few deviances," a gynecologist in Clinic #1 remarked. The interviewees expressed their belief in the present regulatory system as working as intended, that is, to assure patient safety while allowing some private initiatives to increase the competition in the market. The head of Clinic #4 was pleased with the regulatory framework:

> *I believe the Swedish policy works well in this field and in comparison to other countries there has been a willingness to share the regulatory framework when it applies. We used to have shorter freezing times in Sweden, but that could be changed. It used to be prohibited to donate eggs in Sweden but also that has been changed … In comparison to the rest of the world, we have followed the development closely, and there has been this open attitude in Sweden, that is my belief. (Gynecologist and entrepreneur, Clinic #4)*

A gynecologist in Clinic #1 shared this affirmative view and contrasted the situation in Sweden and Northern Europe with India:

> *The systems work well in Sweden and in Northern Europe in general so there is not much space left for less serious companies. I visited India, and there you can observe worrying tendencies. You can get basically anything as long as you pay for it … Most unserious activities, I'd say, there are clinics doing all kinds of stuff that would be considered unethical in Sweden. (Gynecologist and head of clinic, Clinic #1)*

Parts of the Swedish policy were dependent on the European Tissue Directive, enacted in 2004 (see Directive 2004/23/EC of the European Parliament and of the Council), regulating all handling of human tissue in Europe. Also this directive was favorably received by the interviewees: "All donation of human tissue or treatment of human tissue outside of the body is strictly regulated which is very good," the gynecologist in Clinic #1 said.

Despite this wide acclaim of the Swedish and European regulation of assisted fertilization, there was a need for continually modifying and adjusting the regulatory framework to emerging social issues and concerns. For instance, if certain patient groups were denied assisted fertilization on the basis of medical conditions (e.g. handicapped women) there was always the risk that they would pay for the treatment abroad and then the Swedish healthcare system would still have the responsibility for the pregnant woman and her yet-to-be-born baby:

> *[Then] they go to Lithuania or Russia or someplace else to get the treatment. Is that better? In what way have we helped the patient by preventing her from getting it here? … if they go to Russia they get three or four embryos and then they return to give birth to triplets and all are born in week 24 and all of them die. How does that help the patient? When we are prohibiting them from coming here to get the help. We would have done it so much better. (Gynecologist, Clinic #5)*

This kind of "medical tourism" is becoming a growing concern calling for international monitoring bodies and regulatory frameworks (see, for example, Connell, 2006). Especially when it comes to sick or handicapped patients, physically unfit to endure a pregnancy or to become parents, the medical doctors making the assessment face a difficult situation inasmuch as the patient denied the treatment may pay for it abroad where physicians less concerned with patient safety and long-term individual and social costs may provide the therapy. One of the interviewees explained the difficulties the physician is facing in these assessments:

> In Sweden, it is the doctor deciding who is treated and how it should be organized … Some tricky decisions emerge at times like when a couple is denied the treatment. If there are medical conditions that can be invoked, it isn't that complicated and then your colleagues can assist you whether the patient has cancer or severe back injuries and should avoid getting pregnant, but when it comes to social issues such as drug addiction [it is more complicated] … A few times, it has been the case that patients that should not be treated have been accepted and that the newborn child has been taken care of even from the very birth. (Gynecologist, founder of Clinic #7)

One of the midwives in Clinic #1 accounted for these situations:

> It has happened that a multi-disabled woman comes here with her personal assistant to make an egg procurement to get pregnant. Her husband may work part-time and spend half the week taking care of her, but how is that supposed to work? I think they will love their child just as much as anyone else, but how is that coming out practically, I ask myself? (Midwife, department director, Clinic #1)

These apparently complicated cases apart, there were some minor concerns that needed to be handled in the everyday work. For instance, in the Swedish regulatory framework, the couples seeking assisted fertilization help, heterosexual as well as homosexual, need to be registered at the same address for at least one year, i.e. they should live together in a "family-like relationship." However, in the major cities where there is a endemic shortage of apartments and housing facilities, it may be that one of the two still owns an apartment that he or she sublets while remaining registered on the address. In the early stages of a relationship, there is always a risk of abandoning a first-hand contract for an apartment, especially in Stockholm, since it would take years to acquire a new apartment once the first one is lost. Such tricks of the trade, all-too-familiar for all younger people trying to navigate the Swedish housing market, makes the "proof of shared homestead" a bit complicated: policies do not reflect actual living conditions. "It could be the case that they have been living together for three years but that he is registered on another address he's subletting, an apartment he doesn't want to sell, for instance. So that is a crux, him being registered elsewhere but they have been living together for three years," a midwife and department director in Clinic #1 explained.

These minor issues were commonly resolved but there were more far-reaching concerns that called for more debates and decisions in both the authorities regulating and monitoring the healthcare sector and the Swedish parliament, the *Riksdag*. First, there was the issue whether single women should be eligible for the therapy. According to Swedish laws, here being concerned with the child being born, there should be two parents. For a long period of time, only heterosexual couples qualified for the therapy but gay and lesbian activist groups staunchly lobbied for a change in policy, and in 2006, lesbian couples became eligible for assisted fertilization therapy. For the critics of the present policy, the norm of having one nuclear family—or the modified version of it, with two women as the caretakers—is an antiquated moralist belief that needs to be overcome. The psychologist interviewed in Clinic #8 addressed her concerns, pointing at couples with previous children being disqualified for the therapy:

> I do not approve of some of these [regulations], like the rule that you cannot be eligible if you have children on your own. That does not feel like 2011; what if you have children from previous relationships? … It is only the nuclear family that matters, and that is not very modern, I'd say. (Psychologist, counselor, Clinic #8)

Another inconsistency in the policy was that terminally ill patients, for example, could be eligible for the therapy while single women were not because "they were single parents":

> There is some part of the legal documents, perhaps pertaining to [egg] donations, that they have applied to the case of assisted fertilization more broadly, prescribing that you "need to have two parents until becoming an adult," or something similar. But how does that work when it comes to treatment of couples where the male is suffering from some form of cancer? In such cases, we freeze the sperm, for instance. When applying this rule, there are few chances of helping any of these couples [where the father may decease]. So why do we freeze the sperm in these cases? (Psychologist, counselor, Clinic #8)

Today, Sweden has among the highest rate of single-person households in the world. As a consequence of the feminist movement and women entering work life, more women than ever are capable of supporting both themselves and their children economically, and in this situation the demand for sharing the parenting responsibilities with a man or another woman is unnecessary. In addition, women tend to become parents at a later age, especially women with academic education, and since both men and women tend to find their partners later in life as they spend more time educating themselves and making a career, assisted fertilization for single women may help further advance the liberation of women from traditional values and morals.

According to representatives of the monitoring bodies and policy-making communities, the decision to deny single women the right to assisted fertilization therapies is not as much a matter of conservative moralist beliefs as it is a concern for the child. In the event of fatal accidents, terminal illness, or similar events, there is no other parent to care for the child. Regardless of the credibility of such arguments and the statistical evidence of such deaths at a relatively young age, the policy decision is indicative of the concern for the unborn child; becoming a parent is by no means a human right but the child being born has all the rights of any other citizen. In situations where such rights may be complicated to fulfill, the urge to become a parent is sidelined. Regardless of policy discussions and decisions being made, some of the interviewees expressed their personal belief in this matter:

> I think it should be allowed [for single women to get assisted fertilization treatment] because there are so many single mothers so it does not make a difference if I decide I want a child regardless of me living single or together with a man. But I wish the donor to be known. When the child has grown up, it needs to have the chance of knowing. (Biomedical scientist, Clinic #6)

A gynecologist, the founder of Clinic #7, argued that the exclusion of single women from the therapy is "an anomaly," that is out of joint with the times. As a consequence of this policy, Denmark, having a less strict policy that makes single women eligible for assisted fertilization, has been the place where single women may be inseminated. Since Sweden and Denmark in many ways have similar economic, social and cultural conditions, it is somewhat embarrassing for Swedish healthcare politicians that Sweden is forcing single women to leave the country to get the therapy they want. Potentially, a new healthcare policy may eventually change this situation. For the time being, in 2013, this is an issue acquiring little media attention but as the possibilities for adoption from, for example, China and Vietnam have been reduced significantly on the basis of national policies, it may be that there is a willingness to negotiate the present regulatory framework.

Issues of Controversy: Social Freezing, the Uses of Embryos and Gestational Surrogacy

One possibility for enhancing fertility in an age of postponed parenthood is the practice of what has been called *social freezing*, that is, when a younger woman, say 20–25 years old, retrieves eggs from her ovaries to store them in a freezer for later use. As the eggs mature with age, the fertility drop after the age of 35 could be overcome as eggs are fertilized 10 to 15 years after they have been retrieved. For some of the interviewees, social freezing had great potential but called for a new attitude among especially younger women. For others social freezing was not a very appealing scenario for handling declining fertility as it puts further pressure on younger women to plan their lives years and even decades in advance. One gynecologist saw social freezing as an inevitable tendency in the contemporary period, only being in its early stages as a legitimate and widespread social practice:

> Undoubtedly social freezing will increase. That is one thing I have considered myself. And my conclusion is that why not? Studies show that it is socioeconomically beneficial if a twenty-five year old freezes her eggs and saves them. If she returns when she's thirty-eight, then the eggs are still young. (Gynecologist, Clinic #5)

Such a pragmatic view of social freezing was not shared by all interviewees. One of the professors in reproductive medicine, having daughters of her own, did not approve of a widespread use of social freezing because she thought it would put even more pressure on younger women. Instead, she welcomed a new attitude toward having children at a younger age and named social policies including, for example, higher economic compensation for students becoming parents as ways to resist the postponement of parenting. Another interviewee argued against social freezing as a form of medicalization, but argued that under certain conditions, such as in the case of cancer, it could be justified:

> Social freezing gives me the creeps … Should we really medicalize life to that extent? … But there are cases I can accept but those are less "social" than

"medical" [freezing] as in the case of people getting cancer. (Gynecologist, founder of Clinic #7)

Another issue that was discussed among the interviewees was how to handle the embryos being put in the freezers in assisted fertilization clinics. The ability to freeze both oocytes, sperm and embryos have in many ways revolutionized reproductive medicine; women suffering from cancer, for example, and entering a chemotherapy program may save some of their eggs that would otherwise be ruined by the therapy. However, as possibilities emerge, so too do controversies. For instance, if five eggs are retrieved from a woman and fertilized, one embryo is transferred to the womb while four are stored in a freezer. If she manages to get pregnant in the first treatment cycle, there are still four embryos in the freezer. Eventually, she may choose to use them to get a second child in a private clinic but in many cases the embryos are never used.

The Swedish policy changed quite recently and today clinics may store the embryos for five years. After five years the embryos are destroyed. For the representatives of the assisted fertilization clinics, this is a conspicuous waste of biological specimens. They advocated two alternative scenarios: either the embryos are "donated" to other couples suffering from poor fertility or they are used in scientific work (e.g. stem cell research). Today, the first alternative is illegal and the second requires the patient's consent. The interviewees also called for longer storing periods, pointing at the need for harmonizing with the rest of the Nordic countries: "This regulatory framework [regarding freezing] is very delimiting ... Why on earth is this done now when the countries around us have increased to ten years? In Finland it's ten years; in the UK, ten years," a gynecologist in Clinic #5 said. A gynecologist in Clinic #6 advocated what he referred to as the "adoption" of embryos:

Q: This issue with donating embryos?

A: Well, we want that to be legalized. Right now, we keep all these frozen embryos that we will throw away after five years ... What you may call an adoption, adopting embryos, is much better than adopting small children that are already born. (Gynecologist, founder of Clinic #7)

Also the head of Clinic #4 said that he believed that it was a common belief in the field that embryos should be possible to donate. One of the professors and entrepreneurs in reproductive medicine pointed at an alternative use, as biological specimens that could be used in stem cell research, of course after informed consent of the patients:

> *We have tens of thousands of embryos in freezers here in Sweden but we mustn't keep them longer than five years. What can we do with them after that? Is it better to throw them away than to use them in embryonal stem cell research? We believe it is better to use them. And we do have legislation permitting that with the consent of the patient. (Professor and entrepreneur, Clinic #4)*

The interviewees were fully aware of the difficulties facing common-sense thinking when apprehending alternative uses of embryos and they were commonly repeating that the embryos would "end up in the waste-bin" unless they could be used more productively elsewhere. The use of embryos in research work is perhaps one of the most emotionally sensitive areas in reproductive medicine as it is associated with practices potentially in conflict with the dignity of human life.

In addition to the single women and the alternative uses of embryos, the issue of gestational surrogacy was addressed by the interviewees as disputed. In Sweden, unlike many other countries including the United States and Israel, gestational surrogacy is banned in any form. Although the interviewees saw many of the arguments supporting this policy as being legitimate and sound—the scenarios of Indian "surrogacy mother camps" was a disturbing image of the trade that needed to be avoided at all costs—they thought that the policy was too strict. The interviewees argued there were a few cases where surrogacy could be permitted, for instance if a woman would agree to carry her sister's fetus in a situation of illness or other physical limitations. "Surrogacy is prohibited but they are investigating it right now and I believe and hope it will be permitted under certain and quite stern conditions," a gynecologist and the founder of Clinic #7 argued. He continued, pointing at how surrogacy is portrayed in relatively unfavorable terms in the media: "Surrogacy has gotten some attention in e.g., TV and it looks quite discomforting, at least from the outside where they almost keep these young women in some kind of kindergarten but with women with the babies in their bellies" (gynecologist, founder of Clinic #7). Again, the recurrent theme of treating assisted fertilization in its many forms as artifice and a violation of the "natural order" is resurfacing as soon as gestational surrogacy is discussed:

> *There are also prejudice and folk beliefs that matter; for instance, regarding surrogacy. That isn't allowed in Sweden and the main argument as far as I have*

understood is that you shouldn't be able to rent a womb ... there are actually
a number, not too many but a few, that for some reason lack a functioning
womb. They could have suffered from some disease or been in a car accident or
whatever, leading to the situation where they cannot have a child. If they have
functioning ovaries this women may have a sister that could consider carrying
the child. And if they really want to do all this, why can we not handle this kind
of treatment here in Sweden? (Gynecologist, Clinic #5)

The interviewed psychologist argued that surrogacy may be increasingly debated in the near future as gay couples were advancing the question of the right to parenting: "Right now there are discussions regarding homosexual men's possibilities for becoming parents that will shed more light on surrogacy" (psychologist, counselor, Clinic #8). Lesbian couples are today eligible for assisted fertilization therapies and in some quarters of the gay community there is an interest in liberalizing the Swedish legislation. Historically, shifts in policy have occurred after periods of controversies and it may be that surrogacy will also be permitted under certain conditions and the strict control of authorities.

Surrogacy is an eminent example of what Zelizer (2005) speaks of as the "purchase of intimacy." In the case of adoption, it is a child being cared for by the state that is being adopted by the parent(s) and, in the case of assisted fertilization, it is either individual gametes or donated gametes that are being manipulated and brought back to the womb, but it is the female patient's own body where the embryo is transferred. In gestational surrogacy, the embryo is instead transferred to a third party, the woman serving as the carrier of the fetus, and consequently there is yet another acting and thinking subject involved.

Emotionally, donated gametes such as egg and sperm may be more easily conceived of as passive inert matter even if the egg and the sperm accommodates the vitalist components producing human life, but the woman carrying the embryo and fetus in a more direct and conspicuous way intervenes in the socially and culturally sanctioned triad of mother–father–embryo/fetus/child. In addition to this violation of the "intimacies" of human reproduction as a family matter, it is an intervention colored by racial, socioeconomic and gendered differences. In the reporting of surrogacy, the women providing surrogacy are either working-class women (Goslinga-Roy, 2000: 133), women of color (Pande, 2009), or, most likely, both. Surrogacy is thus a close to perfect image of how the economically endowed classes are capable of exploiting Third-World women to do the work that career women are unable or even potentially unwilling to do. For Thomas Frank, the emerging market for surrogacy, most noteworthy in India where women may make as much money as 10 years' income for a family by serving as a surrogate mother (Pande, 2009), is the ultimate triumph of neoliberalism and its emphasis on economizing virtually any natural or social resource. Pande (2010: 970) consequently speaks of surrogate mothers as a new form of "clinical work," "the mother-worker," that similar to all other forms of organized work is the outcome of socioeconomic and managerial procedures: "[T]he perfect commercial surrogate, like the perfect laborer of global production, is not found ready-made in India. The perfect surrogate—cheap, docile, selfless, and nurturing—is produced in the fertility clinics and surrogacy hostels." Pande also emphasizes the enormous differences in access to resources between the two parties involved, i.e. the clients and the clinical laborer:

> *At each stage of the disciplinary process, the mother-worker duality is manipulated in ways that most benefit the mode of production, from the recruitment of guilt-ridden mothers to the disciplining of poor, rural, uneducated Indian women into the perfect mother-workers for national and international clients. (Pande, 2010: 970)*

At the same time as this new form of clinical labor needs to be scrutinized (see, for example, Vora, 2009; Smerdon, 2008), Bailey (2011: 726) emphasizes that the redefining of surrogacy work into what she calls "sexualized care labor" is a sensible but important step toward "reducing the stigmatized harms associated with surrogacy work."

While critiques against the commodification of sexualized care labor are valid and pointing at a disturbing tendency in the international markets for assisted fertilization that needs to be handled, there are other stories being told of how couples are making use of surrogacy as a last resort to fulfill their dreams of becoming parents (Cohen and Athavaley, 2009). In addition, studies of surrogate mothers such as Elly Teman's (2010) ethnography of Israeli surrogate mothers—Israel having among the most liberal policies in the world regarding surrogacy for various complex political reasons—points at some of the emotional labor involved in the work. There is a need for keeping a distance between the couple and the surrogate mother (see also Snowdon, 1994), but there is no evidence of conspicuous exploitation in the Israeli system. Still, at the end of the day, what the Swedish assisted fertilization clinics represent is neither a fully re-regulated market, nor an Israeli-style policy but merely a slight liberalization of the regulatory framework enabling surrogacy in very few occasions, e.g. in cases of former cancer patients losing their reproductive capacities or in cases where the woman is too weak to carry her baby.

This brings us to the question of how the field of practice and the political system are interrelated and communicating. When interviewing a member of the Swedish parliament, a physician working for many years to both promote and regulate assisted fertilization, she agreed that even though there were general concerns regarding assisted fertilization and similar technoscientific advancement both among the members of the parliament and the population at large, the sheer weight of the technoscientific research community and what they are capable of producing makes it complicated to resist its demand for changes in policy:

> *There are many things that we [politicians and legislators] have refused to pass because our gut-feelings told us so and then 30, 40 years later they are in place. It is a matter of social groups articulating the issue, turning it into a debate, and then there is a traditional investigation and the discussions in the political quarters start and all of a sudden the gut-feeling says something different. (Physician, Member of Parliament of Sweden)*

Small and incremental step-by-step changes in policy gradually normalize for instance clinical work in the field of reproductive medicine and, today, it would be fair to say that assisted fertilization is a widely recognized and legitimate clinical practice. Only a few peripheral religious factions playing a marginal political role in Swedish politics and in public debates, opposed to liberal abortion policies, have at times expressed their concern regarding a too liberal legislation. For instance, when lesbian couples were made eligible for assisted fertilization therapy, these right-wing groups were opposed to the decision, regarding it a violation of the institution of the family sanctioned by God. Some of the interviewees, the leading figures in the field and the entrepreneurs starting many of the clinics, agreed that they were actively influencing the political system to accomplish their objectives:

> *We told them [politicians] just enough so they could enact the regulations ... They couldn't enact regulations regarding issues they did not know were biologically possible ... So all this with egg donations, embryo donations, and preimplant genetic diagnostics, none of this could be predicted and anticipated ... In the same manner, they were not able to foresee the freezing of embryos ... We had this conflict with the authorities when we told them we stored embryos from patients with tumors being under chemotherapy and radiation therapy*

and at risk of losing their fertility, telling them that we won't destroy their embryos because when the patients heal they may want to get pregnant. So we were on the verge of losing our accreditation but then they changed the law to a five year period of freezing. (Professor in reproductive medicine, entrepreneur, Clinic #4)

Being skilled institutional entrepreneurs, the leading proponents of assisted fertilization understand that the political system can only digest and process relatively limited and confined issues one at a time, and therefore they seek to advance the policy work step-by-step. Even though the quote above may give an impression that shrewd scientists are manipulating gullible politicians, that is not the case as there is an ongoing and open communication regarding the medical and biological possibilities enabled by reproductive medicine between politicians and researchers. Above all, there are strong professional beliefs and norms that ultimately regulate what activities are conducted: "I usually say that there are things you can do, things you want to do, and things you are allowed to do in a country," the professor in reproductive medicine and entrepreneur claimed. That is, not all technoscientific and medical possibilities are exploited while some of them might be if they are supported by the national policies.

In summary, even though assisted fertilization has been institutionalized and is today a widely recognized clinical practice, demonstrating many benefits, there are still certain issues and concerns that need to be addressed in the policy work. Assisted fertilization may approach a mature state after more than 30 years of clinical practice but it is still a moving target as both new social demands are articulated and the technoscientific and medical possibilities are extended. The debates regarding the possibilities of assisted fertilization are therefore most likely to continue.

Private and Public Clinics in Sweden

By and large, the differences in practice and policy seem to be social and culturally determined rather than differing between public and private clinics. One of the most counter-intuitive findings in the study was the relatively small differences between the private and the public clinics in Sweden. Politically, the public healthcare clinics and the private clinics were supposed to complement one another as the public clinics handled couples with no previous children and patients up to a certain age, while the private clinics served older couples and couples with one child or more as well as those who wanted and could afford additional treatment cycles after unsuccessful treatment in the public system. The interviewees in both private and public clinics did not see any conflicts between the two types of clinics. "The traditional procedure is that doctors enter the university clinic, get the training, do their research work, defend their dissertation, and start private clinics to make some money. That is how it works," a gynecologist in Clinic #5 argued, pointing at the tradition of the medical field where private clinics have been part of the professionalization of medicine. "In principle, any resident doctor in gynecology can start up a clinic if he or she only follows the regulations," the head of Clinic #1 said, indicating the relatively low entry barriers for physicians to run their own clinic. The private and the public clinics had a relatively peaceful co-existence, many of the interviewees suggested, and took pride in their ability to collaborate across organizational and institutional boundaries: "In Sweden, there is a total transparency, there are no closed doors between the private and the public clinics as in many other countries where they barely speak to one another," a gynecologist and founder of Clinic #7 said.

However, some of the interviewees argued that the reasons for private clinics to exist were to be sought in the political system's ambition to externalize the costs for assisted fertilization:

> The only reasons for the private clinics to exists is that they have better service, shorter waiting times, and can accept the patients that the strict Swedish legislation exclude from the public clinics … What I mean is that the reason for the strict legislation is to avoid having to pay for what the public wants, making half of the industry private. (Professor and entrepreneur, Clinic #4)

Another concern regarding the roles of the private and the public clinics was the importance of basic research conducted in the public clinics, serving to further advance know-how in the field. Said the head of Clinic #1: "Of course, there are private clinics demonstrating excellent performances … but I believe they have a hard time keeping themselves updated." A biomedical scientist in Clinic #6 emphasized that it was important that the "big university clinics" received research grants so they could continue their research: "The big university clinics … are leading the way. They test new things and then the private clinics follow suit when they can see that it is confirmed that there are good results produced and the method is safe, and so forth" (biomedical scientist, Clinic #6). In contrast, the biomedical scientists argued, "because there is almost no money" for research in the private clinics, an increased reliance on private clinics would potentially have long-term negative effects for reproductive medicine and assisted fertilization as basic research would be less prioritized.

The head of Clinic #4 addressed the same topic, being somewhat cynical about recent developments in the field and the increased emphasis on short-term profitability in his own clinic that he started: "I can only tell from my point of view how they manage it, and it is more and more becoming a profit-generating machine. There is no development in any way, any longer. They declare they are interested in research—and it may be that I am too critical—but I don't think they are" (gynecologist and entrepreneur, Clinic #4). He continued:

> Those managing these major private [clinics today], they do not have their roots in medicine in one way or another ... not in the same way that we once did when we started all this. It has changed and the business weighs more heavily ... It is the same tendency in most parts of the world. If you look at Australia, the large IVF clinics have become business consortia ... there are venture capital firms backing them ... the money is given more weight now than it used to. (Head of clinic, Clinic #4)

As a consequence of this loss of a scientific ethos in the clinics and the emergence of investor capitalism entrepreneurship in the field of assisted fertilization, the head of Clinic #4 did not anticipate a bright future for research in the private clinics: "I believe the private IVF activities will produce a lower share of the scientific development, that is my prediction. There will be much more emphasis on the universities in the future. I am fully convinced of that." For some interviewees, it was self-evident that the public clinics should take care of the research work because the university hospitals and medical schools were hosting all the leading researchers and had the responsibility to train and educate physicians. From this perspective the role of the private clinics was primarily to assist the research work as much as practically and economically possible:

> It is our responsibility to take care of research and development and be an active part in those fields. When it comes to the private clinics, some of them are quite ambitious in participating in research projects or at least participating in the development work. But that is the nature of the game; say, in cosmetic surgery, where would you guess the research work is conducted, in the university clinic or the private clinic? Of course, in the university clinic you have all the PhD

candidates and the professors, the connections to the research world. If there is
someone driving the field, it is them. (Gynecologist, Clinic #5)

Besides the issue of research work, the interviewees were asked if they saw
any risks in private consortia or investors trying to pursue a low-cost version
of assisted fertilization. A gynecologist in Clinic #1 did not perceive the private
clinics as any kind of threat to safe and effective assisted fertilization. When
asked if he could anticipate any entrepreneurial activities reshaping the field in
the near future, he responded that such issues had been surfacing every now
and then during his entire career in the field of assisted fertilization:

Q: So there are no risks that international companies come here and dump the
prices, like a low-cost competitor to put it a bit drastically?

A: That is an interesting question. I've heard that for twenty years, that "Now,
they're coming here, dumping the prices and offering low cost IVF," but I
haven't seen it. Not yet! (Gynecologist and head of clinic, Clinic #1)

Rather than "dumping the prices" or in any other way seeking to "cut corners"
to enhance profitability of the activities, the private clinics were praised by
some interviewees for demonstrating how effective the activities could be done
when a few key processes are targeted and carefully designed: "It is a good
thing that there are private alternatives, where they work very efficiently and
they use this 'conveyor belt principle' because then you can treat a great number
of patients in a short time at lower cost. There are benefits with that type of
clinics, but there need to be the research and education activities because some
of these patients are quite complicated" (lab researcher, Clinic #2). The shared
view is thus that the private and the public clinics complement one another
and that they are the outcome of various political decisions seeking to reconcile
various objectives. The public clinics make assisted fertilization available for
a broader group of patients and handle the education, training and research
in reproductive medicine, and the private clinics provide a complementary
and highly effective service for couples having one or more children and
for couples where the female client is older than prescribed by the regional
healthcare policies.

Differences in Policy Between Sweden and Abroad

One issue pertaining to the national policy was the differences in the clinical work and the divergent assessment of risks between Sweden and other countries, most noteworthy the United States that in many ways was portrayed as a market wherein patient safety was overruled by economic interests under the guise of "the freedom of choice" of the patient. The interviewees were pleased with the Swedish and European regulatory framework and praised much of the work conducted in Northern Europe. At the same time, there was a lingering concern that "less serious clinics" would put patient safety in peril by, for example, transferring more than one embryo to the uterus. "There are many clinics [abroad] performing very well, just as well as in Sweden. But there are less serious clinics ruled by the money. And then there is a higher risk that the patients will suffer," a biomedical scientist and head of Clinic #2 said. He continued: "I think it is related to how the country is governed … in Finland, is very ambitious." As opposed to the case of Finland, he was less positive toward the clinical practice in the United States: "We were quite shocked about what they were doing abroad [in the United States]. Some of them were still talking about and doing things we abandoned fifteen years ago. And they were like 'Look what we found here!'" (Biomedical scientist, head of Clinic #2).

This view was shared by several interviewees, all with experience from visiting clinics in the United States. A gynecologist in Clinic #1 pointed out that the transfer of numerous embryos was commonplace as the patients paid for getting pregnant:

> If you visit the US, you hear these horrors stories, how they return two, three, four, five [fertilized] eggs without hesitating. I believe that is deeply unethical. We know that twins are more complicated deliveries than single deliveries and when it comes to three [babies] things get very complicated. (Gynecologist and head of clinic, Clinic #1)

Another interviewee argued that the differences in healthcare policy lead to risks for the patients: "If you can only afford one treatment cycle in the US, then you can just as well transfer two or three embryos and their multiple birth frequency is something like 25 percent while we have around 5 percent today in Sweden" (professor in reproductive medicine, entrepreneur, Clinic #4). Also the gynecologist in Clinic #1 pointed at the commercial interest regulating the clinical work:

In the US, they have no publicly funded system for assisted fertilization. It is all private. "Hot cash" rules. That is, they have little interest in running large scale research studies and so forth, because cash is all that counts ... These large randomized studies that are really what matters when it comes to the validation of the research ... that is what we are doing here in Europe ... They have separated the research from the clinical work. (Gynecologist and head of clinic, Clinic #1)

Another interviewee, a gynecologist, shared this view of the American practices and notices that there was a substantial difference in professional standards and different views regarding the economization of healthcare work:

In the US it is quite different because there you pay quite a bit of money and there are young women living off egg donations. We think that is immoral. When I talk to colleagues in the US they tell me "What are you talking about, what is immoral about that?" They just don't understand and we disagree. (Gynecologist, founder of Clinic #7)

The violation of certain professional standards, resting on clinical evidence, was thus a major concern for the Swedish clinicians and researchers. There are solid and undisputed clinical evidence of multiple births being more risky for both the woman giving birth and for the babies. One of the gynecologists recalled the early days of clinical practice when twin births were around 40 percent in assisted fertilization:

I remember the first years I was working. Back then we had a twin-frequency of about 40 percent. 30 percent was quite common. But that leads to all kinds of complications. Now, we have a frequency that is lower than in the population. So we are quite careful about that. In more than 95 percent of our patients, only one embryo is transferred. (Gynecologist, Clinic #5)

Over the years, the multiple transfers have been abandoned as the risks were regarded as being too significant to ignore. Still, in the United States where the patients are asking for multiple embryos to be transferred and since they are, first, paying customers expecting to have their demands fulfilled and, second, the private clinics are promoting themselves on basis of their "success rate" and multiple transfers are regarded as increasing the chances of births, multiple embryo transfers are conducted on a regular basis regardless of the risks. Such conspicuous ignoring of clinical evidence is unsettling for the Swedish clinicians and researchers.

In this case, two different institutional logics predominating in healthcare management clash. On the one hand, the institutional logic of "patient-centered care" emphasizes the central position of the patient and his or her demands and expectations. This institutional logic is conceiving of the healthcare process not as a faceless bureaucracy or assembly-line activity wherein the patient is the input variable being processed in sequential, and department-based, work processes. In the patient-centered care logic, the patient is located at the center of operations and the patient's concerns and wishes should be recognized. In many ways, this institutional logic is a market-based model of healthcare. The other institutional logic is that of "evidence-based medicine" wherein only therapies supported by clinical statistics providing significant efficacy and safety evidence should be applied. Evidence-based medicine is thus a profession-centered institutional logic as only therapies supported by evidence defined on the basis of professional expertise are qualified therapies. For instance, alternative medicines unable to demonstrate adequate evidence of efficacy and safety are excluded.

In the case of multiple embryo transfer, the Swedish interviewees criticized their American colleagues for letting the patient decide how many embryos to transfer, indicating that the capacity to produce pregnancies is regarded to be more important than eventual complications during delivery. The delivery is in many cases taking place in other parts of the American healthcare system and consequently the decisions made in the assisted fertilization clinic are separated from the delivery of the babies. The evidence-based medicine logic prescribes that the professional physician should make informed decisions on the basis of available research results regardless of financial and economic implications. Apparently, the two national systems for organizing assisted fertilization operate along divergent paths. Said a biomedical scientist in Clinic #6:

> It is too much of a factory [in some clinics abroad]. It doesn't feel like that would work here in Sweden, I don't think so. After all, it is human material being used … When you work with humans, it is quite complicated to turn it into some kind of routine work … because there are unpredicted events happening all the time. That is also what makes this job exciting … one woman is not like the other … At the bottom line, it is a matter of how the individual and how she responds. (Biomedical scientist, Clinic #6)

In general, the interviewees pointed at the effects of the close monitoring of the activities and the various arrangements set up to safeguard a qualified therapy. In all of the healthcare regions, there were ethics committees set up to handle certain issues surfacing in the day-to-day work: "I believe that in Scandinavia there is quite satisfying handling of the ethical issues. In this region, we have this ethics group discussing specific cases that might be in the margin. This group is composed of different professions ... but of course we can never know if we are getting the correct answer," the head of Clinic #1 said. One such issue was for instance how to evaluate patients with different health conditions. "We wish to see more clear directives in that field," a gynecologist in Clinic #1 said.

In summary, there are differences, the interviewees argued, between the public healthcare policies and the market-based assisted fertilization work wherein the latter prioritize successful pregnancies over patient safety. These different policies to some extent separate the international professional field into two camps defending their own positions, which, potentially, weakens the professional status of reproductive medicine and its clinical branch, assisted fertilization.

Summary and Conclusion

Assisted fertilization is an excellent example of how technoscience and society are what Jasanoff (2005) calls *co-produced*, mutually constituted and entangled. The advancement of reproductive medicine and assisted fertilization as clinical practice have from the outset been regulated and monitored in detail, but at the same time the political and regulatory framework needs to continually respond to and accommodate recent shift in practice and new technoscientific possibilities produced in the research work. At the same time, social and cultural changes regarding, for example, the postponement of parenting in Western society impose new challenges for the life sciences.

While assisted fertilization in the early 1980s had to deal with patients being infertile or sub-fertile because of sexually transmitted diseases such as chlamydia, informational campaigns have reduced this category of patients in number but instead there is a growing group of obese female patients facing fertility problems. The research on obesity has revealed a number of accompanying health conditions including a number of metabolic diseases such as type 2 diabetes and cardiovascular diseases and an increased incidence for various forms of cancer, but also fertility appear to be affected by being overweight.

In addition to strictly medical conditions (e.g. increased rates of obese patients in the assisted fertilization clinics), economic and cultural changes such as the increased economic independence of women have led to new family structures—the presence of single-person households are among the highest in the world in Sweden—which renders traditional norms and attitudes if not obsolete at least not universally applicable or uncontested norms. Consequently, the increased demands from single women to take advantage of assisted fertilization treatments have been brought into the policy discussions. The exclusion of single women from therapies that couples are eligible for does not primarily rest on medical considerations but is strictly a social and cultural matter, arguably shaped by traditional norms and beliefs proposing the need for a nuclear family structure to support and raise a child. Technoscientific possibilities, scientific research, political regulation and social conditions are thus mutually interrelated, co-produced and folded into one another in the field of reproductive medicine and assisted fertilization. Controversies and debates are in many cases constituted as layers of considerations that need to be taken into account to formulate viable and socially legitimate policies. For instance, if embryos stored in the freezers are to be donated or "adopted" by other couples or brought into embryonal stem cell research activities rather than being destroyed after five years of storage, there are significant ethical, economic, social and cultural aspects that need to be addressed and publicly debated.

In the case of Sweden, there are relatively few controversies in the field of reproductive medicine and where regulatory control or consumer power do not play a role in regulating the practices, there appear to be strong professional norms that reproduce assisted fertilization as a safe and effective (given the difficulties and ambiguities facing the researchers and clinicians) therapy benefitting the largest possible number of clients in the population. After 35 years of operation—in 2012, the first baby born on the basis of assisted fertilization in Sweden, the fifth in the world, can celebrate her 30th birthday— assisted fertilization has reached maturity. Yet, there is much to be learned regarding human reproduction, not the least to learn to know why roughly half of the couples are leaving the clinics without being able to fulfill their dream of becoming parents. "[It is a] relatively new field. Thirty years [of practice] is nothing," the psychologist contended.

PART III
Analysis

7

The Management of Assisted Fertilization

Introduction

> *The Nobel Prize … that is like the best Nobel Prize ever. I was so happy about it. I know [Robert Edwards] has meant a lot for people … I haven't been the least interested in the Nobel Prize before … But here [points at her son] is one of his products!*
>
> *Female former assisted fertilization patient*

> *I think [Robert Edward's Nobel Prize in Medicine and Physiology] really makes a difference: It is a recognition of a field that I believe is interesting. For many reasons: all of the Western world needs children; the population is ageing and there are fewer and fewer children, and in the present life style women become older before they are trying to get a child … Even the sperm quality is deteriorating in the entire Western world for some reason … Therefore I believe it is a very important part of health care to be able to treat involuntary childlessness and the Nobel Prize was a recognition of the field we are working within.*
>
> *Gynecologist, head of department, Clinic #1*

There is an ongoing debate in organization theory and management studies quarters on the "relevance" of business school research (Kieser and Leiner, 2009; Palmer et al., 2009; Khurana, 2007; Gulati, 2007; Bennis and O'Toole, 2005; Pfeffer and Fong, 2002; Starkey and Madan, 2001; Pfeffer, 1993). Critics claim that business school research does little to inform practitioners and that it is marginal in social policy-making. In comparison to the field of economics, for example, expanding its domain of jurisdiction over the last decades (Fourcade, 2009), management studies appear poorly integrated and have few straightforward analytical models that can guide practice and policy-making.

Proponents of business school and management research, on the contrary, claim that it is precisely this capacity to capture and apprehend manifold organizational practices that justifies the study of management work. Unlike economics, based on quantitative methods and formalistic models, at times predicting economic occurrences but in most cases either influencing social action or explaining events *ex post*, management studies deals with contingent and contextualized social action, and such practices do not lend themselves to "social laws" in the same manner as aggregated social phenomena.

Regardless of the debates over the relevance of management studies, there is a need for more detailed studies of social practices rooted in the life sciences to understand how the organization of society is accomplished on the basis of the ability to combine technoscientific research, clinical practices, legal frameworks and regulatory control, and cultural resources. In this final chapter, some of the contributions from the study will be examined in detail, emphasizing the need for organization researchers to examine how the life sciences are transforming themselves into services and commodities in the contemporary era. As has been suggested in the second part of the book, materiality plays a key role in constituting not only the life sciences and the technosciences more broadly but also in constituting society as what it is in the late modern or hypermodern times. Life science and technoscience is not what is "outside of" or "additional to" the regular social order but instead society is assembled, as we learn from actor-network theorists such as Bruno Latour, on the basis of the capacity to constitute social systems "from the bottom up" rather than "top down." In our case, assisted fertilization clinics may appear as very specific domains of expertise where certain and highly specialized know-how are used to accomplish certain objectives, but in fact such clinics are part of the regular, run-of-the-mill society that we tend to by and large take for granted. The awareness that the field of reproductive medicine is potentially capable of handling infertility problems is part of the common-sense understanding of human reproduction and many patients, our interlocutors have argued, are genuinely surprised and even mildly shocked to learn that assisted fertilization clinics are not capable of accomplishing pregnancies in all cases.

The technosciences have undoubtedly helped mankind become the master of nature inasmuch as machines and technologies are helping human beings accomplish things inconceivable just a few generations ago. As the initial wonders at the technological marvels produced vanish, technologies gradually become infrastructural and taken for granted, being no longer sources of veneration and excitement but merely everyday resources. Similarly, in the life sciences, the capacity of curing illness is always experienced as a true wonder by the individual patient but for the majority of people such accomplishments are just assumed after a period of time. Learning that there are limitations also for the technosciences may at times become an event of disillusion as the sciences have been remarkably successful in promoting the idea of their triumph over nature. Given such ideological superstructure of the technosciences, the surprise shown by certain assisted fertilization patients when they learn that they cannot be helped because of their age may be less confusing: after all, they have learned both to rely on and trust the sciences as capable of dominating nature.

Organization theory and management studies here play a role in serving to disentangle and dismantle the various elements and components inherent to the technoscientific assemblages at work on everyday bases. For instance, reproductive medicine research and assisted fertilization work in the clinic is by no means simply a matter of controlling, examining and manipulating human reproductive materials but is equally a matter of organizing administrative routines, enacting legal and regulatory frameworks, negotiating schemes for economic and financial compensation between organizational units, hiring counseling competence to help the patients cope with their therapy, and so forth. That is, life sciences are not confined to the laboratory spaces but as soon as they are commercialized and brought into society they become organizational fields wherein a series of activities are developed in tandem with the medical expertise.

If there is a social value in business school research, it lies precisely in this capacity to analytically apprehend the system of resources and relations that are mobilized in sites such as assisted fertilization clinics. While the technosciences, the life sciences being no exception, may appear secluded and protected from the immediate public gaze, they are in fact, as the science and technology studies demonstrate, fundamentally open to social interests and concerns. Especially when being brought to the market or into the clinics, the life sciences need to be able to demonstrate an adequate degree of efficacy and safety to legitimate themselves. This combination of highly specialized, even esoteric expertise and know-how and the uses of relatively mundane artifacts such as chairs or dishes make healthcare clinics evocative places; it is as if the mundane artifacts per se are animated with some kind of vitalist force as they are associated with the advanced expertise. Naturally, such images of healthcare clinics as sites of magic are deceiving and incapable of the accomplishments of the life sciences, but an organization theory perspective may be in the position to explain how the esoteric and the mundane are capable of jointly constituting social practices that in themselves are capable of making remarkable accomplishments.

That is, an organization theory perspective on the work of assisted fertilization clinics, for example, is to some extent disenchanting the technosciences as everyday practices are examined in detail. The work of the life sciences is then no miracle work but highly disciplined and controlled work under determinate conditions. The technosciences owe much to innovative and creative individuals, capable of making scientific breakthroughs on the basis of hard work or serendipities, but the remainder of the success of the technosciences is to be explained by its capacity of being organized into functional units and fields, carefully corrected by new empirical evidence and overseen by regulatory bodies and determined by legal frameworks and policies.

This book has been written with the ambition to demonstrate for the reader how assisted fertilization work is precisely what is being developed in the intersection between technoscientific possibilities and know-how, social needs, and legal frameworks. While these three analytical categories are by no means once and for all separated but are rather mutually constitutive, assisted fertilization as clinical practice is developed on basis of the capacity of combining these resources in fruitful and productive ways. Again, with all respect for the accomplishment of the technosciences per se, what makes assisted fertilization a durable, legitimate social practice is its capacity to organize heterogeneous resources into specific arrangements and organizational fields. In this final chapter, we are pointing at some of the theoretical and practical implications from such a perspective.

Materialism and Organizing

In Chapter 2 of the book, some space was dedicated to the analysis of the concept of materiality in both the science and technology studies literature and in organization theory more specifically. In the field of feminist theory, the concept of "new materialism" has been proposed as an alternative to all theoretical framework derived from the so-called linguistic turn in philosophy and social theory over the period since the end of World War II. The new materialism is an analytical framework rooted in both pragmatism (e.g. the work of Karen Barad) and post-structuralist thinking (e.g. Elizabeth Grosz's writing on Darwinism and process philosophy) that seeks to overcome the ignorance of materiality in social studies and gender theory. The literature on science and technology studies has from the outset been preoccupied with understanding how both laboratory technologies, equipment and biological specimens such as model organisms and genetically modified animals are constituting what Rheinberger (1997) calls experimental systems. Such experimental systems are in turn regulated by both professional norms and beliefs and legal frameworks enacted by non-scientific juridical bodies. In this perspective, the technosciences and the life sciences more specifically are based on the use of heterogeneous technological and biological systems that to some extent always already include their own theoretical assumptions. Given the loss of verificationist epistemologies, the principal source of legitimacy for the sciences is their *performativity*—what they are capable of accomplishing. As a consequence, the question whether a theory is true or not is of less interest than what human beings are capable of accomplishing with a specific theory. The technosciences are thus legitimized on the basis of what they are capable of accomplishing rather than being "true" in some foundational sense of the term. *Verum ipsum factum*, "truth is what is done," Vico says (cited in Gramsci, 1971: 302–364).

In organization theory, the concept of materiality has been introduced as the study of uses of technologies (e.g. information and communication technologies), as the study of sociomaterial practices, or as imbrications between social and material resources. Recent studies published by Wanda Orlikowski (2007) and Lucy Suchman (2002), for example, propose that the organizing is a matter of effectively bundling material and social resources and that "practices"—a key term in sociology—are always *sociomaterial* practices, i.e. it is not analytically meaningful to separate "the material" from "the social" as they are always already implied in one another. In general, there is an increased interest for theories of materiality in organization studies and the literature include a wide variety of studies of how materiality plays a role in organizing and social practices. For instance, a growing literature on the uses of visual media suggests that the capacity of seeing as a professional, to execute professional vision, is a matter of using advanced computer-based media such as computer tomography technologies. In the contemporary period, vision is always already bound up with advanced technologies.

ASSISTED FERTILIZATION AS SOCIOMATERIAL PRACTICE

The present study contributes both to the science and technology studies literature addressing materiality and to the organization theory literature on sociomaterial practices and imbrications. The study demonstrates that assisted fertilization is outlined as a series of encounters and operations beginning with the examination of the patients' reproductive capacities and ending with a pregnancy reported to the clinic. Throughout the work process, various forms of material resources including advanced technologies such as freezers and microscopes but also mundane but specialized goods such as plastic containers and pipettes are used. Still, the assisted fertilization work is by no means reducible to the materiality put to use but throughout the process social interaction, communication, regulations, ethical guidelines and professional judgment inform, structure and shape the day-to-day work. Clinical assisted fertilization work is thus unfolding as the informed and qualified use of material resources under determinate conditions to accomplished specific goals and objectives, that is, to fertilize the human reproductive materials and to return the most qualified embryo to the patient's womb. Such findings are nothing new in the field of science and technology studies, a corpus of texts that reports a significant number of empirical studies of laboratory practices and technology development projects. Such studies reveal that even seemingly robust experimental systems or technological systems are in fact relatively fragile constructs, relying on the professional capacity to balance approximations and trade-offs to make the system functional.

No experimental systems or technological systems are devoid of ambiguities or breakdowns but what makes the systems work as well as they mostly do are the professional skills of the laboratory researchers, technicians and engineers making the informed decisions that help maintain the systems. For the outsider, a clinic or a laboratory may appear as a black box, a secluded and self-regulating sociotechnical system, but once entering such domains it becomes obvious that there are always discussions and debates regarding how to handle practical concerns. For instance, the embryo selection process, the final stage before the embryo is brought back to the womb, does not rely on the use of some strict technology-generated metrics, such as a method for measuring the "quality" of the embryo and giving the embryologists a "green light" to proceed. Instead, the selection of the embryo is based on individual and collective capacities for making visual inspections. In many cases, such selection procedures were uncomplicated and implied little discussion, but in the case of lower quality of the embryos the choice was more complicated and even in cases where so-called low-quality embryos were selected, they could still lead to pregnancies.

Reproductive medicine and assisted fertilization rest on solid and undisputed know-how but nevertheless the final selection of embryos is partially based on aesthetic judgment. This does not in any way disqualify such procedures but it arguably testifies to the fragile and unstable nature of all technoscientific systems. Even the most prestigious laboratories capable of producing the most praised theories and theorems suffer from breakdowns, malfunctioning equipment, deviant data points, enigmas, and so forth, that is, occurrences and events that testify to the fact that there are no self-perpetuating and self-enclosed experimental systems that operate outside of human oversight, control and management (Vaughan, 1999). When humans create nature in the laboratory setting, it is a form of artifice mimicking nature (Rheinberger, 1997; Fujimura, 1996; Lynch, 1995; Knorr Cetina, 1981) and consequently there are always certain conditions and factors that need to be eliminated to be able to conduct the experimental work. Similarly, in the engineering sciences, the mathematical calculations need to be translated into actual design choices and in the process to move from "paper to machinery" ambiguities and uncertainty are built into the system (Downer, 2011; Perrow, 1984).

Such ambiguities and uncertainties are not indicative of poorly functioning or unaccomplished practices but are rather testifying to the actual accomplishments made by the professional category of engineers over the last century. Despite having no comprehensive understanding of certain technological systems, they have been able to construct and put to use a long series of technologies that have changed human lives. Similarly, in the field of assisted fertilization, the actors tend to deplore the difficulties involved in reaching a performance ratio beyond the 60 percent success rate. For the ambitious clinician and researcher, failing four out of 10 times is an unsatisfying performance. But such self-criticism tends to obscure the fact that six out of 10 couples and women undergoing the therapy actually become parents. For many, not the least the parents themselves, this is a remarkable accomplishment. In the history of human reproduction, there have been only quite vague ideas about how conception and fertilization occurs, and in many cases common-sense thinking and sexist beliefs (e.g. the Aristotelian view of women as passive incubators for the active male sperm, already containing all the qualities of the future baby) have informed not only the obstetrics teaching but also its clinical practices. Today, reproductive medicine has managed to map human reproduction and is in the position to intervene safely into the process. Still, much remains to be known but in the meantime there are new hopes for sub-fertile and infertile couples and single women.

SOCIOMATERIAL PRACTICES IN THE LIFE SCIENCES

Speaking from an organization theory perspective, the study brings another case study of sociomaterial practices and procedures of imbrications to the table. Many studies of sociomaterial practices take place in the study of information and communication technologies, that is, computer-based new media that in various ways assist and complement human beings in their day-to-day work, helping them retrieve, compile, compute and circulate data and information. Such activities are in many ways complementing and extending the capacity for human cognition and information and communication technologies are certainly playing a key role in the contemporary era to serve as *aide-memoires*. At the same time, such technologies and devices are always external to the human body, accessed through human–computer interfaces (see, for example, Dourish, 2004). In contrast, the sociomaterial practices in the healthcare field directly intervene into material substratum of the human body. Endocrinology (i.e. hormone therapy) and surgery procedures (during the egg retrieval) are for instance two domains of expertise being mobilized in the assisted fertilization work.

There is arguably a difference between sociomaterial practices in the form of how to sort out and make use of incoming emails (Barley et al., 2011; Wajcman and Rose, 2011; Edenius and Styhre, 2006) as a knowledge management procedure, and sociomaterial practices in the form of actively manipulating a female patient's ovulation process. The theoretical models and concepts are the same but the degree of *intensity* differs between the cases; being overburdened by incoming email can be a stressful experience but it is an experience of a different kind than having the endocrinology system manipulated. Regardless of these differences, the analytical framework examined in Chapter 1 is still useful in organization studies in both cases. One of the principal differences between computer-based sociomaterial practices and medical sociomaterial practices is that regulatory frameworks and ethical considerations play a more prominent role in the latter case. Computers are technological artifacts that demand little regulation (even though their uses may demand policies and guidelines) while human bodies are sacred objects that must not become experimental grounds unless being closely monitored and regulated (as in the case of full-scale pharmaceutical studies). As a consequence, we may propose a weak or secondary and a strong or primary case of sociomaterial practices wherein the former deals with artifacts and technological systems that operate outside of the human body and the latter include various forms of interventions and manipulations of the human body.

Needless to say, the line of demarcation between the one and the other is a permeable and fluid one; much medical technological instruments used in healthcare work are operating external to the body but the information they provide—the inscriptions of corporeal qualities and conditions into medical metrics and ratios—inform the decisions made by the physicians. Regardless of such analytical difficulties, ultimately embedded in the ontological and epistemological difficulties involved when constructing binary distinctions ("either/or"), much of the literature on sociomaterial practices belong to the category of secondary sociomaterial practices. One of the reasons for this emphasis on the study of computer-based media is perhaps the difficulties involved in getting access to healthcare organizations that need to take into account the patients' interests and needs. However, in the future we hope to see more cases of primary sociomaterial practices reported in the field of organization studies.

Implications for Practice

It is hard to draw any specific conclusions regarding the day-to-day management of assisted fertilization clinics on the basis of the study reported in this volume. Instructing the professional groups accomplishing the work in the clinics is undoubtedly beyond our competence. At the same time, there are a few more general lessons to be learned from the case of the development of assisted fertilization as a clinical branch of reproductive medicine.

First, when speaking in entrepreneurial terms, it takes much effort, energy and determination to develop a new institutional field and it is therefore complicated to predict and anticipate the effects of the life sciences developed today and how they will transform into new clinical practices and commercial therapies in the future. As has been pointed out in a number of cases, reproductive medicine was initially very much oriented toward controlling and limiting human reproduction to resist the population explosion discussed in the 1950s and 1960s. Only a highly innovative and entrepreneurial spirit is capable of turning such widely endorsed and praised scientific programs upside down when proposing that the same know-how that gave us pharmaceutical contraception may in fact be used to enhance human fertility. One can only imagine the skepticism or potentially even hostility facing the pioneers of assisted fertilization medicine such as Robert Edwards when he and his colleagues developed and promoted their research programs in the late 1960s and 1970s. As for instance Max Weber has repeated time and again, capitalism is propelled by the irrationality and charisma of entrepreneurs unable to comply with "common knowledge" and "sound and robust evidence" but who seek their own ways to accomplish the objectives they have set for themselves. *Ex ante*, such entrepreneurial figures may appear as crackpots and oddballs having the wrong ideas about things; *ex post*, they may be heroic figures being able to see what no one else saw at that point in time.

While renowned entrepreneurs like Richard Branson and Steve Jobs are commonly praised as innovative thinkers and businessmen, they had the advantage of working in nascent fields, the record industry and the emerging computer industry, relatively unregulated territories at the time. In comparison, Robert Edwards worked in medicine, perhaps the most prestigious scientific domain in the modern period, also being preoccupied with clinical evidence and safety concerns. Starting entrepreneurial activities in such domains, in many cases downright critical of any attempt to develop new procedures and experimental practices unless accompanied by solid evidence regarding efficacy and safety, is arguably a much bigger challenge.

A common narrative in the pharmaceutical industry, for example, is that today's regulations are so much more detailed and lack the capacity to apprehend ambiguities that they used to have, and consequently many drugs that are today staple therapies would not have qualified for registration in the new strict regulatory regime (Styhre and Sundgren, 2011). Similarly, to develop assisted fertilization as a clinical practice, at some point in time there is a need for actually conceiving a baby and giving birth to it. Such events can never be anticipated or accompanied by solid evidence as they mark the starting point for a new domain of clinical expertise. As suggested in Chapter 3, the development of assisted fertilization as a clinical practice and therapy was, in the case of Sweden and most likely elsewhere too, accompanied by skepticism or even hostility.

The pioneers of assisted fertilization therapies were thus facing both the skepticism of the professional community of physicians arguing that either the resources plowed into this new domain would be used more productively elsewhere, or that the lack of clinical evidence was a major obstacle for the project, but also something worse, namely common-sense thinking. Such thinking proposed that what the world needs is not *more* but *less* babies, a conclusion inferred on the basis of aggregated statistics taking little notice of variations across populations and social strata, but also imposed a general prohibition against "playing God," i.e. to actively examine and intervene into human reproduction. The common-sense view of assisted fertilization research thus both disqualified its objectives and undermined its moral and ethical legitimacy. One of the consequences was the use of derogatory terms such as "test-tube babies" in media and public discussion.

However, like all genuine entrepreneurs the pioneers of assisted fertilization therapies were motivated by what they thought was a good idea and paid little attention to public opinion. At the same time, the views of the proverbial "man on the street" matter as public opinion may be reflected in policies and regulatory frameworks being enacted by political bodies. For instance, in the case of Sweden, the ideology of the heterosexual nuclear family structure as the principal family organization form has strongly informed and shaped the policies. In Sweden, the Christian right is a relatively small community, accounting for only 3–4 percent of the voters, and yet, for example, lesbian couples were only eligible for the therapy in 2006, 24 years after the birth of the first baby born on the basis of assisted fertilization therapy. Still today, single women are denied the therapy. In public debates, it has not been claimed that lesbian women would be less qualified parents but the focus has been throughout on the unborn baby's rights. Since homosexuality is still to some extent a controversial topic even in seemingly liberal countries such as Sweden, it took 24 years to enact new policy regarding lesbian couples. This indicated that also medicine needs to be aligned with public opinion and especially the professional beliefs represented in policy-making bodies.

Speaking of assisted fertilization in entrepreneurial terms is thus a very rich and informative case of how entrepreneurship is of necessity developed in the face of uncertainty and the justified true beliefs of incumbent authorities. While entrepreneurship is in many cases advanced by its proponents (e.g. politicians, interest organizations, entrepreneurship researchers) as what is always of necessity a heroic act of putting the social world as taken for granted into question, there are many cases of failed or misconceived entrepreneurial activities but as the history is written by the winners, such follies are forgotten or buried under the accomplishments of the successful entrepreneurs.

In the case of assisted fertilization, many factors contributed to the advancement of the therapy: a shift in understanding of the "overpopulation problem," the development of hormone therapies, the development of new technologies (e.g. the vaginal ultrasound technology), a shifting family structure wherein especially women tended to become parents at a later age, and the relatively high degree of genital diseases (e.g. chlamydia) leading to infertility among women, etc. Still, the Swedish entrepreneurs in reproductive medicine had to struggle to open the first clinics as politicians claimed assisted fertilization was still some kind of "luxury medicine." It is somewhat ironic that the Social Democrat politicians accepted public clinics only *after* the opening of private clinics in Stockholm and Gothenburg in the mid-1980s in an attempt to provide assisted fertilization therapies not only for the economically endowed classes but for all citizens. As suggested by one of interviewees (cited in Chapter 3), the fact that the Social Democratic Party political program would never tolerate only private clinics was actively manipulated to break the stalemate.

Expressed from the perspective of socialized medicine, even during market liberalization and when opening up for private initiatives, there is a mutual role to be played by the state and the public sector. The case of assisted fertilization in Sweden shows that such enterprising and entrepreneurial actors are not undermining the role of public healthcare, and vice versa. If there is still something like a "third way" in politics and for the bioeconomy, it is in this capacity to balance the public healthcare and private alternatives.

In summary, then, the case of the development of assisted fertilization therapies and clinics is in many ways exemplary of successful individual and collective entrepreneurship; it contains obstacles to be passed, great possibilities, and a social need to be fulfilled. At the same time, one must avoid panegyric praises of the pioneers of assisted fertilization therapies and not write hagiographic accounts of individual contributions but there is little doubt that many people—one child in every school class and his or her parents on average—owe much to these researchers and entrepreneurs. In addition, students of entrepreneurial activities may study the case of assisted fertilization if they want to learn how entrepreneurship is conducted in the face of both uncertainty and hostility.

Second, the case of assisted fertilization contributes to managerial practice in terms of emphasizing how advanced organizational activities are composed as the combination of material resources, professional expertise and know-how, institutionalized procedures and rules, and an ongoing conversation with an external society regarding the usefulness of the activities orchestrated by the organization (e.g. the clinics). Institutional theory conceptualizes organizations as open systems with permeable and fluid boundaries vis-à-vis the environment (see, for example, the seminal paper of Meyer and Rowan, 1977).

Developing and managing assisted fertilization clinics, the case suggests, means that there is a disjunction between what one is capable of accomplishing on the basis of medical expertise, what one is allowed to accomplish, and what one might want to accomplish. The development of reproductive medicine and assisted fertilization therapies has occured in a dynamic relationship to the policies and regulation enacted and put to use. Policy-makers consult experts in reproductive medicine and assisted fertilization but also need to take into account other, non-scientific issues and concerns. The outcome is a national and international regulatory framework that is relatively well functioning according to the representatives of reproductive medicine. At the same time, there is much frustration over the inability to fully exploit the medical opportunities as for instance embryos cannot be donated, single women are not eligible for the therapy, and embryos stored in freezers need to be destroyed after five years of storage.

The case thus suggests that the concept of management cannot only be reserved for the day-to-day work in the clinics but also involves various forms of communication work and politics aimed at influencing both public opinion and policies. The assisted fertilization therapies were not developed in isolation from wider social and economic interests but were embedded in such social concerns. The technosciences and the life sciences more specifically are not developed in subterranean territories but are rather constantly related to and gaining their impetus from social needs and demands. As suggested in Chapter 3, assisted fertilization therapies were successfully developed as they enabled certain solutions to a perceived social problem, that of infertility. On the aggregated level, such infertility may appear as a minor concern, but for the couple struggling to become parents that is not the case—for them, this is a major existential predicament.

Successful managerial work in fields such as assisted fertilization clinics is thus a matter of being able to shift focus from the outside to the inside and orchestrate and support decision-making that safeguard the legitimacy and consequently the longevity of the organization. In such a view, managerial work always contains a certain element of politics as the institutional setting strongly influences the internal operations of the organization. To make a theoretical statement, the study supports the institutional theory view (and more specifically, the institutional theory literature recognizing agency in organizations, for example, the literature on institutional work or institutional entrepreneurship), as it emphasizes the organization's environment as an important managerial factor to consider.

Biopolitics, the Bioeconomy, and the Management of Life

The study also contributes to an ongoing debate on what Michel Foucault in the 1970s started to speak of as *biopolitics*, the political project to not only govern populations through social politics and various forms of civil engineering programs such as housing and infrastructure investment, but to actively govern the population from the middle of the nineteenth century on basis of the emerging sciences of demographics, criminology and medicine (Foucault, 2008). Foucault (1997: 73) defines biopolitics as "[t]he endeavor ... to rationalize the problems presented to governmental practices by the phenomena characteristic of a group of living human beings constituted as a population: health sanitation, birthrate, longevity, race." Foucault's concept of biopolitics is relatively wide and imprecise but it has generated a significant body of literature (Lemke, 2011; Prasad, 2009; Esposito, 2008; Waldby and Cooper, 2007; Marks, 2006). Esposito (2008: 16) suggests that the Swede Rudoph Kjellén was the first to use the term "biopolitics" as an extension of "geopolitics" in 1905, and today, after more than 100 years of advancement of the life sciences, the term biopolitics is no longer a marginal term in the social science vocabulary but is rather central to social organization, leading to all kinds of regulatory and self-monitoring activities including paying attention to, for example, "neurological fitness" (Schüll and Zaloom, 2011; Pitts-Taylor, 2010), sexual performance (Åsberg and Johnson, 2009; Fishman, 2004; Mamo and Fishman, 2001), and weight control and regulation (Dickson, 2011; Monaghan et al., 2010; Throsby, 2009). In this new biopolitical regime, the subject's body is constantly attended to, problematized, and inscribed with certain qualities and norms. In addition, deviations from prescribed bodily standards are handled by what Clarke et al. (2003) speak of as *biomedicalization*, that is, what may originally have been regarded as social concerns become individual disorders that demand medicalization—pharmaceutical therapies.

The term biopolitics is in this view bound up with the term *biopower* (Foucault, 2007), the employment of specific knowledge and expertise to handle and control populations. However, in both Foucault's texts and in continental philosophy and social theory more broadly, the concept of power is a term accommodating various meanings. In French, German and Latin, there is a distinction between what may be best described as "repressive power" and "enabling power," power that excludes and delimits and power that is productive and creative. Foucault uses the terms *puissance* to denote the former and *pouvoir* to denote the latter. In German, *Macht* and *Herrschaft* are corresponding terms, and in Latin Spinoza, for example, distinguishes between *potestas* and *potentia* (Deleuze, 1988: 97–104; Weik, 2011). As Foucault has emphasized throughout his body of work, power has the capacity of being both repressive and creative and the one focus must not obscure the other. Much writing on biopolitics and biopower stresses the *puissance* of biopolitics, its disciplining, regulatory and controlling qualities. In addition, it is important that the bioplitics is also what is helpful and supportive for human beings living in the contemporary society.

The term *medicalization* (Shostak and Conrad, 2008; Conrad, 2007, 1992; Blech, 2006) widely used in medical sociology proposes that the biotechnology and pharmaceutical industries have been able to establish their therapies as legitimate and practical solutions to a variety of disorders and medical conditions, and that such medicalization implies, almost of necessity, a form of manipulation of authorities, decision-makers, professional groups and patients. Such a critical view may be justified at times, but it is also important to recognize that the many contributions from experimental medicine and pharmaceutical research are also enhancing quality and longevity of life. Grand terms such as biopolitics and biopower unfortunately tend to obscure the day-to-day accomplishments in clinics and laboratories—Karl Weick (2001) uses the handy term "small wins" to denote such events—and impose the view of all biopolitical programs and initiatives as being inherently oppressive. Such a one-sided understanding of the term power, perhaps ultimately grounded in a dour critical theory view of contemporary society, only emphasizing the repressive qualities of power, was arguably not what Foucault called for. Being a close follower of Nietzsche, Foucault knew that power can both repress and enable, do good and do harm—it is, as Nietzsche put it, "beyond good and evil."[1]

The study reported in this volume is therefore to be understood as a contribution to the literature on biopolitics and biopower by emphasizing the creative and positive qualities of power. Assisted fertilization is a form of

---

1   "The concept of power, whether of a god or of a man, always includes both the ability to help and the ability to harm," Nietzsche (1967: 193) writes. In a much-cited passage, Foucault further develops this view of power within his analytical framework: "Power would be a fragile thing if its only function were to repress, if it worked only through the mode of censorship, exclusion, blockage and repression, in the manner of a great Superego, exercising itself only in a negative way. If on the contrary, power is strong this is because, as we are beginning to realise, it produces effects at the level of desire—and also at the level of knowledge. Far from preventing knowledge, power produces it" (Foucault, 1980: 59). That Nietzsche is perhaps the single most important figure in post-World War II continental philosophy is indicated by the fact that figures as diverse as Georges Bataille ([1945] 1992), Jacques Derrida (1979), Martin Heidegger ([1961] 1987), George Simmel (1991) and Michel Foucault wrote books or longer essays about Nietzsche's philosophy.

power/knowledge aggregate in the Foucauldian sense of the term (Foucault, 1980) and for some patients it may be regarded as intimidating to undergo the therapy and certain social groups may disapprove of the entire field of research altogether on the basis of, for example, theological teachings. At the same time, the capacity to understand and to be able to retrieve, manipulate and store human reproductive materials is in essence a productive use of knowledge and power; it helps women and men despairing in their hope to become parents fulfill their dreams. Parenthood does not come without costs and efforts as female patients undergo stressful hormone therapies, endure examinations and egg retrieval procedures, and live with the worries regarding the possibilities for getting pregnant, but despite the ordeal it is still an opportunity for overcoming a natural loss of fertility that is greatly appreciated.

The study reported in this volume is therefore making a contribution to the debate on biopolitics and biopower, and terms derived there from including bioeconomy (Rose, 2007; Copeman, 2009), biolabor (Clarke et al., 2009), bioethics (Hedgecoe, 2010; Salter and Salter, 2007), and biocapital (Sunder Rajan, 2006). The life sciences are translated into commercial therapies and services and are thus subject to financial and managerial interests but that does not of necessity make them repressive. An organization theory perspective, anchored in a business school research agenda recognizing commercial interests in any entrepreneurial activity, is arguably in a good position to strike a balance between the critical view of commercial life science and biopharmaceuticals and analytical perspectives. The commercialization of the life sciences and assisted fertilization therapies is by no mean unproblematic as it is today primarily benefitting citizens in welfare states while larger populations in poorer parts of the world could only dream of being able to pay fees in the range of 10,000 US dollars for such therapies. However, when the therapies have been developed within the public healthcare sectors in welfare states in the Western world, much has been learnt and accomplished and taking such know-how to new markets and social groups is today basically a matter of political priorities and entrepreneurial skills; the required know-how regarding efficacy and the safety of the therapies is already in place.

Foucault's term biopolitics also captures a fundamental condition in the contemporary era, the reliance on technoscience in general and the life sciences in particular in everyday life. The term is not an overtly critical view of the contemporary period wherein a paranoia over the advancement of the life sciences and what may be accomplished may overshadow actual accomplishments and contributions to human well-being. As for instance Sarah

Franklin (2001) and Rosi Braidotti (2008) have remarked, today, regardless of its many accomplishments, the public's trust in the technosciences is *lower* than it used to be a few decades ago, testifying to a series of concerns regarding controversial scientific projects such as cloning (Franklin, 2007) and the development of genetically modified organisms (GMOs) (McAfee, 2003). The case of assisted fertilization therapies is — with the exception of a few groups being critical of such practices — widely recognized as an important contribution from the life sciences. In comparison, say, the use of genetically modified (GM) crops in the food industry is much more widely criticized. The study therefore contributes to the biopolitics literature that recognizes a productive view of power.

Implications for Organization Theory: A Life Science Research Agenda

In organization studies, a reductionist epistemology is commonly used wherein either technology *or* institutional rules, *or* professional expertise, etc., is targeted. The social organization of the social sciences prescribes that different schools and research traditions emphasize a highly specialized view of their object of study (as in the expression "I do transformational leadership studies"). Such a functional division of labor encourages expertise and a sense of community within specific quarters of the scholarly fields, further translated into research conferences, interest groups and specialized journals, but this functional organization also gradually undermines a more integrated and comprehensive view of how organizations and managerial work are actually unfolding in the day-to-day practice. The classic metaphor of the blind men and the elephant wherein the different interpretations of the elephant's body parts leads to insightful comments, yet provides no full overview of the magnificent animal, applies; the elephant of clinical assisted fertilization work thus needs to be understood as a social system composed of different sub-systems, technologies and equipment, specific domains of expertise (e.g. the counselor's role is different from the gynecologist's), and so forth, while at the same time all these resources constitute an integrated system that cannot be fully understood unless they are related to one another. The study thus emphasizes that a proper object of study is not only individual professional groups or the technologies they make use of but the integrated organization system. While reductionism is a scholarly virtue in certain research programs, it may be a more problematic procedure in other research projects.

As a consequence, this study calls for more research not only in the field of the life sciences but in all spheres of society taking into account a wider set of factors in the research design. More specifically, ethnographic methods are suitable for capturing both the totality and details in any organization or professional field. Zaloom's (2006) study of financial traders, Ho's (2009) study of investment bankers, Fine's (2007) study of meteorologists, Leidner's (1993) study of salespersons and fast food restaurant staff, and Anteby's (2008) study of "grey zone activities" in a French aeronautics manufacturing company are a few cases that examine social worlds in their full scope. Further studies in this methodological tradition are welcome and would be able to shed further light on, for example, the translation of life science know-how into clinical practices.

Summary and Conclusion

The contemporary society is offering a life world for humans wherein their entire existence is subject to specific regimes of expertise and knowing. While the medieval man had recourse to religious beliefs, mythology and folk psychology to make sense of everyday existence, today, in the age of technoscience and critical reflection and a general skepticism toward ideas that are not grounded in proofs and evidence, there is less room for speculation or myths. Such a life world is paradoxically abandoning one form of determinism—that of God's will and the human condition inscribed by the deities—to embrace another, that of the world being wholly determined by a certain order of things—in physics, medicine, chemistry, and so forth. For the contemporary person, chance is playing just as small a role as it did for the medieval human: the world is essentially constituted in specific *intelligible* ways.

Scientific ideologies assume that the world is lending itself to scientific exploration. Still, in some cases, for instance the human genome mapping project, which promised to lay bare the innermost secrets of human life, the capacity to produce new therapies has by and large been disappointing. The human genome is too small to fully explain the difference between, say, a human, a primate or a plant, but still too complex in terms of how different gene sequences are transcribed into the proteins constituting the amino-acids and is thus preventing a mapping of the relations between gene sequences and medical disorders, for example. The emerging field of proteomics, studying such transcription processes, may be the next step in revealing the role and mechanisms of the human genome, but such a research program is merely in its earliest stages.

During the last 15 to 20 years, there has been a remarkable growth of life science know-how, while at the same time there are relatively few new innovative drugs being registered by the multinational pharmaceutical companies, testifying to the difficulties involved in understanding for instance cancer and neurodegenerate diseases such as Alzheimer's disease and Parkinson's disease. The creative crisis of big pharma is potentially an indicator of the new challenges for experimental medicine. Remarkable accomplishments have been made to fully understand inflammatory and viral diseases and in fields such as endocrinology and cardiology there is a substantial understanding of the generic processes of the human body.

To shift the focus from experimental medicine to reproductive medicine and assisted fertilization work in the clinics, researchers and clinicians today know how to retrieve, manipulate, store and transfer reproductive materials, and adequate technologies have been developed to assist such procedures as far as possible. Still, there is much to be learned regarding the processes of human reproduction, knowledge that may help move the performance ratio above the 60 percent level accomplished today in certain clinics. For instance, andrology (the study of the male endocrinology and reproductive capacities) researchers examine the role of the chromatin in the sperm and try to figure out if the density of the chromatin is related to male infertility. In the case of the female reproductive apparatus, the role of the endometrium and the womb more generally would be of great interest to further explore but unfortunately there are few safe and ethical research methods for such a research program. Today, it is possible to stimulate ovulation and to retrieve eggs that can be fertilized through the ICSI method in cases of low sperm count and/or motility, but the quality of the embryos being grown remain largely an issue that remains to be explained. Some embryos are even in shape and divide as predicted in the standard models, while others are less qualitative. Still, in some cases low-quality embryos do not lead to pregnancies while, on the contrary, in other cases low-quality embryos can lead (although at a lower rate) to pregnancies.

Expressed differently, assisted fertilization clinicians have to work with the reproductive materials they are provided with but they still have a problem to fully predict and to understand why certain embryos develop into fetuses while others do not. Assisted fertilization clinicians are thus working on the basis of a partial and incomplete understanding of the human reproduction process. Regardless of such limitations they are in a position to help roughly half of the couples and single women seeking assistance to become parents. Such accomplishments are based on a variety of factors including advances in reproductive medicine, technological development, the long-term collection of statistics and data from which relationships between different factors can be examined, and the enactment of international standard operation procedures. In other words, only one part of the success of assisted fertilization therapies can be explained by the scientific understanding of human reproduction, i.e. the theoretical modeling of reproduction. The rest is a matter of being able to organize a series of activities that taken together stabilize a clinical practice that is both transparent for outsiders and that can dynamically respond to external changes and new insights (Morlacchi and Nelson, 2011). In other words, life science know-how and any other form of technoscientific knowledge being produced in laboratories and research teams are not really able to exist outside of the material resources and practices that transform the know-how into actual activities and operations, i.e. performances. That is, we do not have transcendental theories on the one hand and material resources on the other, dragging behind the formulation of theories, but on the contrary theoretical models and material resources are mutually constitutive, being inextricably entangled in the day-to-day work.

Hence the importance of what Karen Barad (2007) speaks of as *intra-action* and Rheinberger (1997) names *experimental system*, two epistemological models of technoscientific production that do not reduce experimental practices to their elementary components but rather theorize how the study of nature or life is always a matter of mobilizing and enrolling heterogeneous resources. In an organization theory perspective, capable of examining the totality of such resources as an integrated system of materialities, practices, theories, professional ideologies, and so forth, it is neither determinism nor superior intellectual capacities of brilliant researchers (even though the role of such figures needs to be recognized at some point) that propels assisted fertilization work in the clinics, but precisely the capacity of assembling and compiling heterogeneous resources. The assisted fertilization clinic is not machinery operating by magic or some innate force but is rather a patchwork of materialities and practices that are recreated in every instant of the work, that is, professionals in collaborating with technologies and reproductive materials and other relevant resources. Earlier sociomaterial studies have often studied what we have labeled as weak or secondary practices wherein they are dealing with artifacts and technological systems which operate outside of the human body. This study contributes to developing theoretical concepts by also distinguishing a strong or primary case of sociomaterial practices which includes various forms of interventions and manipulations of the human body.

Seen in this way, the study contributes to the literature on sociomaterial practices or a practice-based view of organizations more broadly, starting from the very bottom and gradually establishing itself by the alignment of people and stuff. With a metaphor derived from geology, a geological formation may appear immutable and eternal ("as old as the hills"), but a closer look reveals that the rocks and stones have been developed and modified during hundreds of thousands of years and under various conditions. Similarly, organizations may appear just as solid and opaque but closer scrutiny shows that organizations too are outcomes from historical processes and various accomplishments and failures. Hewlett Packard was started in garage in Palo Alto, California, and Facebook in Mark Zuckerberg's dorm room at Harvard, and most major corporations have their own versions of such creation stories, in many cases having their roots in the most modest of conditions. "By nature all things must have a crude origin," Vico (1999: 138) says.

A challenge for organization studies is to fail to see how what is seemingly constituted as an integrated and complex, at times even fulfilled, structure is in fact made up of materialities and practices. Such failures are what Gilbert Ryle (1949) speaks of as "category mistakes," the inability to see how integrated structures are related to everyday practices, i.e. a disjunction between the whole and the parts. Grand names like "the Roman empire," "NASA" or "the liberal society" may play a role in common-sense thinking and everyday rhetoric to denote certain conditions and relations but failing to see that, for example, the Mediterranean power developed with the eternal city of Rome as its center was in fact constituted by the various agencies and undertakings throughout the territory during centuries (e.g., cattle breeding on the Iberian peninsula and the tax collected on the basis of such trade) is an exemplary category mistake.

Similarly, reproductive medicine and assisted fertilization need to be understood as sociomaterial practices, as the day-to-day activities that are constantly modified and improved as new know-how and facts are developed or reveal themselves for the actors. Assisted fertilization *qua* clinical practice is thus an organized, joint accomplishment resting on the capacity to critically correct practices in the face of emerging knowledge. Hopefully, this volume has been able to portray the work done in the clinics in such a way.

Appendix:
Methodology of the Study

Research Design

The study reported in this research monograph is part of a broader study exploring the commercialization of the life sciences. Including studies of the pharmaceutical industry, biotechnology industry and biomaterial industry, the field of assisted fertilization is yet another field wherein life science know-how is translated into therapies immediately benefitting social actors. The research question was whether reproductive medicine was facing any significant changes regarding competition and technological development? In organization theory and management studies, reproductive medicine and assisted fertilization have been primarily examined as a pricing policy problem (Schmittlein and Morrison, 2003; Kaplan et al., 1992). Besides these contributions, assisted fertilization is relatively unexplored by organization researchers. Studies in the fields of, for example, science and technology studies (Cussins, 1996, 1998) have used ethnographic methods but this study uses a case study methodology (Siggelkow, 2007; Quattrone, 2006; Gillham, 2000; Stake, 1996), including interviewing, participant observations, and the uses of internal and public documents. The empirical materials presented here are mainly based on interviews with a number of actors engaged in assisted fertilization work. In addition to the personal qualitative interviews, information materials, textbooks, news articles and websites were examined.

Data Collection

At the time of the study and in the Swedish setting of reproductive medicine there were six public and ten private clinics offering assisted fertilization treatments. According to the legal regulations, only the public clinics or clinics that had a contract with a university hospital were allowed to offer treatments involving donation of eggs and sperm, hence the treatment options varied at the different clinics. In total it is estimated that around 150–200 people are employed working directly with assisted fertilization in Sweden.[1] In the latter half of 2010, a letter of intent containing information about the study and asking for permission to conduct interviews was sent to 10 of the clinics, three public and seven private. After further communication and reminders, often directed at specific persons and using recommendations from previous interviewees, interviews were secured with representatives from all three of the public clinics, four of the private clinics and retired representatives from an additional private clinic.

Securing some of the interviews took several months and involved repeated communication attempts. One private clinic asked for more detailed, written information about the study and then never replied to further communication, despite our attempts to contact them. Other times our letter of intent was passed around between the heads and different managers in the clinics, leaving a trail of forwarded messages in the eventual responses that we got. The heads of the clinics that sent the question directly to a few possible interviewees often resulted in quicker replies, since the head of the clinic had then also implicitly or explicitly signed off on participation in the study. Some interviewees recruited further colleagues at their own clinic, depending on who was available on the days that we were coming to visit. Only in one case the head of the clinic answered and declined participation for the whole clinic, due to lack of time. Researchers working in the medical field of assisted fertilization were the recipients who most often refrained from answering our request altogether. Perhaps this was due to lack of time and many other engagements or a lack of support for qualitative research, the reasons can only be speculated about.

All interviews were carried out in person and most were conducted at the clinics. Visiting the clinics, seeing the location and layouts, waiting in the waiting rooms among the patients, noticing the art on the walls and so on, this all contributed to a feeling for the context. The first to answer our request was the head of a public clinic and we were able to organize interviews with several different representatives of this clinic quite quickly, despite a heavy load of research, teaching and clinical duties being part of their work. This clinic, as the other public clinics, was located in a large hospital building near the gynecological department. The atmosphere in these clinics was typical of

---

1   The size of a clinics vary but, for example, one medium sized clinic employs six gynecologists, six midwives or nurses, eight employees working in the laboratory from different professions, one psychologist or social worker, an assistant nurse and two secretaries.

hospital wards, with bright lighting, a sterile interior design, long and wide corridors and practical but rather robust, unfashionable and uncomfortable furniture. Most interviews were conducted in the private or shared offices of the employees, in a conference room or in a treatment room.

To give even more detail concerning the environment, we noted that in one of the waiting rooms there were humorous posters advertising for egg and sperm donors. In another public clinic instead a more solemn roll-up displayed the research findings of a study conducted at the clinic and on a table there was a textbook on assisted fertilization for medical students. The most common literature in the waiting rooms was otherwise the typical fashion, decoration and entertainment magazines and newspapers. The first public clinic we visited had posted pictures in the corridor showing babies and postcards from previous patients, adding a more personal touch to the atmosphere. In the other clinics these pictures could be found in the back-offices of the employees. At one of the private clinics Rebecka was given a guided tour of the laboratories and offered a look in the microscope at a growing embryo. This involved first dressing up in protective clothing, such as the hats and shoes that are worn in operation theaters. The embryologist guide explained about the degree of cleanliness, the amount of time spent cleaning and the special set up of the ventilation in the laboratories to keep the amount of dust and microbes to a minimum in the air. She was also shown the binders with detailed forms for documenting the handling and development of each embryo.

The second clinic to participate was a small private clinic, also quite typical of a private healthcare setting. Here the location was away from the hospital in a comfortable office building with stylish interior decoration, calming music in the waiting room and an impressive aquarium. On the table in front of the comfortable couch there was a "guest book" with notes from patients. The thoughts and feelings of the people who had waited there before were documented in short greetings, including hopes, worries, despair and thankfulness when the treatment had succeeded. Another private clinic had toys in the waiting room, for children who accompanied the parents. For nearly all patients at the public clinics, the attempted pregnancy was the first, so children in the waiting rooms were not expected.

The interviewees whom we met often recommended further interview subjects (e.g. pioneering figures and others contributing to research and development in specific areas within the discipline), making the recruitment of interviewees unfold according to a "snowball methodology." However, as the study developed, we made choices concerning which type of clinic, the profession and previous experience of the interviewees that we would like to include and directed our letters and phone-calls toward these categories of people, in order to gain variation. Several of the interviewees were in or had been in leading and managerial positions, or were founders and co-owners of the private clinics with long experience in the field. A variety of professional categories in the field were selected, including physicians (i.e. gynecologists), employees in the laboratories, researchers, midwives, nurses, administrators and a psychologist. In addition, one policy-maker—a member of the Swedish Parliament—and two patient couples were interviewed. To find the patients we first tried contacting the national association of IVF patients, which works to inform and lobby for the rights of assisted fertilization patients. We asked to interview the board and to find couples through them. After several unsuccessful attempts, we finally resorted to recruiting the couples using informal contacts through our friends and colleagues. The first two couples that we asked were willing to participate, probably in part to be nice and help us with the study, but also because they believed that the topic was important. Ways of improving the care at the clinics was something that both couples discussed at some point during the interview, but also their appreciation of the possibility of getting the treatments. These interviews took place in their homes and were emotional to perform, particularly with the couple who had been unsuccessful with the treatment and who were still struggling to become parents through adoption. These meetings gave an increased insight into the importance and intensity of the treatments to the patients involved.

We also attempted to find an interviewee representing the National Board of Health and Welfare, which is the regulatory authority for assisted fertilization clinics in Sweden. However, this proved impossible since the one person who was specialized in the IVF area declined and his assistant only answered questions through email, mainly referring directly to the legal documents that can be found online.

The interviews were based on a semi-structured interview guide, including questions concerning interviewees' careers, their view on the development of the discipline and important milestones and breakthroughs, the organization, technology and regulation of the clinics, ethical considerations, current important research areas and possible future developments. The patient couples were asked to explain the process they had gone through and what it had been like for them. The psychologist was asked about her work, the types of patients she met and what their experiences were like. The Member of Parliament was asked about the processes leading up to and following the initiation of new laws, and about possible future changes to legislation. Most interviews lasted one hour, they were all recorded digitally and transcribed verbatim by a professional transcription bureau. The interviewees are presented in Table A.1.

Table A.1   Interviewees participating in the study

	Public	Private	Total number of interviewees
Physicians/gynecologists, with or without PhD	3	6	
Laboratory employees, with or without PhD	7	2	
Midwives, information specialist	2	1	
Psychologist	1		
Policy-maker, regulatory body	1		
Patients		4	
Total	14	13	27

Analysis of the Empirical Material

The interview transcripts were read by two senior researchers–the authors– individually coding passages in terms of their content (Spradley, 1979). The initial categories chosen were related to the broad themes of infertility being described as a medical problem, the use of scientific practices and scientific advancement, performance and factors related to the success rates of the treatments, know-how and training, the relationship between private and public, policy and regulation, pricing, ethics, the market and its future and finally social issues and demand factors. A secondary coding was then performed and aimed at categorizing the interview excerpts under what Van Maanen (1979) calls *second-order concepts*, that is, theoretical or analytical categories. These categories were "scientific and clinical know-how," "regulatory frameworks," and "reproductive technologies," that is, the broader categories used to structure the empirical data. While previous studies offered relatively little guidance on how to structure the data into second-order observations, these three categories discriminated the interview material into three interrelated but mutually dependent categories. A broad selection of illustrative excerpts from the original interviews that fell into each second-order category was then used for the empirical chapters of this book.

Bibliography

Abraham, John (2010), Pharmaceuticalization of society in context: Theoretical, empirical, and health dimensions, *Sociology*, 44(4): 603–622.

Abraham, John and Sheppard, Julie (1999), Complacent and conflicting scientific expertise in British and American drug regulation: Clinical risk assessment of Triozolam, *Social Studies of Science*, 29(6): 804–843.

Adler, Paul S. (2005), The evolving object of software development, *Organization*, 12(3): 401–435.

Agamben, Giorgio (1998), *Homo Sacer: Sovereign power and bare life*, trans. by Daniel Heller-Roazen, Stanford: Stanford University Press.

Ahmed, Sara (2010), Imaginary prohibitions: Some preliminary remarks on the founding gestures of the "new materialism," *European Journal of Women's Studies*, 15(1): 23–39.

Alac, Morana (2008), Working with brain scans: Digital images and gestural interaction in FMRI laboratory, *Social Studies of Science*, 38(4): 483–508.

Almeling, Renee (2007), Selling genes, selling gender: Egg agencies, sperm banks, and the medical market in genetic material, *American Sociological Review*, 73(3): 319–340.

Angell, Marcia (2004), *The truth about the drug companies*, New York: Random House.

Anteby, Michal (2008), *Moral gray zones: Side production, identity, and regulation in an aeronautics plant*, Princeton: Princeton University Press.

Åsberg, Cecilia and Johnson, Ericka (2009), Viagra selfhood: Pharmaceutical advertising and the visual formation of Swedish masculinity, *Health Care Analysis*, 17(2): 144–159.

Attewell, Paul (1990), What is a skill?, *Work and Occupations*, 17(4): 422–448.

Bachelard, Gaston ([1934] 1984), *The new scientific spirit*, Boston: Beacon Press.

Bailey, Alison (2011), Reconceiving surrogacy: Toward a reproductive justice account of Indian surrogacy, *Hypatia*, 26(4): 715–741.

Barad, Karen (1998), Getting real: Technoscientific practices and the materialization of reality, *Differences*, 10(2): 87–128.

Barad, Karen (2003), Posthumanist performativity: Towards and understanding of how matter comes to matter, *Signs: Journal of Woman in Culture and Society*, 28(3): 801–831.

Barad, Karen (2007), *Meeting the universe halfway: Quantum physics and the entanglement of matter and meaning*, Durham, NC and London: Duke University Press.

Barad, Karen (2011), Erasers and erasures: Pinch's unfortunate "uncertainty principle," *Social Studies of Science*, 41(3): 443–454.

Barley, Stephen R. (1986), Technology as an occasion of structuring: Evidence from observations of CT scanners and the social order of radiology departments, *Administrative Science Quarterly*, 31: 78–108.

Barley, Stephen R. (1990), The alignment of technology and structure through roles and networks, *Administrative Science Quarterly*, 35: 61–103.

Barley, Stephen R. and Bechky, Beth (1994), In the backroom of science: The work of technicians in science labs, *Work and Occupations*, 21(1): 85–126.

Barley, Stephen R., Meyerson, Debra E. and Grodal, Stine (2011), E-mail as a source and symbol of stress, *Organization Science*, 22(4): 887–906.

Bataille, G. ([1945] 1992), *On Nietzsche*, New York: Paragon House.

Beaulieu, Anne (2002), Images are not the (only) truth: Brain mapping, visual knowledge and iconoclasm, *Science, Technology and Human Values*, 27: 53–86.

Beck, Melinda (2008), Ova time: Women line up to donate eggs—for money. *Wall Street Journal*, December 9.

Bennett, Jane (2010), *Vibrant matter: A political ecology of things*, Durham, NC and London: Duke University Press.

Bennis, Warren G. and O'Toole, James (2005), How business schools lost their way, *Harvard Business Review*, 83(5): 33–53.

Bernard, Claude ([1865] 1957), *An introduction to the study of experimental medicine*, trans. by Henry Copley Greene, New York: Dover.

Beunza, Daniel and Stark, David (2004), Tools of the trade: The socio-technology of arbitrage in a Wall Street trading room, *Industrial and Corporate Change*, 13(2): 369–400.

Beunza, Daniel, Hardie, Iain and Mackenzie, Donald (2006), A price is a social thing: Toward a material sociology of arbitrage, *Organization Studies*, 27: 721–745.

Beynon-Jones, Siân M. (2012), Timing is everything: The demarcation of "later" abortions in Scotland, *Social Studies of Science*, 42(1): 31–52.

Bjuresten, Kerstin, Hreinsson, Julius, Fridström, Margareta, Rosenlund, Björn, Ek, Iingar and Hovatta, Outi (2003), Embryo transfer by midwife or gynecologist: A prospective randomized study, *Acta Obstetricia et Gynecologica Scandinavica*, 82(5): 462–466.

Blauner, Robert (1964), *Alienation and freedom: The factory worker and his industry*, Chicago: University of Chicago Press.

Blech, Jörg (2006), *Inventing disease and pushing pills: Pharmaceutical companies and the medicalization of normal life*, trans. by Gisela Wallor Hajjar, London and New York: Routledge.

Bloomfield, Brian P. (1991), The role of information systems in UK National Health Service: Action at distance and the fetish of calculation, *Social studies of Science*, 21: 701–734.

Bloomfield, Brian and Danieli, Ardha (1995), The role of management consultants in the development of information technology: The indissoluble nature of socio-political and technical skills, *Journal of Management Studies*, 32(1): 23–46.

Blum, Virginia L. (2005), *Flesh wounds: The culture of cosmetic surgery*, Berkeley: University of California Press.

Braidotti, Rosi (1994), *Nomadic subjects: Embodiment and sexual difference in contemporary feminist theory*, New York: Columbia University Press.

Braidotti, Rosi (2002), *Metamorphosis: Toward a materialist theory of becoming*, Cambridge: Polity Press.

Braidotti, Rosi (2006), *Transpositions: On nomadic ethics*, Cambridge and Malden: Polity Press.

Braidotti, Rosi (2008), In spite of the times: The postsecular turn in feminism, *Theory, Culture and Society*, 25(6): 1–24.

Brewis, Joanna and Warren, Samantha (2001), Pregnancy as project: Organizing reproduction, *Administrative Theory and Praxis*, 23(3): 383–406.

Briggs, Laura (2010), Reproductive technology: Of labor and markets, *Feminist Studies*, 36(2): 359–374.

Broadhurst, Susan (1999), The (im)mediate body: A transvaluation of corporeality, *Body and Society*, 5(1): 17–29.

Brody, Howard (2007), *Hooked: Ethics, the medical profession, and the pharmaceutical industry*, Lanham: Rowman and Littlefield.

Brooks, Abigail (2004), "Under the knife and proud of it": An analysis of the normalization of cosmetic surgery, *Critical Sociology*, 30(2): 207–239.

Brown, Bill (2010), Objects, others, and us (the refabrication of things), *Critical Inquiry*, 36: 183–216.

Bud, Robert (1993), *The uses of life: A history of biotechnology*, Cambridge: Cambridge University Press.

Bullough, Vern L. (1994), *Science in the bedroom: A history of sex research*, New York: Basic Books.

Burri, Regula Valérie and Dumit, Joseph (2008), Social studies of scientific imaging and visualization, in Hackett, Edward J., Amsterdamska, Olga,

Lynch, Michael and Wajcman, Judy, eds, *Handbook of science and technology studies*, 3rd edn, Cambridge and London: MIT Press, pp. 297–317.

Butler, Judith (1993), *Bodies that matter*, London: Routledge.

Butler, Judith (1999), *Gender trouble: Feminism and the subversion of identity*, London: Routledge.

Bynum, William F. (1994), *Science and the practice of medicine in the nineteenth century*, Cambridge: Cambridge University Press.

Bynum, William F. (2008), *A very short introduction to the history of medicine*, Oxford and New York: Oxford University Press.

Çalişkan, Koray and Callon, Michel (2009), Economization, part 1: Shorting attention from the economy towards the processes of economization, *Economy and Society*, 38(3): 369–398.

Callinicos, Alex (2009), *Bonfire of illusions: The twin crises of neoliberalism*, Cambridge: Polity.

Callon, Michel, Millo, Yuval and Muniesa, Fabian, eds (2007), *Market devices*, Oxford and Malden: Blackwell.

Canguilhem, Georges (1988), *Ideology and rationality in the history of the life sciences*, Cambridge and London: MIT Press.

Canguilhem, Georges (1991), *The normal and the pathological*, New York: Zone Books.

Canguilhem, Georges (2008), *Knowledge of life*, trans. by Stefano Geroulanos and Daniela Ginsburg, New York: Fordham University Press.

Carruthers, Bruce and Espeland, Wendy (1998), Money, meaning, and morality, *American Behavioral Scientists*, 41(1): 1384–1408.

Cartwright, Lisa (1995), *Screening the body: Tracing medicine's visual culture*, Minneapolis and London: University of Minnesota Press.

Cheal, David (1988), *The gift economy*, London and New York: Routledge.

Cioran, Emil M. (1998), *The trouble with being born*, New York: Arcade Publishing.

Clarke, Adele (1990), Controversy and the development of reproductive sciences, *Social Problems*, 37(1): 18–27.

Clarke, Adele E. (1998), *Disciplining reproduction: Modernity, American life sciences, and the problem of sex*, Berkeley: University of California Press.

Clarke, Adele E., Shim, Janet, Shostak, Sara and Nelson, Alondra (2009), Biomedicalizing genetic health, diseases and identities, in Atkinson, Paul, Glasner, Peter and Lock, Margaret, eds, *Handbook of genetics and society: Mapping the new genomics era*, London and New York: Routledge, pp. 21–40.

Clarke, Adele E., Mamo, Laura, Fishman, Jennifer R., Shim, Janet K. and Fosket, Jennifer Ruth (2003), Biomedicalization: Technoscientific transformations of health, illness, and US biomedicine, *American Sociological Review*, 68: 161–194.

Cochoy, Franck (2009), Driving a shopping cart from STS to business, and the other way around: On the introduction of shopping carts in American grocery stores (1936–1959), *Organization*, 16(1): 31–55.

Cohen, J., Trounson, A., Dawson, K., Jones, H., Hazekamp, J., Nygren, K.-G. and Hamberger, L. (2005), The early days of IVF outside the UK, *Human Reproduction Update*, 11(5): 439–460.

Cohen, Margot and Athavaley, Anjali (2009), A search for a surrogate leads to India. *Wall Street Journal*, October 8.

Cohn, Simon (2004), Increasing resolution, intensifying ambiguity: An ethnographic account of seeing life in brain scans, *Economy and Society*, 33(1): 52–76.

Collins, Randall (1979), *The credential society*, New York: Academic Press.

Connell, John (2006), Medical tourism: Sea, sun, sand and ... surgery, *Tourism Management*, 27(6): 1093–1100.

Conrad, Peter (1992), Medicalization and social control, *Annual Review of Sociology*, 18: 209–232.

Conrad, Peter (2007), *The medicalization of society*, Baltimore: Johns Hopkins University Press.

Conrad, P.O. and Potter, D. (2000), From hyperactive children to ADHD adults: Observations on the expansion of medical categories, *Social Problems*, 47: 559–582.

Coole, Diana and Frost, Samantha, eds (2010), *New materialisms: Ontology, agency, and politics*, Durham, NC and London: Duke University Press.

Coopmans, Catelijne (2011), "Face value": New medical imaging software in commercial view, *Social Studies of Science*, 41(2): 155–176.

Copeman, Jacob (2009), Introduction: Blood donation, bioeconomy, culture, *Body and Society*, 15(1): 1–28.

Currah, Andrew (2007), Managing creativity: The tension between commodities and gifts in a digital networked environment, *Economy and Society*, 36(3): 467–494.

Cussins, Charis (1996), Ontological choreography: Agency through objectification in infertility clinics, *Social Studies of Science*, 26: 575–610.

Cussins, Charis (1998), Reproducing reproduction: Techniques of normalization and naturalization in infertility clinics, in Franklin, Sarah and Ragoné, Helena, eds, *Reproducing reproduction: Kinship, power, and technological innovation*, Philadelphia: University of Pennsylvania Press, pp. 86–101.

Daemmrich, Arthur (1998), The evidence does not speak for itself: Expert witnesses and the organization of DNA-typing companies, *Social Studies of Science*, 28: 741–772.

Das, Veena (2000), The practice of organ transplants: Networks, documents, translations, in Lock, Margaret, Youg, Allan and Cambrosio, Alberto, eds, *Living and working with new medical technologies: Intersections of inquiry*, Cambridge: Cambridge University Press, pp. 263–287.

Daston, Lorraine (1995), The moral economy of science, *Osiris*, 10: 2–24.

Daston, Lorraine (2008), On scientific observation, *Isis*, 99: 97–110.

Davis, Kathy (2002), A dubious equality: Men, women and cosmetic surgery, *Body and Society*, 8(1): 49–66.

DeGrandpre, Richard (2006), *The Cult of Pharmacology*, Durham, NC: Duke University Press.

DeLanda, Manuel (1997), *A thousand years of nonlinear history*, New York: Zone Books.

DeLanda, Manuel (2002), *Intensive science and virtual philosophy*, London and New York: Continuum.

DeLanda, Manuel (2006), *A new philosophy of society: Assemblage theory and social complexity*, London and New York: Continuum.

Deleuze, G. (1983), *Nietzsche and philosophy*, trans. by Hugh Tomlinson, New York: Columbia University Press.

Deleuze, G. (1988), *Spinoza: Practical philosophy*, San Francisco: City Lights Books.

Derrida, Jaques (1979), *Spurs: The style of Nietzsche*, Chicago: University of Chicago Press.

Dickenson, Donna (2008), *Body shopping: The economy fuelled by flesh and blood*, Oxford: Oneworld.

Dickson, Andrew (2011), The *jouissance* of the lard(er): Gender, desire and anxiety in the weight-loss industry, *Culture and Organization*, 17(4): 313–328.

Directive 2004/23/EC of the European Parliament and of the Council of 31 March 2004 on setting standards of quality and safety for the donation, procurement, testing, processing, preservation, storage and distribution of human tissues and cells. *Official Journal L 102*, 07/04/2004 P. 0048–0058.

Dourish, Paul (2004), *Where the action is: The foundation of embodied interaction*, Cambridge, MA: MIT Press.

Downer, John (2011), "737-Cabriolet": The limits of knowledge and the sociology of inevitable failure, *American Journal of Sociology*, 117(3): 725–762.

Dreyfus, Hubert L. and Dreyfus, Stuart E. (2005), Expertise in the real world context, *Organization Studies*, 26: 779–792.

Dumit, Joseph (2004), *Picturing personhood: Brain scans and biomedical identity*, Princeton: Princeton University Press.

Dunn, Mary R. and Jones, Candace (2010), Institutional logics and institutional pluralism: The contestation of care and science logics in medical education, 1967–2005, *Administrative Science Quarterly*, 55: 114–149.

Edenius, Mats and Styhre, Alexander (2006), Knowledge management in the making: Using Balanced Scorecard and e-mail systems, *Journal of Knowledge Management*, 10(3): 86–102.

Espeland, Wendy Nelson and Stevens, Mitchell L. (2008), A sociology of quantification, *European Journal of Sociology*, 49(3): 401–436.

Esposito, Roberto (2008), *Bíos: Biopolitics and philosophy*, trans. by Timothy Campbell, Minneapolis and London: University of Minnesota Press.

Fauser, Bart C. and Edwards, Robert G. (2005). The early days of IVF, *Human Reproduction Update*, 11(5): 437–438.

Feldman, Martha S. and March, James G. (1981), Information in organizations as signal and symbol, *Administrative Science Quarterly*, 26: 171–186.

Fine, Gary-Alan (2007), *Authors of the storm: Meteorologists and the culture of prediction*, Chicago and London: University of Chicago Press.

Fishman, Jennifer R. (2004), Manufacturing desire: The commodification of female sexual dysfunction, *Social Studies of Science*, 34(2): 187–218.

Fleming, Peter and Spicer, André (2005), How objects believe in us: Applications in organizational analysis, *Culture and Organization*, 11(3): 181–193.

Flusser, Vilém (2002), *Writings*, edited by Andreas Ströhl, trans. by Erik Eisel, Minneapolis and London: University of Minnesota Press.

Foucault, Michel (1973), *The birth of the clinic*, London: Routledge.

Foucault, Michel (1980), *Power/knowledge*, New York: Harvester Wheatsheaf.

Foucault, Michel (1997), *Ethics, subjectivity and truth: Essential works of Michel Foucault, vol. 1*, New York: The New Press.

Foucault, Michel (2007), *Security, territory, population: Lectures at the Collège de France, 1977–1978*, trans. by Graham Burchill, Basingstoke and New York: Palgrave.

Foucault, Michel (2008), *The birth of biopolitics: Lectures at the Collège de France, 1978–1979*, ed. by Michael Senellart, trans. by Graham Burchell, Basingstoke: Palgrave.

Fourcade, Marion (2009), *Economists and societies: Discipline and profession in the United States, Britain, and France, 1890s to 1990s*, Princeton and London: Princeton University Press.

Frandsen, Ann-Christine (2009), From psoriasis to a number and back, *Information and Organization*, 19(2): 103–128.

Frank, Arthur W. (1995), *The wounded storyteller: Body, illness, and ethics*, Chicago: University of Chicago Press.

Frank, Thomas (2008), Rent-a-womb is where market logic leads. *Wall Street Journal*, December 10.

Franklin, Sarah (1998), Making miracles: Scientific progress and the facts of life, in Franklin, Sarah and Ragoné, Helena, eds, *Reproducing reproduction: Kinship, power, and technological innovation*, Philadelphia: University of Pennsylvania Press, pp. 102–117.

Franklin, Sarah (2001), Culturing biology: Cell lines for the second millennium, *Health*, 5(3): 335–354.

Franklin, Sarah (2007), *Dolly mixtures: The remaking of genealogy*, Durham, NC: Duke University Press.

Franklin, Sarah and Roberts, Celia (2006), *Born and made: An ethnography of preimplantation genetic diagnosis*, Princeton and London: Princeton University Press.

Fraser, Miriam (2002), What is the matter of feminist criticism?, *Economy and Society*, 31(4): 606–625.

Fraser, Miriam (2003), Material theory: Duration and the serotonin hypothesis of depression, *Theory, Culture and Society*, 20(5): 1–26.

Fraser, Miriam, Kember, Sarah and Lury, Celia (2005), Inventive life: Approaches to a new vitalism, *Theory, Culture and Society*, 22(1): 1–14.

Friese, Carrie and Clarke, Adele E. (2012), Transposing bodies of knowledge and technique: Animal models at work in reproductive sciences, *Social Studies of Science*, 42(1): 31–52.

Fujimura, Joan H. (1996), *Crafting science: A sociohistory of the quest for the genetics of cancer*, Cambridge, MA: Harvard University Press.

Fujimura, Joan H. (2006), Sex genes: A critcial sociomaterial approach to the politics and molecular genetics of sex determination, *Signs*, 32(1): 49–82.

Galison, Peter (1997), *Image and logic: A material culture of microphysics*, Chicago and London: University of Chicago Press.

Gauchat, Gordon (2012), Politicization of science in the public sphere: A study of public trust in the United States, 1974 to 2010, *American Sociological Review*, 77(2): 167–187.

Gherardi, Silvia (2010), Telemedicine: A practice-based approach to technology, *Human Relations*, 63(4): 501–524.

Giancotti, Emilia (1997), The birth of modern materialism in Hobbes and Spinoza, in Montag, Warren and Stoltze, Ted, eds, *The new Spinoza*, Minneapolis: University of Minnesota Press, pp. 49–63.

Gieryn, Thomas F. (1983), Boundary-work and the demarcation of science from non-science: Strains and interest in professional ideologies of scientists, *American Sociological Review*, 48(6): 781–795.

Gillham, Bill (2000), *Case study methods*, London and New York: Continuum.

Gimlin, Debra (2007), Accounting for cosmetic surgery in the USA and Great Britain: A cross-cultural analysis of women's narratives, *Body and Society*, 13(1): 43–62.

Gimlin, Debra (2010), Imaging the Other in cosmetic surgery, *Body and Society*, 16(4): 57–75.

Ginsburg, Faye and Rapp, Rayna (1991), The politics of reproduction, *Annual Review of Anthropology*, 20: 311–343.

Golan, Tal (2004), The emergence of the silent witness: The legal and medical reception of X-ray in the USA, *Social Studies of Science*, 34: 469–499.

Goslinga-Roy, Gillian (2000), Body boundaries, fiction of the female self: An ethnography of power, feminism and the reproductive technologies, *Feminist Studies*, 26(1): 113–140.

Gramsci, A. (1971), *Selection from prison notebooks*, New York: International Publishers.

Greene, Jeremy (2006), *Prescribing by numbers: Drugs and the definition of disease*, Baltimore: Johns Hopkins University Press.

Griesemer, James R. (1992), The role of instruments in the generative analysis of science, in Clarke, Adele E. and Fujimura, Joan H., eds, *The right tools for the job: At work in twentieth-century life sciences*, Princeton: Princeton University Press, pp. 47–67.

Griesemer, James (2006), Genetics from an evolutionary perspective, in Neumann-Held, Eva M. and Rehmann-Sutter, Christoph, eds, *Genes in development: Re-reading the molecular paradigm*, Durham, NC and London: Duke University Press, pp. 199–237.

Grosz, Elizabeth (2004), *The nick of time: Politics, evolution and the untimely*, Durham, NC: Duke University Press.

Grosz, Elizabeth (2005), *Time travels: Feminism, nature, power*, Durham, NC: Duke University Press.

Gulati, Ranjay (2007), Tent poles, tribalism, and boundary spanning: The rigor-relevance debate in management research, *Academy of Management Journal*, 50(4): 775–782.

Gunning, Tom (1995), Tracing the individual body: Photography, detectives, and early cinema, in Carney, Leo and Schwartz, Vanessa R., eds, *Cinema and the invention of modern life*, Berkeley: University of California Press, pp. 15–45.

Hacking, Ian (1983), *Representing and intervening*, Cambridge: Cambridge University Press.

Hacking, Ian (1992), The self-vindicating of the laboratory sciences, in Pickering, Andrew, ed., *Science as practice and culture*, Chicago and London: University of Chicago Press, pp. 29–64.

Hackman, W.D. (1989), Scientific instruments: Models of brass and aids to discovery, in Gooding, David, Pinch, Trevor and Schaffer, Simon, eds, *The uses of experiments: Studies in the natural sciences*, Cambridge, New York and Melbourne: Cambridge University Press, pp. 31–65.

Hallyn, Fernand ([1987] 1990), *The poetic structure of the world: Copernicus and Kepler*, New York: Zone Books.

Hamberger, Lars and Wikland, Matts (2010), Nobel Prize to Robert Edwards, *Acta Obstetricia et Gynecologica Scandinavica*, 89(12): 1502–1503.

Hanson, Norwood Russell (1958), *Patterns of discovery: An inquiry into the conceptual foundations of science*, Cambridge: Cambridge University Press.

Harré, Rom (2002), Material objects in social worlds, *Theory, Culture and Society*, 19(5/6): 23–33.

Harris, Henry (1999), *The birth of the cell*, New Haven: Yale University Press.

Harvey, David (2010), *The enigma of capital and the crisis of capitalism*, London: Profile Books.

Healy, David (2002), *The creation of psychopharmacology*, Cambridge, MA and London: Harvard University Press.

Healy, Kieran (2004), Altruism as an organizational problem: The case of organ procurement, *American Sociological Review*, 69: 387–404.

Hedgecoe, Adam, (2010) Bioethics and the reinforcement of socio-technical expectations, *Organization*, 17(2): 163–186.

Heidegger, Martin ([1961] 1987), *Nietzsche, vol. III: The will to power as knowledge and as metaphysics*, trans. by Joan Stambaugh, David Farrell Krell and Frank A. Capuzzi, San Francisco: Harper and Row.

Helmreich, Stefan (2008), Species of biocapital, *Science as Culture*, 17(4): 463–478.

Henare, Amiria, Holbraad, Martin and Wastell, Sari (2007), *Thinking through things: Theorising artefacts*, London and New York: Routledge.

Heyes, Cressida J. (2009), Diagnosing culture: Body dysmorphic disorder and cosmetic surgery, *Body and Society*, 15(4): 73–93.

Heyes, Cressida J. and Jones, Meredith, eds (2009), *Cosmetic surgery: A feminist primer*, Farnham and Burlington: Ashgate.

Hird, Myra J. (2004), Feminist matters: New materialist considerations of sexual difference, *Feminist Theory*, 5(2): 223–232.

Ho, Karen (2009), *Liquidated: An ethnography of Wall Street*, Durham, NC and London: Duke University Press.

Hobsbawm, Eric J. (1975), *The age of capital, 1848–1875*, London: Weidenfeld and Nicolson.

Holliday, Ruth and Cairnie, Allie (2007), Man made plastic: Investigating men's consumption of aesthetic surgery, *Journal of Consumer Culture*, 7(1): 57–78.

Huxley, Aldous, (1932), *Brave new world,* London: Chatto and Windus.

Ingold, Tim (2000), *The perception of the environment*, London: Routledge.

Ingold, Tim (2010), The textility of making, *Cambridge Journal of Economics*, 34: 91–201.

Introna, Luca D. and Hayes, Niall (2011), On sociomaterial imbrications: What plagiarism detection systems reveal and why it matter, *Information and Organization*, 21: 107–122.

Jasanoff, Sheila, ed. (2004), *Science and ideology*, London and New York: Routledge.

Jasanoff, Sheila (2005), The idiom of co-production, in Jasanoff, Sheila, ed., *States of knowledge: The co-production of science and social order*, London and New York: Routledge, pp. 1–12.

Jeacle, Ingrid (2003), Accounting and the construction of the standard body, *Accounting, Organization and Society*, 28: 357–377.

Johnson, Ericka (2007), Surgical simulations and simulated surgeons: Reconstituting medical practice and practitioners in simulations, *Social Studies of Science*, 37: 585–608.

Johnson, Ericka (2008), Simulating medical patients and practices: Bodies and the construction of valid medical simulators, *Body and Society*, 14(3): 105–128.

Jonvallen, Petra (2006), *Testing pills, enacting obesity: The work of localizing tools in a clinical trail*, PhD Thesis, Department of Technical and Social Change, Linköping University.

Joyce, Kelly A. (2008), *Magnetic appeal: MRI and the myth of transparency*, New York and London: Cornell University Press.

Kaplan, Edward H., Hershlag, Avner, DeChercerney, Alan, H. and Lavy, Gady (1992), To be or not to be? *That* is conception! Managing in vitro fertilization programs, *Management Science*, 38(9): 1217–1229.

Kelly, Susan Elizabeth (2012), The maternal–foetal interface and gestational chimerism: The emerging importance of chimeric bodies, *Science as Culture*, 21(2): 233–257.

Khurana, Rakesh (2007), *From higher aims to hired hands: The social transformation of American business schools and the unfulfilled promise of management as a profession*, Princeton: Princeton University Press.

Kieser, Alfred and Leiner, Lars (2009), Why the rigour-relevance gap in management research is unbridgeable, *Journal of Management Studies*, 46(3): 516–533.

Knorr Cetina, Karin D. (1981), *The manufacture of knowledge: An essay on the constructivist and contextual nature of science*, Oxford: Pergamon Press.

Knorr Cetina, Karin D. (1997), Sociality with objects: Social relations in postsocial societies, *Theory, Culture and Society*, 14(4): 1–30.

Kohler, Robert (1994), *Lords of the fly: Drosophila genetics and experience of life*, Chicago and London: University of Chicago Press.

Kuhn, Thomas S. (1962), *The structure of scientific revolutions*, Chicago: University of Chicago Press.

Lakatos, Imre (1970), Falsification and the methodology of scientific research programmes, in Lakatos, I. and Musgrave, A., eds, *Criticism and the growth of knowledge*, Cambridge: Cambridge University Press, pp. 91–195.

Lakoff, Andrew (2008), The right patients for the drug: Pharmaceutical circuits and the codification of illness, in Hackett, Edward J., Amsterdamska, Olga, Lynch, Michael and Wajcman, Judy, eds, *Handbook of science and technology studies*, 3rd edn, Cambridge, MA and London: MIT Press, pp. 741–760.

Lanzara, Giovan Francesco and Patriotta, Gerardo (2001), Technology and the courtroom: An inquiry into knowledge making in organizations, *Journal of Management Studies*, 38(7): 943–971.

Latour, Bruno (1988), *The pasteurization of France*, trans. by Alan Sheridan and John Law, Cambridge, MA and London: Harvard University Press.

Law, John and Singleton, Vicky (2005), Object lessons, *Organization*, 12(3): 331–355.

Leidner, Robin (1993), *Fast food, fast talk: Service work and the routinization of everyday life*, Berkeley: University of California Press.

Leman, Jonathan (2010), A child is created ["Ett barn blir till"], *SOMA* [Magazine from the Karolinska University Hospital], 4: 1–36.

Lemke, Thomas (2011), *Biopolitics: An advanced introduction*, New York: New York University Press.

Lenoir, Timothy (1980), Kant, Blumenbach, and vital materialism in German biology, *Isis*, 71(1): 77–108.

Lenoir, Timothy (1994), Revolution from above: The role of the state in creating the German research system, 1810–1910, *The American Economic Review*, 88(2): 22–27.

Leonardi, Paul M. (2011), When flexible routines meet flexible technologies: Affordances, constraints, and the imbrications of human and material agencies, *MIS Quarterly*, 35(1): 147–167.

Leonardi, Paul M. and Barley, Stephen R. (2008), Materiality and change: Challenges to building theory about technology and organizing, *Information and Organization*, 18: 159–176.

Leonardi, Paul M. and Barley, Stephen R. (2010), What's under construction here? Social action, materiality, and power in constructivist studies of technology and organizing, *The Academy of Management Annals*, 4(1): 1–51.

Lewontin, Richard (2000), *The triple helix: Genes, organism, environment*, Cambridge, MA: Harvard University Press.

Lipovetsky, Gilles (2005), *Hypermodern times*, trans. by Andrew Brown, Cambridge: Polity.

Lock, Margaret (2002), *Twice dead: Organ transplants and the reinvention of death*, Berkeley, Los Angeles and London: University of California Press.

Longino, Helen E. (1992), Knowledge, bodies, and values: Reproductive technologies and their strategic context, *Inquiry*, 35(3/4): 323–340.

Lowe, Alan (2004), Objects and the production of forms of life: Understanding organizational arrangements from a post-social perspective, *Journal of Organization Change Management*, 17(4): 337–351.

Luhmann, Niklas (1995), *Social systems*, Stanford: Stanford University Press.

Lykke, Nina (2010), The timeliness of post-constructionism, *NORA: Nordic Journal of Feminist and Gender Research*, 18(2): 131–136.

Lynch, Michael (1985), *Art and artifact in laboratory science: A study of shop work and shop talk in a research laboratory*, London: Routledge and Kegan Paul.

Lynch, Michael (1995), Laboratory space and the technological complex: An investigation of topical contextures, in Star, Susan Leigh, ed., *Ecologies of knowledge: Work and politics in science and technology*, Albany: State University of New York Press.

Lyotard, Jean-Francois (1984), *The postmodern condition: A report on knowledge*, Manchester: Manchester University Press.

Mamo, Laura and Fishman, Jennifer R. (2001), Potency in all the right places: Viagra as a technology of the gendered body, *Body and Society*, 7(4): 13–37.

Mann, Susan Archer and Huffman, Douglas J. (2005), The decentering of second wave feminism and the rise of the third wave, *Science and Society*, 69(1): 56–91.

Markens, Susan (2007), *Surrogate motherhood and the politics of reproduction*, Berkeley and Los Angeles: University of California Press.

Marks, John (2006), Biopolitics, *Theory, Culture and Society*, 23(2–3): 333–335.

Marshall, Barbara L. (2009), Sexual medicine, sexual bodies and the pharmaceutical imagination, *Science as Culture*, 18(2): 133–149.

Martin, Luis L. and Kambil, Ajit (1999), Looking back and thinking ahead: Effects of prior success on managers' interpretations of new information technologies, *Academy of Management Journal*, 42(6): 652–661.

Massumi, Brian (2002) *Parables of the virtual: Movement, affect, sensation*, Durham, NC and London: Duke University Press.

McAfee, Kathleen (2003), Neoliberalims on the molecular scale: Economic and genetic reductionism in the biotechnology battles, *Geoforum*, 34(2): 203–219.

Megill, Allan, ed. (1994), *Rethinking objectivity*, Durham, NC: Duke University Press.

Meyer, John W. and Rowan, Brian (1977), Institutionalizing organizations: Formal structure as myth and ceremony, *American Journal of Sociology*, 83(2): 340–363.

Miller, Daniel (2005), Materiality: An introduction, in Miller, Daniel, ed., *Materiality*, Durham, NC and London: Duke University Press, pp. 1–50.

Miller, Daniel (2010), *Stuff*, Cambridge and Malden: Polity.

Mitchell, Robert and Waldby, Catherine (2001), National biobanks: Clinical labor, risk production and the creation of biovalue, *Science, Technology and Human Values*, 35(2): 330–355.

Mol, Annemarie (2002), *The body multiple: Ontology in medical practice*, Durham, NC: Duke University Press.

Monaghan, Lee F., Hollands, Robert and Pritchard, Gary (2010), Obesity epidemic entrepreneurs: Types, practices and interests, *Body and Society*, 16(2): 13–71.

Morlacchi, Piera and Nelson, Richard R. (2011), How medical practice evolves: Learning to treat failing hearts with an implantable device, *Research Policy*, 40: 511–525.

Murray, Fiona (2010), The oncomouse that roared: Hybrid exchanges as a source of distinction at the boundary of overlapping institutions, *American Journal of Sociology*, 116(2): 341–388.

Nietzsche, Friedrich (1967), *The will to power*, New York: Vintage Books.

Nishizaka, Aug (2011), The embodied organization of a real-time fetus: The visible and the invisible in prenatal ultrasound examinations, *Social Studies of Science*, 41(3): 309–336.

Oliver, Richard W. (2000), *The coming biotech age: The business of biomaterials*, New York: McGraw-Hill.

Orlikowski, Wanda J. (2007), Sociomaterial practices: Exploring technology at work, *Organization Studies*, 28(9): 1435–1448.

Orlikowski, Wanda J. (2010), The sociomateriality of organizational life: Considering technology in management research, *Cambridge Journal of Economics*, 34: 125–141.

Orlikowski, Wanda J. and Scott, Susan V. (2008), Sociomateriality: Challenging the separation of technology, work, and organization, *The Academy of Management Annals*, 2(1): 433–474.

Orlikowski, Wanda J., Yates, JoAnne, Okamura, Kazuo and Fujimoto, Masayo (1993), Shaping electronic communication: The metastructuring of technology in the context of use, *Organization Science*, 6(4): 423–444.

Oudshoorn, Nelly (2003), *The male pill: A biography of a technology in the making*, Durham, NC and London: Duke University Press.

Oyama, Susan (1997), Accidental chordate, in Herrstein-Smith, Barbara and Plotnitsky, Arkady, eds, *Mathematics, science, and postclassical theory*, Durham, NC and London: Duke University Press.

Oyama, Susan (2000), *Evolution's eye: A systems view of the biology-culture divide*, Durham, NC: Duke University Press.

Palmer, Donald, Dick, Brian and Freiburger, Nathaniel (2009), Rigor and relevance in organziation studies, *Journal of Management Inquiry*, 18: 265–272.

Pande, Amrita (2009), "It may be her eggs but it's my blood": Surrogates and everyday forms of kinship in India, *Qualitative Sociology*, 32: 379–397.

Pande, Amrita (2010), Commercial surrogacy in India: Manufacturing a perfect mother-worker, *Signs*, 35(4): 969–992.

Pasveer, Bernike (2006), Representing or mediating: A history and philosophy of x-ray images in medicine, in Pauwels, Luc, ed., *Visual cultures of science: Rethinking representational practices in knowledge building and science communications*, Hanover: Dartmouth College Press, pp. 41–62.

Pels, Dick, Hetherington, Kevin and Vendenberghe, Frédéric (2002), The status of the object: Performances, mediations and techniques, *Theory, Culture and Society*, 19(5/6): 1–21.

Perrow, Charles (1983), The organizational context of human factors engineering, *Administrative Science Quarterly*, 28: 521–541.

Perrow, Charles (1984), *Normal accidents*, New York: Basic Books.

Petryna, Adriana (2009), *When experiments travel: Clinical trials and the global search for human subjects*, Durham, NC and London: Duke University Press.

Pfeffer, Jeffrey (1993), Barriers to the advance of organizational science: Paradigm development as a dependent variable, *Academy of Management Review*, 18(4): 599–620.

Pfeffer, Jeffrey and Fong, Christina T. (2002), The end of business schools: Less success than meets the eye, *Academy of Management Learning and Education*, 1(1): 78–95.

Pickering, Andrew (1995), *The mangle of practice: Time, agency, and science*, Chicago and London: University of Chicago Press.

Pickering, Andrew (2003), Interview with Andrew Pickering, in Ihde, Don and Selinger, Evan, *Chasing technoscience: Matrix for materiality*, Bloomington and Indianapolis: Indiana University Press, pp. 83–95.

Pickering, Andrew (2010), *The cybernetic brain: Sketches of another future*, Chicago and London: University of Chicago Press.

Pinch, Trevor (2011), Review essay: Karen Barad, quantum mechanics, and the paradox of mutual exclusivity, *Social Studies of Science*, 41(3): 431–441.

Pitts-Taylor, Victoria (2007), *Surgery junkies: Wellness and pathology in cosmetic culture*, New Brunswick: Rutgers University Press.

Pitts-Taylor, Victoria (2010), The plastic brain: Neoliberalism and the neuronal self, *Health*, 14(6): 635–652.

Porter, Theodore M. (1995), Precision and trust: Early Victorian insurance and the politics of calculation, in Wise, M. Norton, ed., *The values of precision*, Princeton: Princeton University Press, pp. 173–197.

Power, Michael (2004), Counting, control and calculation: Reflection on measuring and management, *Human Relations*, 57(6): 765–783.

Prasad, Amit (2005), Making images/making bodies: Visibility and disciplining through magnetic resonance imaging (MRI), *Science, Technology and Human Values*, 30(2): 291–316.

Prasad, Amit (2009), Capitalizing disease: Biopolitics of drug trails in India, *Theory, Culture and Society*, 26(5): 1–29.

Preda, Alex (1999), Turn to things: Arguments for sociological theory of things, *The Sociological Quarterly*, 40: 347–366.

Quattrone, P. (2006), The possibility of testimony: A case of case study research, *Organization*, 13(1): 143–157.

Rabinow, Paul (1996), *Making PCR: A story of biotechnology*, Chicago and London: University of Chicago Press.

Rader, Karen Ann (2004), *Making mice: Standardizing animals for American biomedical resesearch*, Princeton: Princeton University Press.

Rapp, Reyna (2011), Reproductive entanglements: Body, state, and culture in the dys/regulation of child-bearing, *Social Research*, 78(3): 693–718.

Rheinberger, Hans-Jörg (1997), *Toward a history of epistemic things: Synthesizing proteins in the test tube*, Stanford: Stanford University Press.

Rheinberger, Hans-Jörg (1999), Experimental systems, graphematic spaces, in Lenoir, Timothy, ed., *Inscribing science: Scientific texts and the materiality of communication*, Stanford: Stanford University Press, pp. 285–303.

Rheinberger, Hans-Jörg (2010a), On the historicity of scientific knowledge: Ludwik Fleck, Gaston Bachelard, Edmund Husser, in Hyder, David and Rheinberger, Hans-Jörg, eds, *Science and the life world: Essays on Husserl's "Crisis of European science,"* Stanford: Stanford University Press, pp. 164–176.

Rheinberger, Hans-Jörg (2010b), *The epistemology of the concrete: Twentieth-century histories of life*, Durham, NC and London: Duke University Press.

Riskin, Jessica (2003), Eighteenth-century wetware, *Representations*, 83: 97–125.

Roberts, Celia (2007), *Messengers of sex: Hormones, biomedicine and feminism*, Cambridge: Cambridge University Press.

Rose, Nikolas S. (2007), *The politics of life itself: Biomedicine, power and subjectivity in the twenty-first century*, Princeton and Oxford: Princeton University Press.

Roth, Wolff-Michael (2009), Radical uncertainty in scientific discovery work, *Science, Technology and Human Values*, 34(3): 313–336.

Rouse, Joseph (2004), Barad's feminist naturalization, *Hypathia*, 19(1): 142–161.

Ryle, Gilbert (1949), *The concept of mind*, Harmondsworth: Penguin.

Salter, Brian and Salter, Charlotte (2007), Bioethics and the global moral economy: The cultural politics of human embryonic stem cell science, *Science, Technology and Human Values*, 32(5): 554–581.

Samuel, S., Dirsmith, M.W. and McElroy, B. (2005), Monetized medicine: From the physical to the fiscal, *Accounting, Organization and Society*, 30: 249–278.

Schaffer, Simon (1995), Accurate measurement is an English science, in Wise, M. Norton, ed., *The values of precision*, Princeton: Princeton University Press, pp. 135–172.

Schickore, Jutta (2007), *The microscope and the eye: A history reflection, 1740–1870*, Chicago and London: University of Chicago Press.

Schmittlein, D.C. and Morrison, D.G. (2003), A live baby or your money back: The marketing of in vitro fertilization procedures, *Management Science*, 49(12): 1617–1835.

Schüll, Natasha Dow and Zaloom, Ciatlin (2011), The shortsighted brain: Neuroeconomics and the governance of choice in time, *Social Studies of Science*, 41(4): 515–538.

Serres, Michel (2011), *Malfeasance: Appropriation through pollution?*, trans. by Ann-Marie Feenberg-Diron, Stanford: Stanford University Press.

Serres, Michel and Latour, Bruno (1995), *Conversations on science, culture, and time*, Ann Arbor: University of Michigan Press.

Shapin, Steven and Schaffer, Simon (1985), *Leviathan and the airpump*, Princeton: Princeton University Press.

Sharp, Lesley A. (2003), *Strange harvest: Organ transplants, denatured bodies, and the transformed self*, Berkeley: University of California Press.

Sharp, Lesley A. (2011), The invisible woman: The bioaesthetics of engineered bodies, *Body and Society*, 17(1): 1–30.

Shaw, Jennifer (2012), The *Birth of the clinic* and the advent of reproduction: Pregnancy, pathology and the medical gaze in modernity, *Body and Society*, 18(2): 110–138.

Shenhav, Yehouda (1999), *Manufacturing rationality: The engineering foundation of the managerial revolution*, Oxford and New York: Oxford University Press.

Shostak, Sara and Conrad, Peter (2008), Sequencing and its consequences: Path dependence and the relationships between genetics and medicalization, *American Journal of Sociology*, 114: S287–S316.

Siggelkow, N. (2007), Persuasion with case studies, *Academy of Management Journal*, 50(1): 20–24.

Simakova, E. (2010), RFID "theatre of proof": Product launch and technology demonstrations, *Social Studies of Science*, 40(4): 549–576.

Simmel, Georg (1991), *Schopenhauer and Nietzsche*, trans. by Helmut Loiskandl, Deena Weinstein and Michael Weinstein, Urbana and Chicago: University of Illinois Press.

Simondon, Gilbert ([1958] 1980), *On the mode of existence of technical objects*, trans. by Ninian Mallahphy, London: University of Western Ontario.

Smerdon, Usha Rengachary (2008), Crossing bodies, crossing borders: International surrogacy between the United States and India, *Cumberland Law Review*, 39: 15–85.

Smith, Wally (2009), Theatre of use: A frame analysis of information technology demonstration, *Social Studies of Science*, 39(3): 449–480.

Snowdon, Claire (1994), What makes a mother? Interviews with women involved in egg donation and surrogacy, *Birth*, 21(2): 77–84.

Sommerlund, Julie (2006), Classifying microorganisms: The multiplicity of classifications and research practices in molecular microbial ecology, *Social Studies of Science*, 36(6): 909–928.

Spar, Debora (2006), *The baby business: How money, science, and politics drive the commerce of conception*, Boston: Harvard Business School Press.

Spradley, James P. (1979), *The ethnographic interview*, New York: Holt, Rinehart and Winston.

Stake, Robert E. (1996), *The art of case study research*, Thousand Oaks, London and New Delhi: Sage.

Star, Susan Leigh (1999), The ethnography of infrastructure, *American Behavioral Scientist*, 43(3): 377–339.

Stark, David and Paravel, Verena (2008), Power point in public: Digital technology and the new morphology of demonstration, *Theory, Culture and Society*, 25(5): 30–55.

Starkey, Ken and Madan, Paula (2001), Bridging the relevance gap: Aligning stakeholders in the future of management research, *British Journal of Management*, 12, Special Issue, S3–S26.

Stengers, Isabelle (1997), *Power and invention: Situating science*, Minneapolis and London: Minnesota University Press.

Sterne, Jonathan (2003), Medicine's acoustic culture: Mediate auscultation, the stethoscope and the "autopsy of the living," in Bull, Michael and Back, Les, eds, *The auditory culture reader*, Oxford and New York: Berg, pp. 191–217.

Stiegler, Bernard (2011), *Technics and time, 3: Cinematic time and the question of malaise*, trans. by Stephen Barker, Stanford: Stanford University Press.

Strand, Michael (2011), Where do classifications come from? The DSM-IIL, the transformation of American psychiatry, and the problem of origin in the sociology of knowledge, *Theory and Society*, 40: 273–331.

Styhre, Alexander and Sundgren, Mats (2011), *Venturing into the bioeconomy: Professional ideologies, identity and innovation*, Basingstoke and New York: Palgrave Macmillan.

Suchman, Lucy (2000), Embodied practice in engineering work, *Mind, Culture and Activity*, 7(1–2): 4–18.

Suchman, Lucy (2005), Affiliative objects, *Organization*, 12(3): 379–399.

Suchman, Lucy A. (2007), *Human-machine reconfigurations: Plans and situated actions*, Cambridge: Cambridge University Press.

Sunder Rajan, Kaushik (2006), *Biocapital: The constitution of postgenomic life*, Durham, NC: Duke University Press.

Teman, Elly (2010), *Birthing a mother: The surrogate body and the pregnant self*, Berkeley, Los Angeles and London: University of California Press.

Thacker, Eugene (2010), *After life*, Chicago and London: University of Chacago Press.

Throsby, Karen (2009), The war on obesity as a moral project: Weight loss drugs, obesity surgery and negotiating failure, *Science as Culture*, 18(2): 210–216.

Timmermans, Stefan (2008), Professions and their work: Do market shelters protect professional interests?, *Work and Occupations*, 35(2): 164–188.

Titmuss, Richard M. (1970), *The gift relationship: From human blood to social policy*, London: George Allen and Unwin.

Tober, Diane M. (2001), Semen as gift, semen as good: Reproductive workers and the market in altruism, *Body and Society*, 7(2–3): 137–160.

Turkle, Sherry, ed. (2007), *Evocative objects: Things we think with*, Cambridge, MA: MIT Press.

Twine, France Winddance (2001), *Outsourcing the womb: Race, class and gestational surrogacy in a global market*, London and New York: Routledge.

Van Maanen, John (1979), The fact of fiction in organizational ethnography, *Administrative Science Quarterly*, 24: 539–550.

Vaughan, Diana (1999), The dark side of organizations: Mistake, misconduct and disaster, *Annual Review of Sociology*, 25: 271–305.

Veblen, Thorstein (1904), *The theory of the business enterprise*, New York: Schreiber.

Vico, Giambattista (1999), *New science*, London: Penguin.

Vora, Kalindi (2009), Indian transnational surrogacy and the commodification of vital energy, *Subjectivity*, 28: 266–287.

Wajcman, Judy and Rose, Emily (2011), Constant connectivity: Rethinking interruptions at work, *Organization Studies*, 32(7): 941–961.

Waldby, Catherine (2002), Stem cells, tissue cultures, and the production of biovalue, *Health*, 6(3): 305–322.

Waldby, Cathy and Cooper, Melinda (2007), The biopolitics of reproduction: Post-Fordist biotechnology and women's clinical labour, *Australian Feminist Studies*, 23(55): 57–73.

Warwick, Andrew (2005), X-ray as evidence in German orthopedic surgery, 1985–1900, *Isis*, 96: 1–24.

Watkins, Elizabeth S. (2001), *On the pill: A social history of oral contraceptives, 1950–1970*, Baltimore and London: Johns Hopkins University Press.

Weick, Karl E. (2001), *Making sense of the organization*, Oxford: Blackwell.

Weik, Elke (2011), In deep waters: Process theory between Scylla and Charybdis, *Organization*, 18(5): 655–672.

Wilkinson, Stephen (2006), *Bodies for sale: Ethics and exploitation in the human body trade*, London and New York: Routledge.

Winance, Myriam (2006), Trying out the wheelchair: The mutual shaping of people and devices through adjustment, *Science, Technology, and Human Values*, 31: 52–72.

Witz, Anne (2000), Whose body matters? Feminist sociology and the corporeal turn in sociology and feminism, *Body and Society*, 6(2): 1–24.

Woicehyn, Jaana (2000), Technology adoption: Organizational learning in oil firms, *Organization Studies*, 21(6): 1095–1118.

Woodward, James (1965), *Business organization: Theory and practice*, London: Oxford University Press.

Yates, JoAnne and Van Maanen, John, eds (2001), *Information techology and organizational transformation: History, rhetorics, and practice*, Thousand Oaks, London and New Delhi: Sage.

Zaloom, Caitlin (2006), *Out of the pits: Trading and technology from Chicago to London*, Durham, NC and London: Duke University Press.

Zammuto, Raymond F., Griffith, Terri L., Majchrzak, Ann, Dougherty, Deborah J. and Faraj, Samer (2007), Information technology and the changing fabric of organization, *Organization Science*, 19(5): 749–762.

Zelizer, Vivianne (2005), *The purchase of intimacy*, Princeton: Princeton University Press.

Index